ABRAHAM LINCOLN

The Politician Become a Man

ABRAHAM LINCOLN

The Politician and the Man

BY

RAYMOND HOLDEN

MINTON, BALCH & COMPANY

NEW YORK   1929

Printed in the United States of America by
J. J. LITTLE AND IVES COMPANY, NEW YORK

TO

MY MOTHER

ACKNOWLEDGMENT

I wish to make, for help received in the preparation of this book, grateful acknowledgment of the keen advice and faithful services of my wife, Louise Bogan, and the generous support of my sisters, Marian and Frances Holden.

CONTENTS

PART ONE—THE BIRTH OF A POLITICIAN

PART TWO—THE BIRTH OF A MAN

ILLUSTRATIONS

PART ONE

THE BIRTH OF A POLITICIAN

CHAPTER ONE

A FRONTIER DEBTOR AND HIS WORLD

IN the Old World Napoleon, being dead, had become easy to laugh at. The Continent which he had kept in terror saw the old systems of life dying away. In America, Daniel Webster and John C. Calhoun were alive, and the old systems were still young. But they were, under the skin, dying just the same.

Among the grassy prairies of Illinois, four thousand miles from Europe, the new postmaster of the village of New Salem went stalking about on an absurdly long pair of legs, carrying his mail in his hat. It was the year 1833, the year which emancipated the slaves of the British Empire, but the postmaster of New Salem was not thinking about slavery. He had been born in a slave state and thought little of it, one way or the other. His name was Abraham Lincoln. As he walked or sat on a barrel outside the store that served as a postoffice, he read a book on surveying, or the latest copy of the *Illinois Advocate and State Register*. In the book he read of rods, perches, chains, angles and levels, to be translated into terms of prairie grass. In the newspaper he read of high doings in Washington under the hand of Andrew Jackson, of rewards offered for the return of fugitive Negroes, of the curious bombastic noises being made in Congress, of canals and railroads, money and the prices of produce.

New Salem, Illinois, was a tiny station on the westward march of the European race. Other than in the high thoughts of its founders, there was no reason for its existence. Abraham Lincoln, who, through the efforts of sympathetic friends, had just been installed in the postmastership of that village, to which he had come by accident two years before, was in a bad way. The obscure problems of slavery did not bother him at all. The nationally advertised question of a national bank only a little. But other things bothered him a great deal.

He was twenty-four years old, out of work, heavily burdened with debt as the result of an ambitious but unsuccessful plunge into the local grocery business, still feeling a little persecuted because the people of his own county had, the year before, refused to send him as their representative to the legislature at Vandalia, and utterly at a loss to know how, other than through the exercise of that droll good humor which was characteristic of him, he should go about making a place for himself in the free and easy but often uncharitable world of the pioneer.

As this depressed young postmaster wandered about New Salem in the summer of 1833, with an inch or so of bare leg showing between his socks and his trousers and another inch of something not properly external showing between the top of his pants and his coat, it would have been difficult for a casual visitor to the town to understand his melancholy. For everywhere he went people had a gay word for him, men went out of their way to stop him and speak to him, and frequently, before waving him on his way, could have been seen to be so affected by their contact with him as to double up and give off roars of laughter. And this hale and hearty intercourse was not limited to the more reserved folk of New Salem proper, but extended itself to the roughneck lads of nearby Clary's Grove who had taken a liking to Abraham's penchant for exhibiting his strength, and also to the surprising and barrier-destroying vulgarity of his stories.

But the same qualities which gave Abraham his genius for amusing himself and other people, for catching the light of the common eye and showing it shining back from his own, were sometimes a torment to him. Shining inward with their opposite face they often made him solemn and sad, sent him sometimes around corners to avoid meeting anyone, or walking aimlessly along, talking to himself. It seemed to him at such times that no one ever liked him for the right reason, that nothing he ever did led him anywhere but to other states of poverty and helplessness, never by any chance along the road toward preferment at the hands of those fellow-beings who loved to hear his juicy narratives of common life, his harangues, his jokes, but who never seemed able to take him seriously.

And Abraham Lincoln had left the home of his unpromising father because he intended to be taken seriously. Thomas Lincoln, in spite of a second wife who was a fine rugged spirit and knew how to make something out of nothing, was always moving about aimlessly. Sarah Bush Johnston had had a little property and a lot of the sense of how to care for a family when she married the widower of Nancy Hanks, but you would scarcely know that to look at the household of Lincoln, senior, now. Goose Nest Prairie, in Coles County, Illinois, where the old man was living, was no place for a young man of twenty-four who wanted to get on in the world, even if he could get on with Thomas Lincoln. Besides, it was the third place in which Thomas and Sarah had lived in three years. You could never make anything of raw prairie earth if you kept on running about like stray cattle all the time.

Abraham, coming home from an expedition piloting a flat-

boat load of hogs and supplies down the Big River to New
Orleans the year before had paid a visit to the paternal cabin in
Goose Nest Prairie. One visit was enough. As a paternal cabin it
didn't amount to much. Abraham was through with that sort of
thing. The hut stood in the tall grass of an open, wind-swept
prairie, without a tree or a shrub around it, graced by the presence of neither stable nor outhouse. It was little better than a
hovel, and the other places where the family had lived had
been much the same, sometimes worse. As a homesteader, Thomas
Lincoln simply was not very bright. He had picked out a place
in Indiana once, and lived there till the "milk-sick" and the general itch to be moving drove him out. It was a place from which
you had to go a mile to the spring for water. That sort of thing
was bound to tell in the long run. Abraham simply decided that
there were other ways of living, and that they were meant for
him.

For one thing, Abe liked to be where there were people. He
was as gregarious as a starling. The open, lonely country, the
wood full of screaming, fluttering hordes of wild pigeons, the
creeks with their fish, nights and misty mornings floating quietly
down the Great Mississippi, the glitter of the sun on the Ohio
in his boating days, the jungle-like darkness of the overhanging
virgin forest; these things meant a lot to him. But they were
woven together in his memory like a net into which his consciousness bounced safely when it fell from the trapeze of human
companionship. They were protective, but they were not the
whole act. The high flying was the thing that gave him ideas.
As a matter of fact, it was his one idea.

He did not reflect much. He was like a barrel that was just
a barrel until somebody dipped something out of it. It took conversation and laughter, the look of eyes, antagonism or question,

to make Abraham conscious of what he thought. Somewhere in him was a pattern of darkness and despair to which all his actions kept reverting.

No one ever came close enough to Abraham to know what made that pattern. It was the mark, the effect, of something in his heritage of unknown, early days. It was the bent twig that determined the inclination of his mind's tree. Perhaps his mother Nancy Hanks, bright woman that she was, had bent it by something that she had been, or by having had no known father. Perhaps some reproachful misunderstanding of his own boyish fires had done the deed for Abe. Perhaps it was some disarrangement of interior balance that came in the wake of his too early leap to six-foot stature. No one ever learned. Probably not even Abraham himself.

He was a little shy about his looks, sensitive that he scaled six-feet four in his stocking feet, and yet a little boyishly proud of the strength within his stature. He was bitterly annoyed that he owed people hundreds of dollars merely because the men to whom he and William Berry had sold out their grocery business had skipped the country before the time had come to pay off the note they gave in exchange for the stock and the good will. Abraham was puzzled too about politics, and when he wasn't talking to someone about the how and the why of the two struggling parties, he didn't know that he had any idea what it was all about. Give him someone to talk to and he could convince the listener as well as himself, even of something that he had never had in his head until he began talking. But you couldn't talk all the time.

And here he was in New Salem, himself new, everyone else new, nothing to do but new things, nowhere to go but new places, the romantic life of established places and peoples lying

with its street-lamps, its frilled shirts, its glittering dinner services, its great buildings and fine ladies and carriages, back beyond the Alleghanies, upstream against the current which was
carrying him along.

Abraham thought of pioneer life as an accident of birth,
not as a gift of freshness but as something to be outlived. He
wanted to be among the chosen, the leaders. He badly wanted
to. But he lacked confidence, and his occasional depressions, his
memory of his mother's illegitimacy, and his own distrust of
the passionate pleasure which he took in the sight of girls,
fortified the lack. He remembered his stay in Major Warnick's
house a few years back, in Menard County. He had frozen his
feet in the big snow. The Major was kind, but made Abe feel that
he was considered inferior. This projection of the idea of social
status so that it fell upon Abraham, was as disquieting to the
lank peasant in him as was Polly Warnick's projection of the
sense of her body into the region where a frightened young man
walked watching her and wanting to grab her with his greedy,
clammy hands. Women and mannered society both terrified the
overgrown frontier youth by making subtle demands upon him.

Abraham knew that he must improve himself, make himself
fit to take what he had resolved to get. He did not care much
about books or learning as such, but he wanted to know the face
of things. And that want set him to studying what books he could
get, asking questions of everyone, looking into everything, taking things apart to see what made them go.

It was a little difficult to tell what made New Salem go. It
did not go for very long, but, like a cheap watch, stopped ticking
before it had fairly got to running on time. The Sangamon River,
in spite of the fact that Lincoln had managed to pilot a steam-
boat up it in 1832, never became navigable. The annual incre-

ment of pioneers heaped itself elsewhere and there was no one to trade with. There was no tradition to outwit the logic of economics. New Salem was just a bad guess. It must have been its few inhabitants that made it go. These Abraham could and did know. He had not been a resident of the moribund infant village very long before he knew everyone and everyone knew him.

Very few men with a wide, back-slapping acquaintance fail to think themselves important elements of their community. Lincoln, for all that sense of inferiority which the dark secret of his mind gave him, was no exception to this rule. He conceived of himself now as a person with political possibilities, a man who has got his salt and only needs to get near enough to the bird's tail.

In 1833 Abraham Lincoln conceived of the tail of the bird of politics as feathered with methods of interesting your neighbors. In a frontier community national and international ideas were no part of the scheme of things. You had to tell your friends that you would see to it that the Sangamon River was made navigable if it took an earthquake to do it. You had to make them feel that, by guarding their interests, you would bring prosperity to their doors without any effort on their part. You had to insist that you would see that they were helped when they wanted to bother the government about things like the recovery of stray cattle, and that the government was never allowed to bother them even if their stray cattle knocked down the State House.

Abraham Lincoln of New Salem, believed in what he heard the most people saying. In Sangamon County, unlike most of Illinois, they were upholding the National Bank. Abraham believed in a National Bank. President Jackson was willing to knock the country to bits, if he had to, by way of expressing his distaste for such an anti-popular thing, and for the eastern plutocrats who were back of it and had been back of the finger-in-the-pie Federalist idea ever since the day of Washington and Hamilton.

Although the tradition in Abraham's family, such as it was, was very much on the side of Jackson, life in Sangamon County had led him out of the fold. The pioneers of Sangamon felt that something had to be done to make things different. Lincoln, with his ear to the ground, went with them. Most of the influential men he had met recently, men like William Jones, David Turnham, and William Wood, all leaders of pioneer life, were anti-Jackson men, National Republicans, devoted champions of Henry Clay, although the measure of popular feeling in the nation was illustrated in the election of 1832 when, for president, Jackson received 219 electoral votes to 49 for Clay and 18 for other candidates. Perhaps neither Abraham, nor these influential gentlemen who talked about the "principles of George Washington" understood how completely the National Government had, at the start, been the oyster of the country's aristocrats. Abraham, at least, whose contact with organized civilization had been as limited as that of a child, did not understand what had happened at the presumably Olympian pow-wow in Philadelphia in 1787.

He did not know that the Constitutional Convention had accomplished, not the formation of a government calculated to run in the direction of abstract political science and the doctrines of political philosophers, but of a protective institution made to free business from its hampering obstacles, to stabilize public credit, and to make private property safer than life.* Abraham did not realize that he, as a representative of the poorer classes,

* Beard, Chas. A. Economic Interpretation of the Constitution.

would have found no one in that convention acting for him, nor even interested in him.

He did not understand, having been born in the wilderness and educated in the lore of the backwoods, with trimmings by Parson Weems, what the inauguration of his hero Washington had portended. He could not very well see the nervous General, standing up in 1789 in the presence of Senators and Representatives—in his brown suit, trimmed with metal eagle buttons, his white stockings, his sword and his bag—trying to get one of his hands in his coat front so it wouldn't annoy him by hanging at his side, holding his speech in the other hand and fumbling at it all the time. Abraham would have been puzzled to have been there and, with his usual quick apprehension, to have understood that Washington thought he was being inaugurated president of a colorless, party-less, half-utopian state in which the people should not have very much to say and the politicians should have nothing about which to differ. *

This original notion of the American Republic which had been given to the world, had brought about the conditions which made the National Bank an important issue in the world of politics upon which Abraham Lincoln was entering in 1833. The Confederation under which the American States were governed for ten years prior to the adoption of the Federal Constitution had acquired a national debt of more than forty million dollars, a tremendous sum in the America of the last half of the eighteenth century. To this the government set up by the Constitution in 1789, by a clever bargain, added thirty-odd millions of state debts, mostly to men of wealth, contracted in the course of the Revolutionary War. For the government under Washington, in spite of the fact that the General was a patriot and a

* Journal of William Maclay.

Virginian, was a government in the interests of the merchant princes and manufacturer barons of the seacoast states. And it was to the interest of this group to concentrate power in the hands of the National Government in order to have a centralized agency for the protection of the goose of commerce, busy hatching its golden egg. The southern states, some of whom had already paid their state debts and who cared little about commerce, were very much disturbed at the turn affairs were taking. Perhaps they saw, as one of their leaders, Jefferson, did, how the small farmers, the laborers, the patriot veterans of the war, were, each in their way, being bled by the activities of the great commercial interests.*

These unorganized Americans had been paid for their produce and their services in Continental currency, of which, from the expression, "not worth a continental," we know the value. They had had no choice. The law and the propaganda of the time had forced them to accept these bills.† When the state debts were assumed by the federal government foresighted speculators got busy telling everyone that the government would never redeem the paper it had forced upon the impecunious, and offering to buy it at from two to five shillings the pound. The impoverished holders of this debased medium, many of them starving, were only too eager to get what they could, not knowing that the speculators had picked up information from inner sources that the government was going to redeem the money at par. Thus at even that early date was the man in the street and on the farm being victimized by the professional acquisitor. And, in the time of Washington and Hamilton, that sort of thing was done with-

* Simons, A. M. Social Forces in American History.
† Dewey, D. R. Financial History of the U. S.

out rebuke because most of the sufferers, being debtors without property qualification, could not vote.

As Jefferson said, speaking of the beneficiaries of this painful trickery, "Men thus enriched by the dexterity of a leader would follow of course the chief who was leading them to fortune, and become the zealous instrument of all his enterprises." The speculators did follow and support the Federalist idea as well under Hamilton as later. They followed to the extent, at least, of being willing to see a National Bank established of which the shares could be purchased in the proportion of seventy-five per cent of their value by exchange for certificates of indebtedness, notes, that is, which the government or state had given to wealthy lenders. Almost all of the stock of the bank went curiously enough to the manufacturing and commercial states of the North. And it was the vote of these states in Congress which carried the measure establishing the National Bank.

The original National Bank, and the bank which was rechartered in 1816, after it had been subdued for five years through the efforts of Jefferson and the states who wanted to do their own banking, was unequivocally supported by the business interests of the country and until the election of Andrew Jackson in 1828 had never been called to account for the arbitrary manner in which it used its position, as the fiscal agent of the whole people, to serve the acquisitive rapacity of an unscrupulous few.

By the election of 1832, which Abraham Lincoln, then twenty-one, was old enough to observe, property restrictions upon voting had in most states been abolished. It is not surprising that the popular voice against the dreaded combinations of capital was, in this election, pleasantly overwhelming. Yet Lincoln, because of local interests, believed in the party which the voters had at that time repudiated, the party which, whether openly or not, certainly supported the aristocratic money régime that had been so dear to Alexander Hamilton. But Abraham was not thinking of himself as a supporter of anti-popular tyranny. To him the issues were local, of personal, rather than of national importance. He saw nothing of the background of injustice and knavery which had done so much to create, not only the popular opposition to the Bank, but the grave and irreconcilable feeling of the South, that the North was out for its blood. If he had, the gentle justice of his nature might have been expected to oppose it. At that stage of his career it would have been all but impossible for a young frontiersman to be aware of the crass implications of his nation's early history.

Abraham saw New Salem only, with a side glance at Vandalia and Springfield. He saw Washington's nation as it was in Illinois in 1833. This man Jackson, the first president to get away from the genteel, drawing-room tradition of Europe, or the counting house tradition of New England, brought with him the tang and energy of something Europe could not have understood. But Lincoln understood it, and distrusted it, not as humanity but as leadership. Jackson was a westerner, but was he safe? After all, if you wanted preferment, wasn't it better to try to fit into what existed than to try, perhaps vainly, to lead something new, to make a silk purse out of a sow's ear? You could get a running start that way.

The National Bank furore was a case in point. Good or bad, four years of an administration opposed to that institution, had left money in a very low state. That was hard on westerners. Even if the present western president had thought he was helping them when he opposed the bank, it was hard. No, Abraham was not going to accept Jackson just because he was a frontiersman. You didn't have to accept him. There was Henry Clay.

He thought that opposition to the Bank was a crime, calculated to ruin the country financially. For Jackson's opposition had put the Bank, and hence credit, in a precarious position. He didn't think that it was giving the people's resources over into the hands of the money clique. And Henry Clay was no plutocratic enemy of the common man. He was just a good National Republican. And Abraham was a pretty good National Republican in many ways by this time. It needed but little to make him solid.

President Jackson had certainly, in the previous December, put a firm quietus on the lively sentiments of discord which were being expressed in South Carolina over the right of the Federal Government to collect duties in the ports of a state whose institutions were not benefited by the tariff, and whose social system did not meet with approval everywhere. The Nullification Proclamation was a good thing for the Union which had been founded by the Aristocrats of 1787 and which was now become too comfortable a hide for the organism of the common man of the 1830's to shed. But there were other issues. Abe Lincoln, child of the western prairie, postmaster of New Salem, ex-Captain of volunteers who had gone through the Black Hawk war and never had a shot at a live Indian, defeated candidate for the state legislature, greedy consumer of the newspapers of three states, never let anyone who could tell about it afterwards know what he thought of President Jackson. President Jackson represented the undeveloped country and the common man, breaking a long line of office-holding in the tradition of the Federalists. Lincoln was of the West, and of the mass of the common man, but the way to preferment in Sangamon County was not through the party of Andrew Jackson. And Abe needed preferment very badly.

Anyone who had seen him repairing log cabins, splitting wood, husking corn, milking, or killing pigs, to earn enough money to get bread into his mouth during the past six months would have known without a second look that Abraham needed preferment. It was his friends that helped him. They got him the postmaster's job which brought him a little return. They advised him to study law, they helped him get through Flint and Gibson on Surveying, and Kirkman's grammar in order that he might assist the County Surveyor and thus earn a little more. And every time anyone helped him it was fun for the helper as well as help for Lincoln, because he knew the simple ways of human contact and gave of himself as much as he ever got from anyone.

Abraham was not a very apt young man when it came to books. He would much rather have talked than read, much rather have lain flat on his back than bent over a table. He had to read over everything he wanted two or three times before he got it just right. But, once he had got it, it stayed with him and a little of it was sure to come up the next time intercourse with his fellow beings put the dipper in his barrel. He was no brighter than the next man—years of huddling in lean-tos and cabins here and there along the fantastic line of march of the Kentucky pioneer, with never enough to eat, to wear, to find out, had seen to that—but he was ambitious and persevering and he read, albeit with distaste for the effort, whatever he could lay his hands on. Anything, that is, so long as it represented something more than mere abstract ideas, things which being lacking in himself, did not appeal to him in the wit of others. What he learned, he learned not from the quick anticipation of brilliance but from the slow, painful, draught-horse pull of diligence and determination.

It was as a result of this struggle that Abraham learned the rudiments of surveying, which knowledge had an important bearing upon his career. In the first place he was able to get the job of Assistant County Surveyor, assistant to a New England Irishman named John Calhoun, who curiously enough was not even remotely connected with the southern statesman of that name. In the second place, Abraham's job took him about the county more widely than his postmastership had permitted him to travel. And he took his ready friendliness with him, endearing people to him wherever he went, leaving with them the recollection of an uncommon personality, the possessor of which they would be bound to recognize as a friend even though they saw him in the haughty distance of a political campaign.

At this time, East, West, North and South, everywhere in the British Empire, the slaves were awaiting the operation of the Emancipation Act. The *haut monde* of England was gossiping about William the Fourth. The general public in that ancient land was struggling through mingled emotions to understand what was going on in its first reform parliament. The French, having parted with Charles the Tenth without any especial pain, had abolished the hereditary nobility and under Louis Philippe were about to mourn the death of one who linked their memories with what seemed a greater day, the Marquis de Lafayette. In Germany revolt against the monarchic order had risen and been suppressed and a boy of fifteen named Karl Marx was putting two and two together.

Converging upon the sloping forehead of the postmaster-surveyor of New Salem, Illinois, were the states and territorial possessions of that confederacy called the United States of America, by the grace of God and considerable human chicanery, free and independent. They were made up of some thirteen millions of people, about a quarter of the number black, among whom was distributed very unequally a considerable amount of actual wealth. Most of the wealth, indeed practically all, was in the hands of the members of a few social groups, consisting of the hereditary gentry, the operators of great plantations, the great merchants, and the living beneficiaries of the amazing amount of profiteering which had gone on during the Revolution and the War of 1812. These groups had taken fairly good care to guard their accumulations by mutual intermarriage, and were sitting at comfortable ease on the top of North American society. Beneath them were other groups of potential financial power—manufacturers, shippers and landowners on a smaller scale. Beneath these, only recently become convinced that their day was at hand, were the small farmers, the laborers and artisans, the hewers of wood and drawers of water. And in the South, largely taking the place of these last, were some two and a half million actual slaves. In the West, all about Abraham Lincoln, were the members of the bottom and middle strata of society who had dared to take advantage of that opportunity to shake off the oppressive life of the eastern seaboard which the undeveloped regions beyond the Alleghanies offered.

Abraham Lincoln busied himself among the stumpy, stony farms, the mud wallows, the rubbish heaps, the cabins and shacks of a people in a purely primitive state, helping to mark off their property, one's from another's, and thus to lay out the field for a continuation of the eastern struggle for possession of the earth, that Fortunatus purse without the development of which there would be neither wealth nor the lack of it. Abraham's life and that of his neighbors was on a very elementary scale, but beyond its horizon, on the same chord of planet, was life in differing stages, the states of man's development all existing at the same time, as if the procession of human history were laid endwise about the globe. There was the dining table and liveried-servant life of the seacoast cities, the shirt-sleeve and kitchen-supper life of the middleman and the small tradesman, the loaf and old cheese life of the millhand and the laborer; there was the home-spun, home-made sausage life of the small farmer, the pork-barrel life of the sailor and wharfinger, the numb and lackadaisical corn-pone and hoe-cake life of the slave, under the golden artifice of feudal culture which flourished on the great plantations.

Across the Atlantic, where this golden artifice was first and most widely achieved, civilization had reached so far that a reaction had set in. Society had sent out its running roots into the New World and the head of the plant was dying. The apparent impossibility of maintaining concord among the workers of a society bursting out into seemingly destructive eruptions of machine inventiveness, had brought about violence and hatred and social instability. Men were trying, like the late King Canute, to bid the waves of an irresistible sea to stand back and suffer them to hold the ground merely loaned them by an earlier tide.

Monarchy, the emblem of feudal life, seemed to be tottering in England and on the Continent. The consequences of the French Revolution had begun to herald the day of the bourgeoisie. Disgruntled subjects were leaving their European homes by the thousand, heading for the vast unoccupied and, for the most part, ungoverned lands of North America, there, though they did not know it, to begin anew a cycle which should lead to imperial consolidation. It was the beginning of to-day.

And in that beginning, Abraham Lincoln was a poor anxious, ambitious country boy, with a talent for human contacts and a mind as inquiring as a mouse, biding his time in the besetting nearness of debt and defeat. He went about with his surveying, delivering his letters in person, though he was not required to, talking of everything that came into his head. Everything except the circumstances of the outer world of which he knew nothing. He was building up a following.

He knew nothing about the outer world, but he was none the less anxious to learn and know of it. He had said in a long address to the inattentive voters of Sangamon County the year before, that the state should give everybody an education so that all might study the history of their own and other nations. Abraham wanted to be informed, but he himself did not care much about the business of being educated. He had not had as good an education as many of his contemporaries, chiefly because of a failure to avail himself of opportunities. He could have gone to Robert Owen's communistic experimental colony at New Harmony and worked for the excellent schooling which could have been had there. If he had made half the effort to get into the new Indiana University which he later made to get into public office his name would have been on the rolls before this. He might have gone after 1830 to Illinois, McKendrie, Shurtleff or Knox colleges. He made no effort to do so. Whatever the reasons, he had let these opportunities go by. When he was a boy he had seemed to have no initiative. Now that he was grown and could see the possible values of the opportunities he had missed he was afraid to go back to them. He did not dare to take himself out of the swim, to hide himself in the academic life. He wanted to be on hand for the gathering of the crop of good will which he had been sowing.

He felt that he must pound away at his rut, and keep himself ever in the public eye. And his good nature, his ability to mix with all kinds of people, pleasant and cross, kept him thoroughly in the public eye. So much so, indeed, that in 1834, the people of New Salem of both parties urged him to run as their candidate for the state legislature. He did not need urging, only to be convinced by his elders that the time was ripe.

His wide popularity in the county helped him immeasurably. This, ably seconded by a discreet failure to mention, during his campaign, anything about issues unattractive to the democrats—who by his silence had been led to become his supporters also—and by a realization that proper recognition of the principles of fair play in election brawls would be a popularizing asset, won for Abraham Lincoln his first political victory. There was little opposition. He was, it is true, suspected of having religious beliefs, if any, which had been soured from the cream of frontier orthodoxy by the lightnings of Thomas Paine's "Age of Reason" and Volney's "Ruins," but the voters did not care. They knew he was a good fellow. They believed he was intensely local in feeling, as indeed he was. They felt confident that he would trip up anyone monkeying with the interests of Sangamon County, though it were Andrew Jackson himself.

So Abraham, at twenty-five, was given the right to go from the dead village of New Salem to the mudhole town of Vandalia, the capital, there to represent a couple of thousand simple folk who, like himself, had little or no knowledge of or concern with any but local interests.

CHAPTER TWO

NEW FRIENDS AND OLD CONFLICTS

THE autumn of 1834 saw Abraham Lincoln's stock going up rapidly. After the election of early August he held three offices; that of postmaster of New Salem, that of Assistant Surveyor of Sangamon County, and that of Representative for his district in the General Assembly of Illinois, representing in that body the National Republican voters of his vicinity and also the Democrats. While the shackles were being removed from the slaves of the British Empire, Abraham was rattling his own and stepping out into public life with the very sincere and friendly backing of an important section of the people of Illinois behind him, the majority of whom were the descendants of immigrants from slave states.

Although his taste for serving people and making himself generally useful was indulged by his possession of three practical positions, the emoluments of those positions did not greatly fatten his purse. In fact, it was at this time that the law began to persecute him as a debtor. It took his horse and his surveying instruments to satisfy one of the notes which his confidence in his ability to be a storekeeper had induced him to give out, but which his taste for carelessness had prevented him from paying. This would have been an embarrassing situation for the Deputy County Surveyor had not one of his many ardent friends and supporters, James Short, bought in the equipment and returned it to him. But even with this kind aid there were moments when the thought of debt and deficit set up a burning in his veins.

That burning, however, did not consume the ambition which kept him forever at his books, studying the fundamentals of law, the tricks of surveying, or the outer edges of the world's philosophical opinion. Abraham had in some way picked up from his life in the dirt-floored cabins of his youth, the essentials of that attitude common to a society of relatively equal opportunity, namely the belief that a man's first duty is to improve his social condition. That he had not crystallized this belief before he came to New Salem is apparent from his neglect of the educational opportunities offered him up to that time, but in the last two years it had taken complete possession of him. Now, in the late summer of 1834, it seemed to be bearing fruit. At least he could now call himself, if he wished, the Honorable A. Lincoln.

The young man on the make is very likely, as a general rule, to associate with social improvement the idea of marriage. But in 1834 Abraham was in no position to consider marriage, even if intimate contact with girls had been easy for him, which it decidedly was not. There were plenty of girls in New Salem, and other young men seemed to find little or no difficulty in becoming engaged to them, but Lincoln was still reticent. The women with whom he did allow himself to associate, up to this time, were the matronly motherly type like Mrs. Hannah Armstrong, who would sew his trousers for him and make him shirts.

In the previous year Abraham had boarded in the tavern of James Rutledge, a log house of two rooms and loft, in which lived Mr. Rutledge and nine little Rutledge's, occupying space according to their ages, which ranged from four to twenty-five. Lincoln was one of several boarders who added to the household burdens of Ann Rutledge and her older sister, Mrs. Rutledge

having decided that it would be more profitable to keep house for
the bachelor James Short of Sand Ridge, than for her own dense
family at the Tavern.

In New Salem, quite unlike many other parts of the world,
the difference between the top and bottom of the social ladder
was negligible. The Rutledge's were poor, among the poorest,
and so was Lincoln, but except in so far as lack of circumstantial
dignity depressed them it cannot be said that they suffered from
their poverty. Everyone in New Salem worked hard and apparently thought little of it.

One of the other Rutledge boarders was wealthier than the
rest, having made several thousand dollars in the course of a
thrifty career among the log houses, by buying and selling land,
and by diligent use of a partnership in the only profitable store
in the neighborhood. This fellow-boarder of Lincoln's was John
McNamar of New York, who had come West to make enough
money for the transportation of the impoverished relatives whom
he intended to have follow him. In order that his family and
his family's creditors might not keep too close tabs upon him
and so interfere with the accumulation of sufficient cash, John
had passed in New Salem as John McNeil, an expedient not at
all uncommon among pioneers.

Ann Rutledge, a pretty blue-eyed girl of twenty, short and
plump, capable and vivacious, found time enough in the press
of her household duties to be interested in the promising young
man from New York, whose money and whose part owner-
ship of her father's farm must have enhanced his charms in her
eyes. Certainly she was willing, when John returned to New
York for his family, to consider herself engaged to marry him.

New York, however, was a long way off, and John McNamar
was no quicker than he might have been about making the trip.

He took a fever on the way, which delayed him several weeks, he had trouble with his father's creditors, and his father's ill-health delayed him still more. Furthermore, he either did not write or was the victim of the then common bad-luck attendant upon the use of the frontier mails. Certainly Ann got few letters from him and eventually none. When he returned to New Salem it was too late.

Even in a pioneer community a popular young girl must dislike the appearance of being jilted. Even frontier folk, without the economics of caste and credit to goad them may be tempted to the exciting meannesses of hint and gossip. The people of New Salem certainly did not hesitate to let Ann Rutledge know that they thought her catch had gotten away from her, and Ann, having in the shape of Samuel Hill, her fiancé's partner in merchandising, and in the distant awkwardness of the interested Abraham Lincoln, enough birds in the hand to make the bush seem of little consequence, was able to do some forgetting on her own account. It may have hurt her, but she managed it.

Abraham had never before in his life been thrown so closely into contact for so long a time with so appealing a girlish figure as Ann Rutledge. He had always been able to avoid girls before. He could not escape the constant presence of one who served him and lived day and night under the same roof with him. Then too, the sight of Ann's tenderness for John McNamar may have served for the first time to make him feel that a girl is neither a harpy nor an untouchable angel to the man who is the simple master of his own emotions. Perhaps he unconsciously felt that the bond of this young thing's engagement to his fellow-lodger, put her in the class with those more matronly figures whom he had dared to approach and to esteem. She, too, was set apart.

Whatever it was that loosened his tight grip upon himself,

it had begun to do its work during Abraham's period of boarding at the Rutledge Tavern, a brief period indeed, and followed by no immediate reversal of behavior. At first, in fact, it merely served to give the young and gawky frontiersman, more used to flatboats, axes, wrestling matches and grocery store comedy, than to the amenities of mixed society, a slightly different point of view toward women. It permitted him when he went to call on one of his fostering matrons, Mrs. Bennett Abell, to pay some attention to a large and stately young lady from Kentucky who was visiting in the Abell cabin, one of the kind whom Abraham would have, prior to his residence at the Hotel Rutledge, jumped through a window to escape. For Mary Owens, Mrs. Bennett Abell's sister, was no little china girl to pretend you didn't see. She was a woman of twenty-five, of more than average intelligence, and almost double the size of an Ann Rutledge. Furthermore, she dressed smartly, bringing to the lackadaisical village of New Salem such airs and graces as comparative wealth and educational advantages had given her the taste and means to adopt. If Ann Rutledge, the tavern-keeper's daughter represented for the novice Lincoln the appeal of shy, tender-hearted, red-lipped girlhood, Mary Owens, the blue-grass lady, represented the appeal of mundane, self-confident womanhood. Beyond the appeal of Ann Rutledge was the melting warmth of personal delight. Beyond the appeal of Mary Owens was the possibility of lifelong social elevation. About her hung some of the mystery of suavity and ease of manner to contrast with Ann's direct and undistinguished brightness.

Ann Rutledge was engaged to another man and Mary Owens appeared as definitely betrothed to a kind of life which marked her quite as plainly against the trespass of the uncouth pioneer. Miss Owens' first visit to New Salem was brief, thus removing her personage from the region of its influence upon Lincoln, but leaving behind her the waxing mystery of something not quite understood, which Abraham could not manage to believe was beyond him. The new-born concentration upon Ann Rutlerge which the departure of both Miss Owens and McNamar had effected did not at once swell with the richness of intimate devotion. The situation was a little indefinite. In fact, many of those who lived in close contact with Abraham and Ann were not aware that any sort of understanding existed between them. Everyone pitied Ann the loss of her lover John McNamar, of whom she had been genuinely fond. Everyone liked Abraham and surely would have been delighted to see him get a lovely and popular girl, but the noticeable lack of people who knew anything about his interest in Ann, seems to indicate that no one believed in Abraham's interest in girls. Later events made it seem probable that Abraham was none too confident of it himself.

In the midst of this mild and circumscribed courtship in that little backwoods village on the Sangamon, Abraham borrowed two hundred dollars from Coleman Smoot, saying that the loan was the natural consequence of that gentleman's having voted for him. He bought himself a sixty-dollar suit of clothes, and set out on the stagecoach for Vandalia, the capital and social hub of Illinois. For the first time in his ambitious young life, Abraham Lincoln could feel that he was dressed like a white man. It made him very gay to think of himself, as the stage rolled and creaked through the groves and prairies and over the rolling hills, bearing its uproarious company of legislators toward the well-stocked and expectant tipple-palaces which lined the west bank of the Kaskaskia River down to the southeast of New Salem.

For Abraham Lincoln this was the beginning of a new life, the launching of a vessel sister to that less proud flatboat which had stuck upon Cameron and Rutledge's milldam at New Salem in May of 1831, in the course of a voyage to New Orleans. That voyage had determined his residence during the last three years and a half and so had paved the way for this new outset. Abraham, not at all troubled by the fact that the new clothes he had on had merely added to his burden of debt and could not, by clothing him, make that burden more attractive, was buoyed up by the quadruple success of the past year. He had been made postmaster of New Salem and still held that simple office. He had been appointed, and he remained, Deputy Surveyor of Sangamon County. The people of the same county, Democrats and Republicans alike, had sent him to represent them in the Legislature. And, by no means least, he had been able to look at women for the first time with something not entirely filial in his eagerness. For the first time he had managed not to feel, as an accompaniment to the eagerness, a cold tightness about his heart and an unwilling lack of focus in his eyes. This accomplishment by no means ended for him the tyrannous reign of women over his mind and heart. It was merely a loosening of the sense of secret hurt which lived with him always, and which women were forever baiting.

It was enough to give him an unusual gaiety as he entered the muddy winter streets of dismal and miasmic Vandalia on its bluff between the foggy bottoms of the Kaskaskia and the swampy prairies of the West. The little town, with its ninety-odd houses, only two of which were not of wood, was crowded with legislators and their families, public officials in boots and long coats, lobbyists in wide hats, lawyers with their bags, horses, wagons, sheep, pigs, and all kinds of foot-encumbering fowl.

The streets were entirely unpaved and shin-deep in a mixture of mud and rubbish, the natural forage-ground of the local pork supply. Over this wallow of thoroughfares streamed the fluttering candlelight from taverns and liquor-groceries. There was an atmosphere of excited tension blowing about the town. Voices were brisk and loud on corners and in alleys. Everyone had a pet scheme and everyone else must hear of it and, having heard, must go and have a drink. Here were the forces of pioneer life gathering together for their double attack; the one, forward upon the undeveloped resources of their state, the other, back against the strongholds of position and privilege.

Abraham went the rounds with his Sangamon contingent thrilled, though not in consequence of the astounding flow of liquor, by the spectacle of all these ambitious, scheming, powerful folk, roaring their welcome to a newcomer in the trade of politics. Like many a more experienced legislator he did not understand what it was all about, but he felt an exuberant realization of the glorious tumult of his connection with it. This was what men were best at, and he particularly. Everything about him was quickened and heightened. He could feel his powers overriding the lack of confidence which his financial and emotional difficulties kept nourishing.

A stone's throw from the capital, great trees were still crashing down under the frantic weight of hordes of wild pigeons. Panthers slipped furtively and massively through the thickets, performing their brutal economy as yet unthreatened. Everywhere was wilderness, the rivers undeveloped, the soil barely turned, the villages mere camps. Across this wilderness came, as yet, little of the manufactured products of the eastern seaboard. There was cloth, there was liquor, there were shoes, utensils, books, foodstuffs, but for the most part, liquor being a notable exception, these things came in small quantities, and makeshifts for them were contrived before the hearth of many a pioneer cabin. The wind of organized industry had not yet risen in Illinois and the legislators gathered in Vandalia in December, 1834, could not have dreamed of the sure internal evolution of a new social and political force which was going on in the mills and manufactories of the Middle Atlantic and New England states. If any one of them did realize the changing status of the free workman and the free employer in that region he gave it no more thought than Illinois as a whole was, at that time, giving to slavery, which for all practical purposes was no thought at all.

Not that agitation against slavery had not taken on importance. It had for many decades been a lively source of debate, one which had engaged the attention of the pre-Revolutionary colonists and which was by no means dead forty years after the founding of the republic. But those who believed in the abolition of slavery and were willing to say so in public were still confined to the ranks of those Wilberforcian moralists whose tractable mind's eyes could be focussed exclusively upon one side of a question.

William Lloyd Garrison, that curiously passionate messiah, driven by the occlusive belief that slavery was not, merely, an unfortunate survival of primitive social conditions, but a fearful crime, taking to himself as best an Anglo-Saxon can, the rôle of anarchist, had founded the *Liberator* in 1831, eventually coming to advocate repudiation of the Constitution and dissolution of the Union. Garrison's fervent and radical paper attempted, with small but far-reaching success to inject into public life and political activity the biblical moralities which were dear to the heart of its founder, even if terribly confusing to the decent and sincere

southern slaveholder. Garrison, although his paper had practically no circulation at first, was so vehement that he frightened
the great mass of unfanatical northerners and angered and disgusted the greater part of the South. His influence therefore had,
even as early as 1834, done a great deal to keep the question of
abolition alive and to put it into politics. Furthermore, although
he was unwilling to admit that anyone else could be as firm and
sincere about the matter as he was himself, he had companions
of only a little less colorful frenzy.

Although the North, therefore, carried these nettles in its
pocket and had to be careful how it walked, and the South
could not swallow its rage entirely, the western states, for their
part, believed that there were more important things, and that
slavery would take care of itself. They had been interested in
President Jackson's amazingly firm hand held up in 1832 to
restrain South Carolina, not because South Carolina was a slave
state, nor because of the injury done that state by the tariff of
1828, which was sugar to the industrial North, but only salt to
the wounds of the slave states. What interested them in Old
Hickory's Nullification stand, was the matter of its bearing upon
the rights of individual states. They took great pride in their
sectional importance as foundation stones under the future
American life. And they did not want slavery to be a distraction.
Therefore, when they could, they ignored it.

When Abraham Lincoln entered upon his duties as a member
of the Ninth General Assembly of the State of Illinois on December 1st, 1834, he had never, to any living person, made a
single expression of opinion as to the rightness or wrongness of
the institution which was the basis of the social organization
not only of his native state Kentucky, but of little less than half
of the people of the American nation. Abraham was tender-

hearted, with that timidity which goes with emotional reticence. He had a certain humility. "Why should the spirit of mortal be proud?" became a favorite quotation with him. It is not unlikely, therefore, that even at this time he regarded slavery as an unfortunate arrangement between employer and employed. Even this, however, is uncertain, as he had seen slaves in chains being shipped down the Ohio River and had noted particularly that they were the happiest people on the boat. It was not all a soul-searing cruelty, then, although in 1837 he was able to speak of the institution as an injustice.

Even if he did have misgivings about the position of the Negro he had an excellent sense of how to keep himself in the public eye and he must have known that there was no use whatever of making an issue of something to which his public was so indifferent. Although his silence on the subject of slavery may have been due to an unconscious gesture of his extraordinary genius for perceiving current mouth-and-ear values, Abraham's failure to talk about other more fundamental issues was neither due to tact or inadvertence.

Abraham Lincoln saw the world outward from New Salem, through Vandalia and Springfield, not in the bird's-eye view of time and space which would have let him see how man's need to sustain himself makes of society what hunger makes of the individual man, a hand for grasping and a mouth for taking in food, and how, this being the case, control of the sources of material supply, not hope nor ideal, nor golden rule, is the circumstance which determines the course of a nation's development. In 1834 railroads were still in their swaddling clothes, although their development must have been foreseen by anyone with a mind apt for the problems of national rather than local progress. Abraham, admiring the idea, thought them too expensive, and recommended the all but impossible task of making the Sangamon River navigable.

What the new Representative could not see, was the tremendous effect of certain natural accidents and contingencies along the developing course of American life. Agriculture was still the prime concern of the majority of Americans, and most westerners still thought of human life as essentially an agricultural system. But in the East, across the Alleghanies, things were happening to that system. In the very year of 1834 a new process in the smelting of iron was devised which increased the output of furnaces by almost half. This combined with the recent devices by means of which steam had turned out to be capable of hauling vehicles on rails, all of which required iron in their preparation, immediately set the finger of popular interest pointing at the production of that natural metal, and toward the possibilities of its use to increase the wealth which resulted from manufacturing. For the railroad could be extended more rapidly with a more rapid production of iron, and the extension of it would automatically extend the markets for factory products.

In the background, behind this new instrument of commerce, hovered darkly the cloud which was before very long to resolve itself into a storm of change. It was soon to become apparent that you could not build railroads without money. Where was the money to come from? At first everyone thought that the states, perhaps assisted by the Federal Government, would provide it. But it soon became apparent that there was great possibility of private gain in the financing of railroads and like developments. It was not long before those powerful individuals who recognized the fact and had the means to act upon their recognition, were scheming to keep that gain from being diverted into the impersonal maw of state and federal treasuries. And their schemes were greatly aided by the existence of that perpetually rancorous conflict between the state and the nation which divided the people into those who wanted the Federal Government strengthened at the expense of the state and those who did not. The people, trying to escape the fangs of one wolf were prepared to invite another to attend them.

CHAPTER THREE

THE TENDED TREE BEARS FRUIT

THE United States of America, in pursuit of what was then believed to be their "manifest destiny," were, in the fourth decade of the nineteenth century, hacking away at the great mass of unsettled savage land to their west. Their cutting edge was sickle-shaped, its deepest concavity being at the Mississippi side of western Illinois and its horns running through Arkansas to Texas and through Iowa to Wisconsin. Illinois was then the driving point of advance, where the speed was least but the force very great. Here it was that the two streams of westward migration were meeting and consolidating for further advance. The southern stream, coming from Virginia, Kentucky and Tennessee, had been the first to flow, but the development of the Erie Canal in northern New York and the progress of steam navigation on the great lakes had made it possible for a second or northern current to set in.

In the middle of this decade, the population of Illinois consisted chiefly of pioneers of southern birth. The French of Vincennes and Kaskaskia were on the wane, having scarcely outlasted their entertainment of the Marquis de Lafayette in 1824. The Yankee and the Pennsylvanian had as yet not put in an appearance in anything like force. It was natural, therefore, that the eighty-one members of the Ninth General Assembly of the State of Illinois should have been mostly men of the southern tradition. It is true that most of them had outgrown, if they had ever known, the influences of that southern economy which, under John C. Calhoun, had been making things warm for President Jackson, but they were none the less men who had neither understanding of nor use for the state of mind of the more commercial New Englander. They were building up within themselves a new point of view, neither southern nor northern.

At ten o'clock in the morning of December 1st, 1834, rubbing elbows and exchanging pleasantries with his fifty-four fellow members of the lower house, Abraham Lincoln entered the dilapidated two-story brick capitol at Vandalia and was born into political life, a life that was destined never again to take its shackles from his brain.

Those who ten years before had built the curious edifice in which Lincoln now found himself, milling about with his more experienced but little less excited companions, had built in the true pioneer tradition of living in the minute. They had built profitably but not too well. Now from musty and leak-tarnished ceilings the plaster was flaking off upon the head and the home-spun of the lawmakers who transacted their business beneath it. Bricks were loose in the walls and the floors creaked and sagged under heavy feet until it seemed that the cement of tobacco juice and fallen candle wax was the only thing that kept them from going down. The winter wind from the river bottoms shook at loose window-panes and generally contrived to make its way through them.

Yet, scarcely conscious of this dilapidation, and unwilling to lend his name to any measures for improvement (he voted against a proposition to rent a better room than the all but un-tenable one in which the Council of Revision did its work) sat Abraham Lincoln, taking everything in with the eagerness of a child asked to help hold the hose at a fire. He took his cue, in voting, from Major John Stuart, leader of the Sangamon County delegation and one of the leading Whigs of the state. He was, being a neophyte, consoled by the gift of a place on the most unimportant Committee in the House, that on Public Accounts and Expenditures, a position which, if the honor did not turn his head, must have made the young man feel a bit sheepish, remembering his own sadly confused accounts and expenditures.

Aside from the more or less perfunctory business of recording his vote on measures brought up by his colleagues, Abraham's chief business during this session of the Illinois Legislature was that of watching, listening, and of weighing and balancing what he saw and heard of men and their opinions, of indications of strength and weakness in the lines of parties. He saw how important to the westerner was the question of the public lands, those tracts which had, even before the adoption of the Constitution, been entrused to the care of the government set up by the Articles of Confederation. Devoted follower of Henry Clay as Abraham was, he must have been puzzled to read of the attitude on this very question of Clay's New England colleague, Daniel Webster. Webster, in Congress, at Washington, shortly before, in that magnificent piece of rhetoric which ended, "Liberty and Union, now and forever, one and inseparable," had supported a bill to restrict the sale of public lands, abolish the public lands survey, and practically to put a stop to the easy drift of potential labor into the freedom of the West. Webster was reflecting the sentiments of industrial Massachusetts.

Whatever Abraham thought of this curious paradox expounded at Washington, he did, in January of 1835, introduce a measure in the Illinois House of Representatives, suggesting that

the Illinois members of the National Congress be instructed to
plead for an annual payment to their state of twenty per cent
of the proceeds of the sale of public lands lying within the boundaries of the state. He was trying to advance a pawn which might
be used to checkmate any later opposition to the schemes of
internal improvement which he had in mind. But, unfortunately,
none of Abraham's colleagues paid any attention to his motion.
It was promptly laid upon the table, and he himself had the
good sense to forget it. Perhaps, when the Federal Government
did divide among the states the surplus resulting from its sale
of lands thus paving the way, by over-inflation, for the panic of
1837, Abraham was glad of what had happened.*

During Lincoln's attendance in that enthusiastic school of
the politician, he got his first real inkling of the import of
various national issues, chief among them that poisonous matter
of the National Bank. For a gentleman from Madison County,
a staunch Democrat and an ardent supporter of President Jackson, introduced resolutions favoring Jackson's punitive attitude
toward the Bank bogey man. These resolutions immediately
started a furious wrangle in the House, to which Abraham listened in considerable bewilderment, such bewilderment indeed
that his votes on the various motions involved were confused and
even contradictory. He was trying very hard to consider the
matter, which he was fundamentally unable to understand, in
the light of party alignment. When party alignment was not
clear neither was Abraham. His confused voting was not nearly
so important as the schooling he got in the various methods of
seeking and wielding political advantage, both within the actual
confines of the House and in the all-important lobby outside,

* References to Lincoln's career in the Illinois Legislature are from the Journals of
the Illinois House of Representatives and from Beveridge, Albert J. Abraham Lincoln.
Vol. I.

where a man's talk was unrestricted, and always loud enough to make the candle flames tremble, and to shake more plaster from the ceilings.

The crowded and happy six weeks of this first session of the Ninth General Assembly of Illinois did much to set Abraham Lincoln on the course which he was to follow for the next twenty years, many of whose incidents he was afterwards to look back upon with annoyance, shame and dismay. The first step in that course, when the Legislature adjourned on the 13th of February, 1835, was a return to New Salem, which was like returning to a bread crumb after a dream of cake. Abraham was to miss the talk, the sense of action, the color and excitement of those days in Vandalia and to realize that New Salem was no longer large enough to hold a rising young politician who was making friends among the men of importance in his state and who had begun to make the attitudes and tricks of legislative procedure a part of his way of looking at things. Perhaps, as he rode in the stagecoach back to his all but motionless post office, to his surveying instruments and his relatively unimportant village friends, he looked back with a little shudder half of pride and half of misgiving at the boy that he had been, the untutored son of an uneasy and impoverished frontiersman, the frightened but adoring son of a mother with a past. He wondered a great deal about Nancy Hanks, his mother, who had died when he was only nine. When the twenty-six-year old legislator, in his Springfield tailored suit of clothes, returned to the town which had given him the opportunity to climb out of his past, he found himself believing that mixed with the darkness of his mother's birth must have been the fact that no common man like Thomas Lincoln had given him his character. Well, he thought, there must be no slipping back. The candlelight from the cabins of New Salem, coming around the bend of the wagon track, meant hard, unpleasant work for him. For he had now committed himself more surely than ever to the belief that his political future would be greatly helped by a mastering of the principles of law. For it was obvious, at this stage of American life, that the only great reputations had been made by military leaders, preachers, and finally lawyers. Abraham's experiences as a Captain of volunteers in the Black Hawk "war" of 1832, had convinced him that the military life was not always a sure way to immediate fame, and he had no taste whatever for the ways of the preacher. He had bought a copy of Blackstone's "Commentaries" at an auction. To the law, therefore, being sufficiently urged by friends who recognized how valuable his sense of human values would be in a court room, the young man had turned. And now his return to New Salem must mean a period of terrific study, of Blackstone and other books lent him by John Stuart, in order that he might master the fundamentals of the profession in the quickest possible time. The amazing abundance of lawyers on the frontier did not trouble him at all, for if there were sometimes as many as a dozen to every five hundred settlers, there was an unlimited expanse of land in the offing upon which these settlers had their eyes. And wherever there was land, if men were to dispute title of it with root and rock and neighbor, there must be law, great quantities of the barbed-wire mesh of legality.

This new enterprise was pleasant only because of what it promised for his career. Abraham never enjoyed hard work, though he knew how to get it done and he had no enthusiasm for the law, as such. But the study took some of the flat taste from the draughts of New Salem, which for ten months he had to swallow. But a still greater bubble was provided by his increasing interest in Ann Rutledge. Abraham was actually beginning to find himself emotionally involved. John McNamar was still away in New York, and his correspondence with his New Salem fiancée had ceased. Abraham ought to know. He was the postmaster. If there had been a letter it would have been his hat that carried it out to Sand Ridge, where the troubled Ann was then living.

No letter came, Ann, wanting Abraham, still remembered John. She was afraid to give him up, afraid that the next creak of cart wheels might be under his return to claim her. And yet he had not written her in over a year. Surely that gave her something like release. Abraham was not sure whether it did or not, but he gave Ann to understand that if she could consider her engagement to McNamar broken she might consider something like an engagement to Lincoln begun. Not to take effect immediately. He would have to get himself made a lawyer first. That would mean income, which was necessary. And Ann should have an opportunity of going to the Woman's College at Jacksonville. These conditions were a soothing restraint upon the importunities of Abraham's highly emotional nature. They let him want the girl without fearing that he was yet entirely lost in the want. They left a loophole for him, a thing which, later experiences show, it was almost instinctive in him to provide. In the spring of 1835 he did not know how severely he was to be punished for his caution.

Abraham was now busier than he had been at any previous time. He had the small and scarcely exacting duties of his postmastership, his surveying, his need to read the papers carefully in order to know what was going on in the state and what was to be expected of him at the next session of the legislature, if there should be one. He had the constant bother of the difficult principles of law crying to be got into his capacious but none too ready skull. By no means least, though he may not have realized it, was the unaccustomed strain put upon every bit of him by his increasing devotion to Ann Rutledge. A young man who has held himself aloof from girls, who has even cultivated what he supposed to be a positive and honest distaste for them, cannot come off unscathed when he feels the hard bud of that distaste melting and ripening into the unexpected flower of consent.

Abraham did not come off unscathed. His health suffered and made the work he had to do seem almost too hard to bear. And when Ann Rutledge fell ill of one of those malignant fevers which oppress the dwellers in simplicity when muggy summers come upon them, it must have seemed to Lincoln that he was being made the victim of some distinct and painful persecution. No one will ever know what moments of self-blame and agony he had, thinking, perhaps, that Ann's illness must be due to his importunities upon her unsettled heart. No one will ever know how he may have thought that as his mother, whom he had worshipped, was taken away from him just when he had begun to fear a cabin without her in it, so was Ann Rutledge, at the height of his need of her, being threatened. It looked a little as if Abraham's love was fatal to its object.

In August Ann died, and for a time neither friends, nor law, nor transit, nor postoffice, could get any use out of him. Abraham was beside himself. Some thought that he had gone mad, some that he was just sick. Abraham kept to himself, and the darknesses kept at him like knives. It was ambition that brought him back, with the help of a little rest, and the sympathetic ministration of those few friends who came as near as anyone could to understanding him. He spent two weeks in the cabin of Bowling Green, whose wife tended him as if he had been a child.

The Gentleman from Sangamon County (Lincoln in 1848)

Mrs. Green's tender care made it in time possible for the call of Abraham's eagerness to get on to be heard in him. Back to the village he went, albeit sadly. And his sadness, made so much more depressing by the difficulty of commanding the energy required to do anything, wandered about among the cabins with him, making many of his friends marvel at the change in him. That comparatively few knew of his involvement with Ann must have exposed him not a little to quips and questions that hurt deeply. That even some members of Ann's family doubted the girl's preference for him must have been the bitterest circumstance of all. No one could realize that Ann or no Ann, Abraham's condition was the result of a crisis, physical if not spiritual, just that sort of crisis which no one ever understands to be taking place in a young man.

From this crisis Abraham must have learned something, but whatever things he learned, a knowledge of what women meant to him was not among them. One might have thought that after this tragic incident, as the gigantic figure in its flat soft hat went about wiping the hot dust of New Salem alleys from its cheeks, it would have been resolving into definite arrangement the elements of the tragedy which had taken place. But Abraham could not do that. He was still too insecure, too frightened, and not quite square enough with himself. To everyone else in New Salem he was "Honest" Abe, but to his own heart he was, like many men, deceitful and shifty. And that lack of honesty with himself was to put him through the hoops of another mildly bitter experience in the course of the very next summer.

Meanwhile the months which followed the death of Ann Rutledge and Abraham's collapse were passing by. There was little in them to bring cheer to the young law-student. There was nothing but the now unsweetened business of delivering and

receiving mail, reading people's newspapers before they called
for them at the office, surveying, holding the chain and staring
off across the fields, reading Blackstone, eating and sleeping at
Henry Onstott's tavern—the very tavern where he had first seen
Ann—trying to live up to his gladly earned reputation as a wit
and a master of repartee, talking with everyone and thinking that
there was no longer anything to find out.

This painful existence was terminated in December by a call
from Governor Duncan for an extra session of the Legislature.
Once more Abraham journeyed to Vandalia, perhaps never in
his life so glad of an excuse to move, so glad to have public things
intrude upon his private bewilderment. Perhaps there was a little
bitterness in his approach to the public threshold of the tumble-
down capitol at Vandalia. Abraham had many friends in Springfield, among whom was his political adviser, John Todd Stuart.
Major Stuart was bent upon getting the state capital removed
from Vandalia to Springfield in the interests of Sangamon
County, whose merchants and farmers and professional men
would greatly benefit by the change. It was easy to enlist Abraham's support for this measure.

There was to be a presidential election in 1836, and the question of a continuation of Andrew Jackson's policies would then
be put before the people. The people of Sangamon County had
now become thoroughly Whig, and would oppose the candidacy of Martin Van Buren, but the Democrats were planning
to put resolutions through the House of Representatives which
should indicate the sentiments of the State of Illinois and thus
aid in the national campaign. These resolutions, together with
the Democratic idea of party conventions, which the Whigs, in
a rather unimaginative remembrance of General Washington's
opinion, regarded with loathing, and the business of planting

seeds which should sprout into a crop of votes in favor of the removal of the capital to Springfield when the next General Assembly came to vote on it, were sufficient to keep Abraham Lincoln busy and to take his mind off his troubles and uncertainties.

Abraham, now beginning to realize the power of party alignment as compared with the doubtful value of alignments due to personal friendship, voted automatically for every Whig resolution and against every Democratic motion which had the earmarks of party about it. The plaster of political adherence, which had been poured into him by his friends and his Sangamon County contacts, was beginning to harden. He and Stuart, very shrewdly however, supported measures favorable to other counties whenever the bringing of such a measure to roll call gave them an opportunity to show that it was their votes which had helped. These were some of the seeds which should be asked to contribute their grain when the voting on the removal of the capital to the seat of Sangamon County was taken up.

Thus was Abraham learning to pull an oar in the political boat. He saw how others manipulated the sweep and found no difficulty in appropriating to himself the tricks and the wiles of the experienced.

When the extra session of the General Assembly was adjourned in February, 1836, Abraham returned to New Salem in a frame of mind much better than that in which he had left it the previous December. He was beginning to feel like a man of importance. Sangamon County was going Whig very rapidly, so Lincoln's judgment in casting his lot with that party was vindicated. Furthermore, it was going so strongly Whig that in the 1836 election it would not matter that he had lost, by his spoken attitude in the legislature, the Democratic support which the astute silences of his previous campaign had gained for him. He was beginning to hold political opinions of his own. He had become something of a leader out of the fullness of his original willingness to be led. At least, when the election of 1836 came around, he made the remarkable statement that, "I go for all sharing the privileges of government who assist in bearing its burdens. Consequently, I go for admitting all whites to the right of suffrage who pay taxes or bear arms (by no means excluding females)." *

Abraham was elected, without a struggle, save for an encounter at secondhand with Colonel Robert Allen, who passed through New Salem, remarking as he went that he knew facts which if made public would make it impossible for either Lincoln or his fellow Whig, Ninian W. Edwards, to be elected by the people of the county. Abraham immediately, on hearing of this underhanded attack, came out with a public letter to the Colonel, in which was manifest that straightforward squareness which characterized most of his contacts with the public. Colonel Allen made no answer and thus lost the point of his attack. Lincoln received the largest number of votes of any county candidate. In September he put in his application for a license to practice law.

As Major John T. Stuart, the former Whig leader of the House of Representatives, had not been a candidate for reëlection, being busy with an attempt to get himself sent to the National Congress, Abraham now found himself in the position of floor leader of the Whig party in the lower house of the General Assembly of Illinois. He had said in the course of a campaign talk, "I desire to live, and I desire place and distinction as a politician." Now, recovering from his emotional setback of the previous

* Works, Vol. I, p. 131.

summer, he was very much alive; subject, it is true, to more than usually frequent spells of moodiness, but none the less full of life and determination. And the election of 1836 brought him to the threshold of place and distinction as a politician. But the outward elation with which he was now filled was again to lead him into difficulties. Difficulties which, because of the protecting scar upon his earlier wound, were to hurt him less than the earlier ones, but which were to humiliate him in a way calculated to bring out the undeveloped and unhappy childhood in his heart.

Mary Owens, the Kentucky belle, had returned to New Salem to visit her sister Mrs. Abell. It might have been supposed that Lincoln, having become acquainted with Ann Rutledge and Mary Owens at about the same time and having shown more interest in Ann, would have thought of the impressive and genteel Miss Owens with some distaste after the other's death. But the fact is that to the people of New Salem it appeared that Lincoln was now smitten with the idea of Mary Owens. Abraham himself admitted that he had told Mrs. Abell that if she would get her sister back to New Salem he would marry her. Ann Rutledge was not long in her grave, and there were tongues ready to wag, even in deprecation of the conduct of so true a local hero as Abraham. Abraham was certainly caught up in the meshes of a definite interest in the stately Kentucky girl. Twice he asked her to marry him and twice she put him off. Mary was no fool, and she had seen this lanky suitor very intimately during the summer of 1836. She found that he was, as she phrased it, "deficient in those little links which make up the chain of woman's happiness." She believed in the cult of polish and refinement. Abraham knew nothing of either, however golden might be his heart.

When the Legislature convened at Vandalia in December, Lincoln had to leave New Salem with the sting of his lady's repeated rejection of him clinging like a burr to the otherwise fair surface of his prospects. He must have realized that an inability to be convincing in his proposals, due to the fact that although enamored of Miss Owens he was also afraid of giving over his life to a woman, would be bound to leave him as it had left him, an ardent friend, but a rejected suitor. And it was one thing to feel cautious when that noticeable young woman was in the same village, within easy reach of him, but in the womanless atmosphere of the Vandalia State House, calm reason was a horse of another color. If he had hoped that his absence would stimulate Mary to more interest in him he was disappointed. She did not even write.

For a week Abraham indulged himself in the protective self-pity due a man who does not feel very well. Then he had to do something. He wrote:

Vandalia, December 13, 1836.

Mary:—I have been sick ever since my arrival, or I should have written sooner. It is but little difference, however, as I have very little even yet to write. . . . And more, the longer I can avoid the mortification of looking in the post office for your letter and not finding it, the better. You see I am mad about that old letter yet. I'll try you once more, anyhow.

The new State House is not yet finished, and consequently the legislature is doing little or nothing. The governor delivered an inflammatory political message, and it is expected there will be some sparring between the parties about it, as soon as the two houses get to business. . . .

Our chance to take the seat of government to Springfield is better than I expected. An internal-improvement convention was held here since we met, which recommended a loan of several millions of dollars, on the faith of the state, to construct railroads. Some of the legislature are for it, and some against it; which has the majority I cannot tell. There is great strife and struggling for the office of United States Senator here at this time. It is probable we shall ease the pains in a few days. The opposition men have no candidate of their own, and consequently they will smile as complacently at the angry snarl of the contending Van Buren candidates and their respective friends as the Christian does at Satan's rage. You recollect that I mentioned at the outset of this letter that I had been unwell. That is the fact, though I believe I am about well now; but that, with other things I cannot account for, have conspired, and have gotten my spirits so low that I feel I would rather be any place in the world than here. I really cannot endure the thought of staying here ten weeks. Write back as soon as you get this, and, if possible, say something that will please me, for I really have not been pleased since I left you. This letter is so dry and stupid that I am ashamed to send it, but with my present feelings I cannot do any better.

Give my best respects to Mr. and Mrs. Able and family.

Your friend,
LINCOLN.*

That was not exactly a letter to precipitate a woman's doubting mind. It did not change the situation between Abraham and Mary Owens. But the Legislature was soon able to get down to business in earnest and to involve Abraham's troubled mind to a point which could, at least temporarily, exclude the thought of women.

* Works, Vol. I, p. 133.

CHAPTER FOUR

A JUGGLER HAS HIS HANDS FULL

A THOUSAND miles from Vandalia, in a flourishing if crowded and unattractive city of the Atlantic seaboard, serious events were brewing. The merchants of New York, finding themselves upon a receding wave of illusory prosperity, had begun to see a different kind of breaker ahead. The year 1836 had been of a deceiving glitter to the financial world. Everywhere in the nation, this mirage had spread. The Federal Government, having made the naïve mistake of paying off its national debt, even felt so expansive that it began to divide up the surplus revenue from the sale of public lands and to return it proportionately to the states, a thing which in the previous year Abraham Lincoln had hoped to see come about. The Treasury Department gleefully persuaded itself that nothing could prevent an annual surplus of many millions of dollars, but the last installment due the states was never paid. These were drops in the wave upon which the merchants and financiers of the country had chosen to ride.

Everywhere in the nation this amazing overconfidence was as much in evidence as the exuberant breath of whisky was among the gentlemen at the Illinois capital. Nor were the members of the General Assembly of Illinois, free from the more abstract stimulant. At Vandalia, measures were introduced, and passed providing for the borrowing of millions of dollars on the state's credit, for the undertaking of railroads, canals and other internal improvements all on the grandest imaginable scale, with scarcely a trace of orderly plan. In order to secure the votes of counties whose natural features would exclude them from the benefit of the millennial schemes propounded, it was agreed to pay into the treasuries of those counties two hundred thousand dollars each, in cash. Cash! Why, said the ardent legislators, hiccoughing into their handkerchiefs or coming in from the nearest bar, the bankers of Europe and America will fall over one another in their eagerness to lend the golden state of Illinois money which everyone must be certain will pay at least ten per cent. Men in the lobby with their glasses in their hands could prove that the state could afford to borrow a hundred thousand dollars for internal improvements and never notice it at all. Those mild, if careful, members of the Vandalia madhouse who objected that for a state whose citizens could not for the most part even support their families it was a little indelicate to suggest the making of waterways where even "nature had never attempted it," were shouted down immediately. Nothing could stop the onrush now. The Illinois Internal Improvement Act was passed, saddling upon the state a burden of debt and disgrace from which it took many years to recover. Abraham Lincoln's vote had helped to pass it, though it would have passed even if he had voted "no."

And in New York City, frantic business men worked late behind their oil lamps and candles, in the little gabled brick offices of the lower city. They were trying to figure out that the crash which had begun to seem inevitable, might, like the prosperity of the year before, be merely a mirage. The drays rattled on the cobbles outside their windows, the masts and spars of ships loading and unloading made a fine tracery against the sky at the end of every island street. Warehouses were piled high with goods. But in the books, it was written what the element of time could do. All this potential wealth could not liquidate itself rapidly enough. The value of goods in warehouses shrank like Alice after eating the cake. The momentum of expansion had been too great, and the machine of commerce had not kept pace with it. Right and left the blows fell. Merchants in the metropolis failed for more than a hundred million dollars in a few weeks. The contagion of panic spread throughout the country. The banks began to suspend specie payment, the government, which in the previous year had issued an order insisting that federal revenues from the sale of public lands be paid only in specie, found now that it had no revenues to collect, there being no specie at large. And the national treasury was as empty as Mother Hubbard's cupboard. Several states even went so far as to repudiate their financial obligations, thus still further weakening the all but defunct public credit.

But in Vandalia, with bonfires and whisky and champagne and glasses clattering against walls and ceilings, and brilliant encomiums issuing from the majority of mouths, the panic was as yet unnoticed. The Internal Improvement Act was passed. There were grave protests, from many of Lincoln's friends, in fact; men who saw the trouble that was in store, but even the governor's veto could do nothing, such was the intricate play of bargain and advantage among the greedy citizens of Illinois.

It was at this time that the question of slavery thrust itself into unavoidable notice for the first time since Abraham Lincoln had entered public life. William Lloyd Garrison's *Liberator,* small as its circulation was, had aroused considerable storm both North and South. Abolitionists were making trouble in many places, though in small numbers, aided by a wholesale propaganda of pamphlets and pictures. The southern states saw danger to the union if such things were allowed to go on. They would

not answer for the results of the wrath which might be aroused
by the fanatics of the North. Feeling that something should be
done about it, the South passed resolutions and forwarded them
to the states of the North, where they were received with almost
universal sympathy. Indeed the majority of northern states trans-
mitted messages of good will in reply. The Governor of Illinois
placed before his legislature such of these resolutions as had come
to his notice.

In this form, therefore, was brought before the young Whig
floorleader a compendium of national opinion on the subject
of slavery and the rising agitation against it. Abraham must have
studied these resolutions, presenting as they did all points of
view from mere slick side-stepping to outspoken sympathy with
the trials of the states whose social system was based upon the
institution of slavery. He must have seen that not from any state
in the union had there come or was there likely to come at that
time, any statement of support for the violence and fanaticism of
the abolitionist. When the state of Illinois passed resolutions
condemning abolitionists and national interference with state
rights, in its General Assembly, under Abraham's very nose, he
must have known what he thought.

But Abraham Lincoln in January, 1837, was busy with something else. Under the watchful eye of the lobbying John T.
Stuart, as crafty a politician as you could have found in the
West, he was arranging his strings and his puppets for the play
which at that time meant everything to him. He had apparently
determined to identify himself with the future of the Whig city
of Springfield, and his one concern during this session was to
see that the Democratic Legislature was induced to vote for the
location of the new state capital in that Whig stronghold. That
was no mean task, and the fact that Abraham managed it suc-

cessfully, in spite of powerful and aggressive influences from other cities, well illustrates how much he had learned of the tricks of parliamentary and unparliamentary manipulation in the course of his brief experience as a law-maker.

So deeply concerned was Lincoln with this one issue, that during the entire first session of the Tenth General Assembly, every vote he made on every motion or resolution had a bearing on the result of the final vote on the location of the state capital. He took no part in the debate on the Internal Improvement Bill, although he voted for it, and for many side issues calculated to make other counties indebted to him for his vote. He said nothing in opposition to the Democratic resolutions supporting the Jackson Administration although he voted against them. He said nothing in opposition to the House's resolutions of sympathy with the South which declared that abolition societies were a menace, that the Constitution of the United States guaranteed to the southern states the right to hold slaves, that these states could not be deprived of that right without their consent, and that the Federal Government could not, without breach of faith, abolish slavery in the District of Columbia without the consent of its citizens. Abraham said nothing at this time, although he was one of six of the eighty-three voting members of the General Assembly to vote against their adoption. Until the capital of Illinois had been safely determined by vote of that same Assembly, he was not going to say anything to stir up a distracting fight.

Abraham, with his eye always upon the favors of Springfield, his future home, did rise once, when the State Bank at Springfield was the subject of attack. His friends were closely connected with the bank, and he could not allow any reflection upon it or upon Springfield to go unchallenged. And in the course of the sarcastic speech which he made on this occasion Abraham took pains to mention by name and to flatter with honorable suggestion, the officers of the Springfield Bank and the twenty-four leading men of the state who had had charge of the apportionment of the bank's stock. In this manner did the former strong boy of New Salem, pave the way for his career as a lawyer in the rising city of Springfield.

Late in February, almost at the close of the legislative session, Abraham's tender offices on behalf of Springfield bore fruit. The terrible waste of bargaining which had been indulged in had thrown the balance on the young Whig leader's side, and the voting went his way. Springfield was to be the new capital. A few days later, Abraham's. business having been triumphantly concluded, and there being nothing now to prevent the consideration of other matters, he and Dan Stone, a fellow representative from the County of Sangamon, in which Springfield was located, presented to the House of Representatives of the State of Illinois, the following protest against the resolutions of sympathy with the slave-holding states which had been adopted by the General Assembly six weeks before, with neither Stone nor Lincoln doing more than voting "nay."

March 3, 1837.

Resolutions upon the subject of domestic slavery having passed both branches of the General Assembly at its present session, the undersigned hereby protest against the passage of the same.

They believe that the institution of slavery is founded on both injustice and bad policy, but that the promulgation of abolition doctrines tends rather to increase than to abate its evils.

They believe that the Congress of the United States has no power under the Constitution to interfere with the institution of slavery in the different States.

They believe that the Congress of the United States has the power under the Constitution, to abolish slavery in the District of Columbia, but that the power ought not to be exercised, unless at the request of the people of the district.

The difference between these opinions and those contained in the said resolutions is their reason for entering this protest.

DAN STONE
A. LINCOLN.

Representatives from the County of Sangamon.*

Whatever the differences which Abraham and his colleague had in mind and which seemed to them sufficient to warrant the making of this protest six weeks after the resolutions against which it protested, to the impartial observer at this late day they seem extremely slight. The original resolutions stated that the Constitution guaranteed slavery to the slave states, whereas Abraham and Daniel did not affirm anything quite so definite, and the protest of the gentlemen from Sangamon did style the institution of slavery an injustice and a bad policy, although qualifying that designation by stating that advocacy of the abolition of slavery was worse. It is hard to escape the conclusion that Lincoln and Stone presented this protest merely in fulfillment of some political promise, possibly connected with the securing of votes in favor of making Springfield the capital. It is not probable, however, that Lincoln would have signed a protest calling slavery an injustice unless he had believed it to be so. And although there must have been many other members of the General Assembly who would have agreed with him, there were none, other than his Sangamon colleague, who could be induced to say so publicly. Lincoln did say so, although he waited until

* Works, Vol. I, p. 161.

he got his pet scheme safely through the mill before committing himself.

On the 6th of March, 1827, having done its worst, the youthful General Assembly of Illinois, adjourned the most important session through which it had passed up to that time. The various members made their last rounds of the bars and dining rooms, closed up their bags, and to the infinite chagrin of the town, quitted Vandalia until the next session. For most of them it must have been a noticeable letdown, after the violent and rhapsodic excitement of their three months' frenzy. For Vandalia it was little less than a tragedy, for that unattractive town had done much to make the legislators happy. A few more perfunctory sessions and they would know it no more. The town's prestige was to be transferred to a rival. Vandalia had indulged in a campaign of internal improvement of its own, chiefly consisting in the importation of many of the advantages of culture and luxury, fine wines, new books for the members of the assembly, music teachers, and private tutors for their children. These distinctions could not prevail against the Springfield lobby.

Abraham Lincoln, with a license to practise law before the bar of Illinois, just granted him by the State Supreme Court, returned to New Salem, and to the friends who had raised him from the station of a poor and untried youth to that of a promising and much talked of legislator. He had now made the first notable success of his life, but it was a success whose value could only be judged in terms of the future. It had not made over Abraham's immediate life. He was still up to his ears in a flood of indebtedness which was growing larger rather than smaller. He had no money in his pocket and no prospect of any. And there was his intention to move to Springfield, which must be justified in the eyes of those friends of New Salem who in helping him had been pleased to think that they were helping their village, and there was Mary Owens, that powerful and compelling lady whom he was not sure whether to regard as asset or liability.

Abraham found it possible, in his wanderings about the town during the cold and blustery days, and the damp thawing days of early March, to accumulate a horse and a pair of saddlebags, a great deal of friendly confidence, but no money. And he was not able to come to any definite agreement with the troubling Mary Owens, who kept putting him off, feeling unconvinced of the depth of her affectionate feeling for him. She was afraid that he cared more for her than she for him and, although their natures were by no means incompatible, Mary had her doubts of the fun there would be in living with a man with no manners, no polish, none of those little tender apprehensions which a woman may reasonably expect even from a man of six-feet-four.

Without any definite acceptance of his suggestion of marriage and with a refusal of it which he could not be certain was not a joke the impecunious Abraham set off on his borrowed horse for Springfield, there to make his permanent home and to begin his career as a lawyer in partnership with the well-known politico-legal Macchiavelli of the Sangamon, John Todd Stuart, the handsomest man in Illinois.

Late in March, 1837, Joshua Speed, a good-looking and intelligent young merchant of the frontier, was standing in his general store at Springfield. Stooping through the door came an outrageously tall and gaunt-looking man of twenty-eight, upon whose sloping forehead was set a wide-brimmed felt hat. Over his arm the stranger carried a pair of saddlebags. His trousers and coat were spattered with mud. His face wore a look of trouble and bewilderment. It seemed to Speed that he had never seen so sad a man. But there was something in the traveler's manner that appealed to the storekeeper. It was a fortunate visit for Abraham Lincoln, whose greatest worry at the moment was based upon the lack of quilts and bedding for the bedstead which he had just contracted for with the town's cabinetmaker, and without which he would have no place to lay his head. He asked the storekeeper what the stuff would cost.

Speed was so surprised to see the look of dejection increase in Lincoln's face at the quotation of seventeen dollars, that he began to figure out ways of helping the stranger. That was Abraham Lincoln's quality. Merely to meet him was to want to help him. That was one of the secrets of his command. He was frank, he was abject, his face was unhappily tragic. When he mentioned the fact that, although he was a duly elected member of the General Assembly of Illinois, he had not the money to pay for his bedding, the hearer wanted to make it easy for him. Abraham's ungainly wistfulness seemed, without voice, to demand consideration. He was like a child on a journey, marked for the protection of all men.

Upstairs above his store Joshua Speed had a large room with a large double bed in it, and plenty of covers on the bed. Without hesitation he offered Abraham a half share in the whole. Abraham looked about the store, at the counters piled with goods, at the great friendly fireplace in the rear. He took his saddlebags and walked upstairs, deposited the bags on the floor and came down again.

"Well, Speed, I'm moved," he said, and the melancholy was gone from his face. The disarming friendliness of a boundless relief spread itself in a smile upon his countenance. In the half-comic intimacy of that double bed upstairs, Abraham and Joshua were to learn the farther side of friendship together. And in the half-tragic bustle of little Springfield, whose interests Lincoln had served, but whose heart was not immediately open in return, the New Salem lawyer was to learn for a time the quality of loneliness. There was John Stuart, his partner to be, ever busy with his political affairs, and there was William Butler, whose attention had been attracted by Lincoln's political activity. And there were merchants, men with money, families of the inner circle of Springfield's curious social life, who had heard of the young politician and were grateful for what he had done to help their town. But few of them made any attempt to approach his person. William Butler gave him board at his table and said nothing very serious about repayment. Stuart gave his junior partner all the work of the small office to attend to. This work consisted chiefly in sitting in a rickety chair covered with a buffalo robe, attending to an almost negligible correspondence, the making of occasional legal papers and the few necessary entries in the firm's books. In between the widely separated demands of these tasks was plenty of time to use the same chair and the same buffalo robe for study of the dull but necessary principles of the law. In the meantime, Stuart himself chased about the state after Stephen A. Douglas, trying, and in the end successfully, to get himself elected to Congress over the amazingly powerful little man whom Lincoln was later to encounter.

Several times Abraham tried to write a letter to Mary Owens, leaning like a schoolboy on the frail table which served the office for a desk. But he was uncertain of his attitude and for six weeks did not succeed. In May he managed to write:

. . . This thing of living in Springfield is rather a dull business, after all; at least it is so to me. I am quite as lonesome here as I ever was anywhere in my life. I have been spoken to by but one woman since I have been here, and should not have been by her if she could have avoided it. I've never been to church yet, and probably shall not be soon. I stay away because I am conscious I should not know how to behave myself.

I am often thinking of what we said about your coming to live at Springfield. I am afraid you would not be satisfied. There is a great deal of flourishing about in carriages here which it would be your doom to see without sharing it. You would have to be poor without the means of hiding your poverty. Do you believe you could bear that patiently? Whatever woman may cast her lot with mine, should any ever do so, it is my intention to do all in my power to make her happy and contented; and there is nothing I can imagine that would make me more unhappy than to fail in the effort. I know I should be much happier with you than the way I am, provided I saw no signs of discontent in you. What you have said to me may have been in the way of jest, or I may have misunderstood you. If so, then let it be forgotten; if otherwise, I much wish you would think seriously before you decide. What I have said I will most positively abide by, provided that you wish it. My opinion is that you had better not do it. You have not been accustomed to hardship, and it may be more severe than you now imagine. I know you are capable of thinking correctly on any subject, and if you deliberate maturely upon this subject before you decide, then I am willing to abide your decision.

You must write me a good long letter after you get this. You have nothing else to do, and though it might not seem interesting to you after you had written it, it would be a good deal of company to me in this "busy wilderness." Tell your sister I don't want to hear any more about selling out and moving. That gives me the "hypo" whenever I think of it. Yours, etc.   LINCOLN.*

The streets of Springfield through which Abraham walked to mail this defensive and pleading letter, were, like those of Vandalia, wide and unpaved. There were no sidewalks, only here and there a few loose planks laid down to bridge dangerous expanses impassable without damage because of either mud

* Works, Vol. I, p. 162.

or dust, according to the season. The usual scavengering hogs rooted in the alleys and about the public square. It was a dismal prospect for a lonely young man to contemplate. Things would not be so bad, once the Legislature convened and Abraham went back to Vandalia to fight against a repeal of the state capital law, a thing which the representatives of other counties were sure to attempt. It was still hard for this, the most popular Whig in Sangamon County, to feel like anything but a failure when he was not having direct contact with his fellow beings.

Women did not appear to be troubled when he passed them in the street, however much his own internal arrangements were stimulated by the passage. The clothes which he wore had long since ceased to be new and there was little of the dashing cavalier about their wearer. Human beings dig for their gold only in the most prepossessing spots, so great is their fear of being humiliated by having dug in vain. And Abraham Lincoln, at twenty-eight, was not one of those spots. To the timid, his great receding brow and coarse black hair crowning a face that suggested sorrow, was a terrifying thing. To the timid even among pioneers sorrow suggested God and God suggested hell fire. So the timid passed Abraham Lincoln by. The bold saw only the massive and uncouth ruggedness of his giant frame, and defended themselves against it by thinking it funny. The heart within that frame was stung by avoidance and mockery. It could not bear to be esteemed what it was not, and it was not funny. It was grimly determined to be successful and suave.

Evenings by the fireplace, at the back of Speed's store, it was possible for Abraham to show what he was. Give him a chance to open his mouth to men and they would know him. They would forget his clothes, his figure, and they would not have to forget the horrible daunting melancholy of his look, for it would be gone. The beam of an assurance, taken by assault, from the faces of listeners, could blot it out. Talk, which came to Abraham as easily and as voluminously as water to fish, seemed to carry him beyond himself. His wit and the appetizing depth of his interpretation of the commonness of human life, made him a very real figure to the group of lawyers and less-sanctioned disputers who gathered with Lincoln and Speed around the fire. But these qualities of his personality brought him little discipline, and though they let men see him at his best, they excited him to new ideas and enterprises in which his ignorance often acted as a clog upon the driving force of the ambition which incited him. A controversy in which the pathetically eager young man appears not at his best occupied him during most of that summer of his first year in Springfield.

The law business took him occasionally to other towns on the Judicial Circuit, a special session of the Legislature in July took him to Vandalia, * and a visit to New Salem thereafter took him to the ample and troubling Mary Owens. From all of these things he returned to the remarkable and unpromising business of mud-slinging. Like water which has not had time to find a tranquil level after being poured into its tank, the nation was slopping back and forth, troubled by its own fluid tendencies as well as by the irresistible gravity of economic consolidation. The financial panic which was sweeping the whole world was particularly troublesome in the western states, many of which had, by repudiating their obligations, lost the power of borrowing money cheaply and had in consequence been thrust into the open arms of those private capitalists with money to

* The capital had not yet been moved to Springfield in conformity with the recent act of the Legislature.

lend at high rates. The beneficent socialized state which the founding fathers had envisaged had failed to materialize. Instead it had been sandbagged during the struggle for and against the National Bank. It had lain down never to rise again, while private enterprise walked off with its clothes, ever after to go about in them unsuspected. The nation had begun to reap the results of the bargaining which it had indulged in during the Constitutional Convention of 1787, the South having the flower of the slave system which it had been awarded, the North the golden bough of the tree of commerce, for whose nourishment it had been willing to suffer slavery in those states that wanted it. And that golden bough was growing like Jack's beanstalk, making a thick prison ceiling above the heads of those young men and women who had undertaken factory work as something of an economic lark preliminary to the actual business of life. These young people, who had believed themselves free began to see the tangle closing in above them and to realize for the first time that there was no escape, that they were factory workers for good and all. All his life Abraham Lincoln refused to believe that such a situation existed.

These workers did not see clearly what it was that had brought about the change in their status. They did not see the dragon corporation materializing above the branches like the Cheshire cat. They did not see how everyone must bow down to that dragon and offer it the inch which it should stretch out into a mile of privilege. They did not see, nor did the western prairie lawyer, with an eye to internal improvements, see, how he too must feed the beast. Instead, he wandered about Springfield, or bent over law books in his little office at No. 4 Hoffman's Row, or else he hung about the office of Simeon Francis, editor of the *Sangamo Journal,* the fiercely partisan organ of

the local Whigs. Abraham Lincoln, who saw, better than he
saw the state of life in the nation, what his own prospects required, saw that he must keep in the public eye. It was not
hard for him to make the admiring Mr. Francis more than
willing for him to get his personal publicity through the use
of the columns of the *Sangamo Journal*. Even before moving
to Springfield, Abraham had managed to cast the spell of his
personality over those columns and their editor. Now that the
promising young man had become a notable politician and
a partner of the big chief of all the Illinois Whigs, John T.
Stuart, Francis was willing to give his young friend some share
in the control of the paper's policies.

At this time a matter had come up which made Abraham
very anxious to have a public vehicle of expression. It was a
matter of striking a bushful of birds with the same stone, for it
was a matter of exposing a mean scoundrel, of advancing the
interests of his party, of indulging his taste for satirical invective,
and last but not least of keeping himself in the limelight. With
these things in mind he was quick to take advantage of Editor
Francis's expansive state of mind.

In the columns of the *Sangamo Journal* * he now launched a
voluminous and violent attack upon General James Adams, a
Springfield lawyer who appeared to be in fraudulent possession
of some land belonging to the widow of a former client. At the
same time, General Adams, whose personal popularity in the
county was very great, was running on the Democratic ticket
for judge of the probate court. Lincoln, being no longer on
the fence but a leader among the Whigs, did not need to think
twice to know that General Adams should not be elected. Furthermore, although he never succeeded in convincing either the

---

* *Sangamo Journal.* June & July 1837, v. d.

public or the courts of law, Abraham convinced himself that Adams had forged an assignment to himself of a judgment against the widow's land.

Lincoln and Stuart, together with two other Whig attorneys, set out to finish the General. They filed suit against him, as representatives of the heirs of Joseph Anderson, deceased, the former owner of General Adams' disputed land. The suit never came to anything in the courts, but the echoes of it in the public press reached all over the state, quite as the Whig defenders of widows and orphans had supposed it would. But they had not reckoned upon General Adams's personal following at the polls. In spite of the malicious, though probably justified, campaign which the Whigs carried on against him, the General polled an unprecedented vote. The venomous attack, which had been waged in the columns of the *Sangamo Journal* in the form of anonymous letters, was now continued over Abraham's signature. When, in 1865, Lincoln closed his Second Inaugural Address with the words, "with malice toward none, with charity for all . . . " if he thought of the day thirty years before when he had been laying about him with malicious and uncharitable words, calling General Adams a forger, a traitor to his country, a despoiler of widows and orphans, he must have smiled to himself to understand how far he had gone upon the road of humility and self-possession.

In 1837, however, Abraham was so busy with his vitriol that he had little time to think of anything else. Certainly it kept the rancorous uncertainties of his relations with Mary Owens temporarily out of his heart. When he did think of Mary it was to write her that he thought it would be a good plan if she were to call off the whole thing, engagement or whatever it was. He himself would, if she wished, go through with it, but he felt that she would be better off not to wish it. He did not desire to take the initiative either in calling the engagement on or off.

"Do not understand by this," he wrote, "that I wish to cut your acquaintance. I mean no such thing. . . . What I do wish is that our further acquaintance shall depend upon yourself. . . . " *

If Mary had needed confirmation of her suspicions that Abraham would not be much help as a husband, there, she must have thought, it was, plain as day. Their relationship from that time on did depend upon Mary, and Mary saw to it that it ceased, rather to Abraham's chagrin. He had pictured himself as a noble fellow, releasing from an unwilling heart a rather frightened girl. Now he was undeceived by Mary's attitude of unconcerned finality. He took out his annoyance by writing, flippantly, the history of the affair to the wife of a friend in the hope that the smart and rather unmanly things he said might convince him that he was unaffected by the situation.

This is what he wrote of the woman who had been to him, for more than a year, alternate desire and despair:

. . . It was, then, in the autumn of 1836 that a married lady of my acquaintance, and who was a great friend of mine, being about to pay a visit to her father and other relatives residing in Kentucky, proposed to me that on her return she would bring a sister of hers with her on condition that I would engage to become her brother-in-law with all convenient despatch. I of course, accepted the proposal, for you know I could not have done otherwise had I really been averse to it; but privately, between you and me, I was most confoundedly well pleased with the project. . . . Time passed on; the lady took her journey and in due time returned, sister in company, sure enough. This astonished me a little, for it appeared to me that her coming so readily showed

* Works, Vol. I, p. 165.

that she was a trifle too willing. . . . In a few days we had an inter-
view, and, although I had seen her before she did not look as my
imagination had pictured her. I knew she was oversize, but she now
appeared a fair match for Falstaff. I knew she was called an "old
maid," and I felt no doubt of the truth of at least half of the appel-
lation, but now, when I beheld her, I could not for my life avoid
thinking of my mother;* and this, not from withered features,—for
her skin was too full of fat to permit of its contracting into wrinkles,—
but from her want of teeth, and from a kind of notion that ran in
my head that nothing could have commenced at infancy and reached
her present bulk in less than thirty-five or forty years; and in short,
I was not at all pleased with her. But what could I do? I had told
her sister that I would take her for better or for worse, and I made
a point of honor and conscience in all things to stick to my word,
especially if others had been induced to act on it, which in this case
I had no doubt they had, for I was now fairly convinced that no
other man would have her, and hence the conclusion that they were
bent on holding me to my bargain. . . .

After all my suffering upon this deeply interesting subject, here
I am, wholly, unexpectedly, completely, out of the "scrape"; and now
I want to know if you can guess how I got out of it—out, clear, in
every sense of the term; no violation of word, honor, or conscience.
. . . After I had delayed the matter as long as I thought I could in
honor do (which by the way, had brought me round into the last
fall), I concluded I might as well bring it to a consummation without
further delay; and so I mustered my resolution, and made the proposal
to her direct; but shocking to relate, she answered, No. At first I supposed she did it through an affectation of modesty, which I thought
ill became her under the peculiar circumstances of the case; but on my
renewal of the charge, I found she repelled it with greater firmness
than before. I tried it again and again, but with the same success, or
rather with the same want of success.

* Abraham undoubtedly was not referring to Nancy Hanks Lincoln, but to his
stepmother.

I finally was forced to give it up; at which I found myself mortified almost beyond endurance. I was mortified, it seemed to me, in a hundred different ways. . . . I then for the first time began to suspect that I was really a little in love with her. But let it all go. I'll try and out-live it. Others have been made fools of by the girls, but this can never with truth be said of me. . . .*

* Works, Vol. I, p. 189 ff.

CHAPTER FIVE

THE NOVICE RAISES HIS VOICE

SIXTY miles from Springfield on the banks of the Mississippi, lay the city of Alton, Illinois. It had been one of the unsuccessful candidates for the location of the new state capital and was, in 1837, the wealthiest and most important city in the state. Being on the great artery of North and South travel, and depending for its commercial importance on the maintenance of trade with the South, it was, in sentiment, strongly opposed to any discussion of the abolition of slavery, as indeed were most Illinois cities, though with less reason.

To this busy town, with his printing press and his type, had come Elijah Lovejoy, a preacher from the Calvinistic preserves of Massachusetts, ready to do a little poaching in the less austere regions of the frontier. In November, 1837, Mr. Lovejoy was busy, with all the ineptitude of the bombastic reformer, editing a paper called the *Observer,* a paper devoted to the interests of "righteousness." Righteousness was the Reverend Lovejoy's strong point. He would have the nation righteous if he had to commit crime to make it so. Like William Lloyd Garrison of the *Liberator,* this reformer was one of those who have no eye for obstacles. Both men acted upon a passionate but distressing principle, the principle of implacable hostility. If the foundation of your house turned out to be of base stuff, why, tear it out without committing the venial sin of first removing the house above it to a place of safety. That was their principle.

Lovejoy had not originally been outspoken in favor of abolition but he soon became so. He began to feel bricks falling about
his head as a result of his tugging at the underpinning, and he
immediately began flinging back the bricks into the air as fast
as they fell. When the local citizenry asked him please not to
speak against slavery and slaveholders in quite such violent
terms, he became inflamed and talked more loudly than before.
Mr. Lovejoy went wildly on his way, stung by his passionate belief in the wrong of slavery and without the slightest sense of
the economic conditions which slavery represented, and which,
rather than the bestiality of slaveholders, served to perpetuate the
institution. In glowing terms he insulted the entire South of
which he knew nothing, except by hearsay. He vilified all
Catholics, although he knew as little of them as he did of
Southerners. He glorified in the righteousness which his own
views sustained. The citizens of several towns through which
he had passed made it wise for him to move on. Sometimes they
threw his press into the river, but he always found another. It
was high comedy, for a time; but it was comedy that had little
of the comic about it. And Mr. Lovejoy, always writing new
matter into his part, ended by acting in a tragedy. For he could
not continue with impunity.

On the night of November 7, 1837, a gathering of the citizens of Alton, conscious of their wealth, their success, their
moral standing, exasperated by the editor's incendiary obstinacy
and frightened by his messianic mask, for the last time threw
his printing press into the Mississippi. It was the end of Lovejoy. In an attempt to defend his property against the mob
he fired into it. The mob, only too glad of an excuse, returned his
fire and dropped him where he stood. The emotional fool, driven
by a righteous impulse, became, in that moment, a cry of mar-

tyr in the mouths of wiser and more compelling men, a cry that
brought the ill-chosen activity of the abolitionists more power
than it had ever had before.

While this tragedy was being enacted at Alton, Abraham
Lincoln was busy in Springfield with his vitriol, taking a last
fling at the crooked but unabashed General Adams. Abraham
had lost Mary Owens. The professions of loneliness and sadness
which he had made to her fell back upon him unrequited and
filled with their gnawing mischief the intervals between his
political activity, his legal business and his private studies. But
he was not going to be made a fool of by the girls. There must
be others somewhere, others less formidable than Miss Owens.
Girls in Springfield there certainly were, but they were not
easily approachable by a young man conspicuous for his awkwardness and his lack of manners. There was a little girl of
twelve at the house where Abraham ate his meals. She was William Butler's sister-in-law, Sarah Rickard. For a while, at least,
Abraham could enjoy her girlishness without any fear of com-
plications, and with a certain sense that he was being admired.
He need not think of her as an eligible bride.

Lincoln had recently returned to Springfield from Vandalia,
after a frantic session of the Legislature, convened by the Governor in the hope of undoing some of the damage which Lincoln and his colleagues, in their advocacy of the Internal Improvement Act, had done to the State of Illinois. In this session,
Abraham, in spite of the plain fact that that act was impossible
in every way, voted against repealing it. Perhaps he was stung
to obstinacy by an insult which he had received from a fellow
legislator. General W. L. D. Ewing, Democrat, in the course of
a controversy arising out of the various attempts to repeal the
law which awarded the state capital to Springfield, had called

Lincoln a coarse and vulgar fellow. Perhaps, too, there was gall in the fact that James Shields, Democrat, a distinguished member of the lower house whom Lincoln hated and could not be pleasant to, presented, as a remedy for the terrible financial situation into which the panic of 1837 had forced the state, a bill which was preferred by the house to Lincoln's own. Abraham had begun to realize that as a financier he was a bungler, but he was not yet ready to let his political opponents prove it. And even if he had bungled he had achieved political prominence. That made him the equal of Ewing or Shields. And it made him, in the face of this opposition, vengeful rather than humble.

When he returned from Vandalia to Springfield he was in a very belligerent mood. He was in that state of mind which makes a young man feel that the way out of defeat and humiliation is to pretend that you are neither defeated nor humiliated but that you are, after all, right and that you will prevail. His reason, when faced with crises, was so much shrewder than that of many others, that he was inclined to forget the gaps of ignorance and inexperience which lay like pitfalls in his path. When he met these gaps, walking along his career like a fighting cock, there was nothing to do but pretend that they were not there, or that he had known about them all the time and was contented to ignore them. Perhaps it was in this mood that Abraham addressed the Young Men's Lyceum of Springfield, on the subject of the "Perpetuation of Our Political Institutions." In this speech, chiefly notable for the diligence with which its author contrived to make ten high-flown and rhetorical words do the work of one simple one, Abraham Lincoln made no direct mention of the killing of Lovejoy in Alton, no mention of slavery, no mention of the changes in the state of the nation which had taken place since the national government had been conceived

by the "patriots of '76." Instead he said, "That our government
should have been maintained in its original form, from its
establishment until now, is not much to be wondered at." He
regarded the nation as finished, subject to no more exciting
experiment, no modification. " . . . The game is caught;
and . . . with the catching end the pleasures of the chase." *
He advised regarding the government as already perfected, and
resisting efforts to change or defy its laws.

Meanwhile, the Internal Improvement Law, which Abraham
had helped to pass, was making havoc of the finances of Illinois. In fact, the chief business of the last session of the legislature to meet in the old capital at Vandalia, was the problem of
how to get out from under that Old Man of the Sea. That question, together with the ever present matter of how, where and
for whose benefit to run banks, and the struggle to prevent the
capital from going to Springfield, kept Abraham busy, and in
some degree satisfied, until the spring of 1839. Accompanying
discussion of these problems, which were close to his heart,
came wedges of new and wider issues, which at first he dismissed
with a perfunctory vote or a silence. Since the Lovejoy incident
at Alton the matter of slavery had been given considerable life,
and propositions treating of it in one way or another were introduced into the sessions of the legislature of 1838. To a resolution
that no free state or its citizens ought to "interfere with the
property of slave-holding states . . . guarantied unto them by
the Constitution of the United States, and without which guar-
anty this Union, perhaps, would never have been formed," Lincoln gave his silent assent. He was willing to let it pass.

During the same session, although, as the leader of his county

---

* Works, Vol. I, p. 148. Date in works, however, is wrong. Speech was delivered
Jan. 1838.

delegation, Abraham presented a petition affirming the protests of some six hundred citizens of Sangamon County against the retailing of intoxicating liquors, it was his vote which killed a temperance bill prepared in the House. He also voted against a similar bill prepared in the Senate, a bill which, in spite of his opposition, was passed. It was in support of the fatal Internal Improvement Act that Abraham reached the height of his legislative folly. Instead of admitting that it was a mistake, and, as one of the chief authors of the mistake, helping to make amends for it, he presented a report and resolutions suggesting that the already bankrupt state borrow five millions of dollars to purchase the government land lying within the confines of Illinois. Although some of Abraham's best friends could not tolerate such folly and left his side, his proposal was actually accepted by the legislature. Thus a session which had had, as its chief business, the task of lightening the financial burdens of the State, concluded by accumulating, thanks to Abraham Lincoln, a still greater burden. That was a considerable triumph, and in spite of the unpleasant and inevitable consequences, it put Lincoln very close to the head of his party in the state. And that was where he was going, to the head.

In the meantime, Abraham's law partner, John T. Stuart, had been elected to Congress by a majority of thirty-six votes in a total polling of thirty-six thousand. It was a close shave, but the matter had been arranged by a little trickery here and there. Stephen A. Douglas, the defeated candidate, protested the election, and would undoubtedly have won out, but for a confidential letter circulated by Lincoln and five other Whigs asking the editors of Whig Papers to investigate the possibility of proving any counterbalancing fraud on Douglas's side. As it was, Douglas withdrew his protest, rather to Lincoln's surprise and much to his relief.

Stuart was elected, and that meant that Lincoln would, for a year, at least, bear the burden of whatever business came to No. 4 Hoffman's Row.

Springfield, although extremely grateful to the adroit Mr. Lincoln, clever politician, who had gained for the town the immeasurable advantage of being the state capital, still had very little to say to Mr. Lincoln, eligible bachelor. Occasionally parties were given by the wives and friends of members of the group which met in Speed's store, and Abraham, painfully, but with a punctual eye to the possibilities involved, attended when he could. But his rise from loneliness and social neglect was slow, and it was not attended by the exciting crises which made political life a foil for his sense of futility and inferiority. Abraham loved companionship for its own sake and he would have liked to regard women as equally with men the unembarrassed subject of it. He had already remarked that he saw no reason why women should not vote, and it must have annoyed him considerably to find that they did not return his respectful admiration by finding him desirable and amusing. They liked and admired him, but did not warm to him. It would have been hard for him to believe that they were afraid of him. It was easier to remember taunts like General Ewing's, who had called him coarse and vulgar. Well, he would show them. He would have "place and distinction as a politician." Even the women would come around eventually.

It was ridicule that hurt Abraham most. He could never stand that. When a gentleman of the Democratic faith, Mr. Jesse Thomas, who believed that the Sangamon County delegation in the State Legislature had been guilty of bad faith with the people in promulgating the monstrous Internal Improvement Act, said harsh things about all the delegation and especially

biting things of Lincoln, Abraham broke out with his vitriol
again. Mr. Thomas, surprised and hurt, wilted under the attack
like a pansy in a dry vase. The crowd, more interested in dramatic
performance than in political fact or innuendo, roared its approval of Abraham's violence. And sensing the approval, Abraham enlarged upon his invective. The crowd was delighted
and remembered. That kind of man was one you could understand. Abraham had won another victory, though the recollection of it afterward was always to fill him with something very
like shame.

At this time of his life, there were only two things which
could make the rising young lawyer do things of which he might
later be ashamed. His hatred of ridicule and contempt, when
those attitudes were turned against him, and his devotion to the
party organization upon which his rise depended. In the first
session of the Twelfth General Assembly of Illinois, a peculiar
situation arose. It was one which, Abraham's close connection
with the material interests of the city which was to provide
his livelihood during most of the next quarter century, was of
vital importance to him.

It happened that the Springfield State Bank, darling of the
Sangamon County Whigs, and long the recipient of favors from
the state legislature, held almost all of the scanty funds of the
State of Illinois. And the directors of that bank were very anxious,
in view of the dreadful financial condition of the country, to
keep as much of that money on deposit as they possibly could.
Furthermore, the salaries of all state officers and members of the
legislature were paid in notes of the Springfield Bank. If it had
no money, the legislators would suffer. But, if the current session of the legislature should be allowed to adjourn before the
day on which the law required the next session to begin, there

would be no way of avoiding the resumption of specie payments. Such payments had been suspended by the previous session, the suspension to last until the first meeting of the Twelfth Assembly adjourned. The Whigs, who wanted to spare the Bank the painful necessity of parting with its cash, resolved that by seeing to it that there was never a quorum in the house to vote adjournment, they would keep the session alive indefinitely. If it lasted until the subsequent one pushed it out of existence and took its place it could not be said to have adjourned. Consequently the Springfield Bank would be absolved from the necessity of resuming specie payment.

The Democrats had at that time a majority in both branches of the legislature, but, unless all of them were present, could not master a quorum in the House without some Whigs. Abraham, when the Senate had managed to accumulate a quorum and vote adjournment, passing the resolution along to the House, saw to it that enough Whigs kept away from the session to nullify any possible action. For a number of Democrats were sick. The sergeant-at-arms was sent out about the town and through the lobby to round up such missing members as he could, but he received only threats. Dignified Whigs as much as told him to go jump in the lake.

Abraham Lincoln was jubilant. Night came on. The candlelight flickered on the walls and over the scantily filled benches of the lower house. The sound of winter night rumbled at the darkened windows. The murmur of fugitive voices came from the lobby, with now and then the sound of an angry harangue. Occasionally the weary speaker, that same General Ewing who had called Abraham a coarse and vulgar fellow, and who had defeated him for the speakership, rose to question the members or to receive a motion. Many of the Democrats slept in their

seats. Lincoln, in the dark hollow of his place, whispered to the
few Whig colleagues who had remained with him.

Suddenly the Speaker rose and announced the presence of a
quorum. Abraham, the Whig watchdog, was astounded and no
doubt incredulous. He and his companions found it hard to
believe that enough sick Democrats could have been routed from
their beds to make up for the Whig discrepancy. Perhaps with
some idea that a vote would show the quorum incomplete, Abraham voted and so discovered his mistake. Although his vote
on the adoption of the Senate resolution for adjournment was
nay, it was too late, the motion had passed. Before it had been
made certain, however, Abraham and his friends, in a panic
of fear lest some further vote be taken, opened a window at the
back of the room and dropped out of sight of the House into
the blustery night which was coursing up and down upon the
street outside. *

It was in this boyish and lively manner that Abraham Lincoln was taking his lessons in the art of politics while at the
other end of the winter winds the violence and horror of national disaster was brewing. Perhaps, in Speed's store that evening, Abraham chuckled over his escapade, sharing the bravado
of it with the secure company of gay-hearted and like-minded
Whigs who were always to be found there. But the strange
demon of the hell of economics must have chuckled much more
gleefully, as he stirred the tar-pots of confusion and discord.
For the controversy over the National Bank and indeed the whole
question of the nation's finances, which had culminated in the
panic of 1837 and its subsequent stringencies, turned out to be
a splendid alloy for brimstone. And the recurring question of
slavery, especially in the hands of the newly arisen abolitionists,

* Beveridge, Albert J. Abraham Lincoln, Vol. I, p. 276.

was no mean flux for the sulphurous preparation with which the country was destined to be deluged. It was during the generation just completed, which had paralleled the life of Abraham, the pride of the Sangamon, that the country had taken an entirely new and unforeseen course in its development. And that course would have seemed to almost any public figure of 1787 to be leading straight to damnation.

Those aristocratic merchants and financiers who had fitted up the United States of America as a kind of armored golden coach to be superimposed upon the humble philosophical running gear devised by Thomas Jefferson, had never supposed that their vehicle would be called upon to travel roads of which they knew nothing. But within thirty-five or forty years of the adoption of the Constitution the whole course of American life had shown unmistakable signs of change. The development of rail transportation had begun. The improved iron industry was galloping along in the wake of the steam cars. The Erie Canal had not only opened the near Northwest, but had created a demand for a tremendous amount of unskilled, non-agricultural labor. The cotton gin, invented before 1800, had now begun to show its full effect, having brought the Southern planter into the exporting business, and having, to his sorrow, got him mixed up with Northern capitalists to whom he had to entrust much of his raw material for manufacture. And this increase of trade, cotton spinning on a large scale, added to the North's already great volume of wool, leather, lumber, and shipping business, was bound to change the emphasis in Northern life from agricultural to industrial. Already, in 1840, emigration from some of the New England states to the West had ceased. There was too much activity at home. In twenty years the manufacturing class in Massachusetts had increased four times as much as the

agricultural, and even the slight increase in farmers had begun
to center itself upon thriving manufacturing towns. In New
England, which was doing the bulk of the nation's industrial
producing and•consequently getting the lion's share of the profits,
the agricultural life had already become, as it is everywhere to-
day, definitely subordinate to the factory and the mill.

The more manufacturing there was, the greater the perfection of railroads and steam vessels, which are purely assembled
manufactures. And the greater the perfection of railroads, steam
vessels, and other machines, the wider the field of market. Thus
the change in American life was feeding upon itself and swelling up like Aesop's frog. No one had foreseen it and no one
could control it. The South, which was still in the agricultural
stage, by virtue of the great demand for that agricultural product,
raw cotton (not to mention rice, indigo and tobacco), could
merely rail against the injustice of it. The North, not at all concerned with injustice which left in its mouth the meat end of
the bone of contention, was content to hop around finding new
ways of taking advantage of the situation and of strengthening
its own position.

The West, in whose heart the ambitious Lincoln sat, talking earnestly and amusingly with his friends before a great
fireplace of beech logs, was as yet neither fish, flesh nor fowl.
It was a breeding ground for new Americans, men with ideas
of getting on which were tinged with the hues of hope and free
from the hampering obstacles of tradition and privilege. As a
part of the nation, the West still embodied all stages in the development of human society, from the primitive savagery of the
lean-to pioneer to the relatively advanced, if sadly limited, culture
of the gabled mansion of the thriving city. Every Westerner
knew, especially since Andrew Jackson's presidency, that he had

a perfectly clear chance of sitting on top of the world, but like the sadly muddled Abe Lincoln, he had no means of knowing where to give his allegiance save to political party, and no means of deciding to which political party save in terms of the influence of friends. Abraham Lincoln, like every other son of pioneer parents, was born under a representative government. It is plain that unless there are differing interests among a population there can be no reason whatever for representation. Although they differed little among themselves, the interests of the West were from the first different from those of North and South, their economic as well as their social interests. The economic interests were not at all clearly defined, but the social were definite. The Westerner was neither akin to the industrial aristocracy of the North nor to the family aristocracy of the South. He was a compound of influences taken from both, influences which, as has been shown, seemed to meet on the frontier of central Illinois. To develop sectional importance and to stake it upon what looked like a winning horse was the prime concern of the Westerner returning backwards along the stream of national expansion.

It is not strange, therefore, that Abraham Lincoln, who came to a central point of the frontier with Southern blood in his veins and the additional linkage of Southern birth to turn him toward the feudal, none the less accepted and let himself be carried along by the tide of Northern influence, which though he did not realize it, was based upon the new power of industry, the not new but freshly empowered conceptions of gain and possession, and was to be, as if sprouting from the very root-stock of his ambition, the essence of the future America. We cannot blame a young Illinois lawyer, with a taste for power and a talent for leadership, that he was present as an usher at the mar-

riage of our time with an old mean-spirited, gross-throated, plutocratic villain of an industrial system who has kept his bride
in terror though in affluence. Abraham Lincoln did not invent
the life of to-day. But it would be well, if we are to understand
the amazing career of one of the most remarkable figures that
ever appeared in public life, to remember that he took great
pains to seek out an invitation to the ceremony. At the close of
his career in the Illinois legislature, it had become plain to Abraham that the way to the top did not lead through the South.
Not because the South was cursed with what to many seemed
the inhuman institution of slavery, not because the plantation
system was against the grain of republican life, but because the
dominant caste, linked vaguely in his apprehensive mind, with
dead but Olympian Federalists, spoke at last only from the gilded
places of the North. This predilection on Lincoln's part for a
certain political cast is to some extent explained by a perusal of
his public activities in the Illinois legislature. He was on the side
of the ruling powers in practically all of his alignments—not the
ruling powers in the sense that they were victors in elections
necessarily, for more Democrats than Whigs were victorious in
Lincoln's early manhood, and he ceased early to vote for Democrats even though friends of his. But Abraham never allowed
himself to show any signs of radical thought or action. His
vote was almost always given against the questioning of public
officials suspected of neglect or betrayal of the public interest.
His supposition was, apparently, that anyone in office is entitled
to the benefit of the doubt. The office holder, not the man in
the street, was the ingredient of his demos. In this frame of
mind, he regarded with something like horror, the accusations
hurled against the Springfield Bank, against the idea of a
National Bank, against the Southern slaveholder. Abraham

was, in his thirtieth year, a thorough-going, out-and-out conservative.

The Whig party was the party of conservatism and Abraham
was now high in the councils of the party in his own state. He
had earned the respect and admiration of many of his fellow-
citizens, and was becoming known all over the state, not only
before the fireplace of Joshua Speed's store and in Sangamon
County. But there was trouble ahead, for his success had not
yet extended itself to the field of domestic life, and there he was
to meet something like a defeat whose shadow never left him.

CHAPTER SIX

THE PERILS OF EVASION

IN a sunny second story of a great red brick mansion near Louisville, Kentucky, Abraham Lincoln, the terror of the Legislative Halls of Illinois, lay stretched in bed. The covers of the bed were of fine, well-cared for stuff, there were rich colors in the soft carpet of the floor. The brilliant August sunlight fell upon the polished wood of chairs and table and dresser. Through the opened window came the sound of voices in the garden below. There was the high, bright, tinkling of little Eliza Davis, laughing and chattering as she ran about in her full skirt and pantalettes. There was the soft sound of Negro voices from the slave quarters, the scrape of horses' hoofs pawing at the drive, the voice of the Negro coachman admonishing them, the sound of wind in leaves heavy with Southern sun.

In the great hall downstairs, Mrs. Speed, the widowed mistress of the house, was arranging flowers with the help of her daughter, Mary. Both women wore black, tiers of stiff silk expanding bell-like toward the polished floor. The pleasant walls and ceilings of that spacious place were fittingly generous of silence and dignity. The soft Southern accent of Mrs. Speed and her daughter as they chatted together was a part of the air of the place. It was the ceremony of summer morning in a Southern home, a home of untroubled gentleness.

A well-dressed Negro slave, carrying a tray with a coffee pot, cream pitcher, sugar bowl, and cup, slipped along the upper hall and knocked at Abraham Lincoln's bedroom door. He opened the door and entered the room with a cheery word and a rich Negro smile.* Abraham scarcely turned in bed. He lay back upon his pillow, looking at the ceiling. Gloomily aware of the servant's presence, and a little embarrassed by the obvious servitude, he sat up awkwardly and took the tray. When the door had closed again upon the Negro, Abraham swallowed his coffee and stared out the window through the August morning haze, at the heavy line of distant forest beyond the grain fields of the plantation. The face which looked out was the face of a man haunted and ravaged, the face of a fugitive who, in flight, is always looking backward at the terror that pursues. It was a narrow face, broadened at the top in a low receding forehead which sloped up into a shock of wild black hair. The eyes were small but bright with relaxed agony, circled by darkness that seemed not so much a color of the skin as something coming from their own depths,—a reversal of light. The lines which hung from the great straight nose across the skull-like jaws had their tint of darkness, too. The full, wide mouth with its pallid lips, was drawn and tense like the mouth of someone holding fast to something.

This, in these (to him) unusual surroundings, was Abraham Lincoln, the politician hero of many a doubtfully parliamentary fracas in the capitals at Vandalia and Springfield, in Illinois. Those altercations and argumentations that had kept Abraham, as stone-breaking keeps a convict, from thinking too much of the things beyond him, were over now. In the previous March the legislature of Illinois had adjourned and its most dramatic and picturesque member never sat in it again. His last few months as an active legislator, in spite of an unusually large amount of that sort of business which ordinarily did not fail to arouse and in-

* Speed, J. F. Reminiscences of Abraham Lincoln. 1864.

terest him, had been for Abraham months of pain and anguish,— listless, unhappy drudgery. In January, 1841, he had sent a letter to Washington to Congressman John Stuart, his law partner. He said, "I am now the most miserable man living. If what I feel were equally distributed on the whole human family, there would not be one cheerful face on earth. Whether I shall ever be better I cannot tell; I awfully forbode I shall not. To remain as I am is impossible. I must die or be better, as it appears to me." *

It was in consequence of this misery and suffering that Abraham had been invited to spend the best part of the late summer at the family home of his devoted friend and Springfield bedfellow, Joshua Speed. Now, looking back over his agony from the vantage point of a comfortable hospitality which made no demands upon him, it seemed to Lincoln marvelous that he had been able to survive the last eight months. He had tried to make his political career all in all to him, and he had succeeded in making it very important. But it was not all-important, however much he would have liked to think it so. In spite of his boyish bravado and his resolve not to let women make a monkey out of him, Abraham had once more become emotionally involved. Sadly enough it was his beloved politics that had brought about the involvement. It was a by-product of his legislative activity and his ardent Whig partisanship that had laid him low and brought him to this peaceful convalescence in the Speed home at Louisville.

For Abraham had risen high enough in the social scale of Springfield not only to attend dances but to be permitted access to the home of one of the Whig leaders of the state, Ninian W. Edwards, son of the first governor of Illinois Territory. Joshua Speed had introduced Lincoln into the Edwards household, which

* Lincoln to Jno. T. Stuart. Jan. 23, 1841. Works, I, 235.

was considered in Springfield one of the aristocratic fortresses of the state. Perhaps even Speed, who was a prosperous young man of a Kentucky plantation family, would not have presumed to let Abraham gangle about in so fine a parlor as the Edwards' but for the fact that Lincoln was at the time very well known for his efforts to endow the aristocratic vicinity with a state capital, and was also a partner of John T. Stuart whose mother had been sister to Mrs. Edwards' father.

Abraham and Joshua Speed, though utterly unlike in background, were temperamentally extremely congenial. Each of these two young bachelors, had the idea that there was something rather horrible about unequivocal intimacy with women, and as they lay in their great bed over Speed's store they had often talked over what seemed to them the repulsive problem of marriage, speculating on its real nature, and wondering if it were not too much for a sensitive young man to stand.* They were both of them strong, full-bodied, vigorous men, but like elephants faced with mice, they felt in women the suggestion of some mysterious and overpowering demand, and the feeling troubled them. But they could not, either physically or socially, afford to go in for asceticism. Hence the appearance of both of them at the Edwards mansion, to call upon two young ladies who were visiting the Kentucky matron who presided there.

One of these girls, whom her cousin Ninian had picked out for Speed, was Miss Matilda Edwards, of Alton. The other was Mary Todd, of Lexington, Kentucky, sister of Mrs. Edwards and now, on account of difficulties with a stepmother at home, a permanent resident in the Edwards household, from which another sister had already married Dr. William Wallace of Springfield. Mary Todd, had just finished a very noticeable education in the

* Cf. Lincoln to Speed: Numerous letters, 1842. Works, Vol. I.

select establishment of Madame Mentelle, a French emigrée who
had halted her emigration in the gentle town of Lexington.*
Madame Mentelle must have been reading the accounts of
Americans provided by European travelers of the early 19th century, for she made no mistake in supposing that they were conscious of being a little uncouth and in need of just such a cosmo-
politan veneer as she could supply. With Mary Todd, the veneer
took a particularly hard and bright finish. As a little girl, she had
been something of an *enfant terrible*. Now she had acquired a
precise and accurate speech, a delicate and well-formed handwriting, and an apparent inability to keep from showing that she
could both speak and read French. To the society of Springfield,
which, in order to reach the Edwards' door, had to kick pigs out
of the way, and which was rather conscious of the offal on its
boots, such attainments as Mary Todd possessed seemed highly
desirable, the mark of a natural distinction. And Abraham Lincoln, the most recently elected member of Springfield society, had
not been able to ignore the glitter of the young lady from Madame
Mentelle's, who backed up her glitter with a plump and attractive,
if rather feline, appearance.

If Madame Mentelle had not been able to furnish her pupil with
the proper genius of a human heart, she had at least been able to
provide the stage directions necessary for a great lady. And a great
lady would be an excellent addition to the stock-in-trade of the
frontier politician. Abraham, caught perhaps as much by that as
the fullness of Mary Todd's figure and the sleek whiteness of her
shoulders, repeated his Mary Owens tactics. But this time, he
could not be quite so lackadaisical. There were other suitors in
the field, among them Stephen A. Douglas, the diminutive Lincoln of the Democrats. Perhaps as Abraham, from the Speed's

* Helm, Katherine Mary, Wife of Lincoln.

guestroom, looked back upon the horrible days of his uncertain courtship of his second Kentucky belle, the thought of letting Stephen A. Douglas take his girl away from him brought a grimace of angry determination to the taut mouth. Perhaps a shudder, because things were worse than that. For it was not Douglas who got Mary Todd, but Abraham Lincoln, and the horror that had made him "the most miserable man living," was in the fact that he, Abraham had simply been unable to accept her. He had wanted her and had let her see it, but when she yielded and the suitor's cup was full, something had snapped within him and the fine nectar was turned to gall. Whatever the ceremony which had been arranged for January 1, 1841, whether it was a wedding,* as Mrs. Edwards described it, a mere formal betrothal, or nothing but a New Year's festivity, requiring Abraham's presence as Mary's fiancé (perhaps suggested to him with too much an air of proprietorship), the fact was,—and Abraham had to shudder every time he thought of it,—he had been unable to go through with the ordeal. He had permitted arrangements to be made, but, when the time came, without giving Mary any notice, he had gone away, off somewhere into the country. He had been balky before, but the matter had seemed settled. Abraham had unsettled it again. And he had learned that evasion as well as performance could carry its horror. He had simply gone to pieces.

Eight months later when most of the actual direct suffering was over, Abraham was still not himself. He had not seen Mary since that horrible day, but he had not lost his consciousness of her. Even in his tender care at the hands of Speed and his sympathetic family there was a certain sting,—for Lincoln, uncouth as he was, had a conscience (that failure to rationalize one's acts), and up to a certain point it made him unhappy. He could not, as

* Cf. Statement of Mrs. N. W. Edwards, Beveridge, I, 313-4.

he lay in bed drinking his morning coffee, brought him by a slave, be certain that, back in Springfield, Mary Todd was not lying face down upon her bed crying her heart out, or biting her handkerchief in rage at being jilted. That hurt him almost as much as the painful fact that he now had to make up his mind to leave things as they were or go back and tell Mary that he was sorry and that if she considered herself bound to him, he would marry her anyway. Exactly what he had told Mary Owens, and now Mary Owens was out of the picture. Perhaps, if he went back like a man, this second Mary would say also that she could do without him, in which case he might go freely with a free conscience, about the businesses which it had come to be impossible for him to attend. Freely, provided that freedom did not turn out to have a sting of defeat in its tail.

Something had to be done, that was certain. Abraham knew that he could not go on making himself sick and half-crazy as he had done in his hysterical attempt to escape from the consequences of his delinquency. He was now recovered enough to know what he ought to do, but not to know how to find the will to do it. He had sadly muddled his business as a legislator before the adjournment in March, being absent on many important occasions * and taking no part in the Assembly activities on most of the days when he was present. Nor was it on the cards for him to be reëlected. He had let his law business go completely topsy-turvy, to the patient distress of his partner. But Stuart was Mary Todd's cousin and the firm had been dissolved. Abraham had allowed his friends to become so concerned for him that they went about hiding razors and carving knives and guns wherever such weapons might catch his eye and suggest suicide to him. He had further mystified his friend Speed by apparently paying court

* Jnls, H. R. State of Ill. Session, 1840-41. Also Beveridge, I, 289.

to little Sarah Rickard, now sixteen, the sister-in-law of William Butler, with whom he boarded in Springfield. He had, in fact, surprised even Sarah, by asking her to marry him,* perhaps knowing that she at least, being so young, would be more than likely to delight him by asking him to wait a few years. Sarah must indeed have been flattered, if she was not too frightened to notice, by the juxtaposition in Lincoln's mind of herself and the idea of suicide.

One day late in the summer, when Abraham had rested long enough at the Speed mansion to convince himself that he was not and was not going to be genuinely sick, but was merely allowing himself to be hysterical, he packed up and returned to Springfield, not without considerable discussion with his friend Joshua as to whether women should be married or not. For Joshua, like Abraham, had his emotional difficulties. They were focussed, in his case, not upon Miss Matilda Edwards, but upon a bright-eyed and warm-fleshed young creature of Louisville, Fanny Henning. Fanny was one of those girls whose beauty though decorous and fine, at the same time suggests voluptuousness and undissembled eagerness. That was the sort of girl that would be sure to attract two such timid fauns as Abraham and Joshua. And in the attraction, they would be sure to find a boyish fear of inadequacy, a thing which every boy feels at one time or another but is always sure that no one else ever felt, since no one else could possibly be guilty of the same dreadful sins.

Abraham was getting a little used to the idea of having failed to go through with his emotional "crisis." It gave him some courage to see Speed facing his approaching marriage to Fanny Henning in the same nervous manner. Speed was beginning to build up a rational excuse for treating Fanny to a dose of Abraham's

* Herndon, Wm. H. (and Weik, Jesse W.) Herndon's Lincoln, I, 230.

jilting medicine. He kept explaining to himself and to Lincoln that he was afraid he did not really love her and that no man should marry a woman he was not sure he could give everything to. When Fanny fell seriously ill, Abraham explained to his friend that her illness was undoubtedly a disguised examination paper from the Almighty, sent to resolve the doubts and prove the state of mind of the worried Joshua. Abraham rather naïvely remarked, in a letter to Speed, written after his return to Springfield "Why, Speed, if you did not love her, although you might not wish her death, you would most certainly be resigned to it." * Perhaps what neither Lincoln nor Speed realized was that the agony which the prospective bridgegroom would have to go through if the adorable Fanny lived and continued to be adorable and in need of being married, almost worked to the extent of making that same bridegroom think that it would perhaps be better after all if she were to die.

Back in Springfield, Abraham set himself to try and catch up the loose threads of the old life which the great Todd-Lincoln disaster had so sadly torn and snarled. Judge Stephen T. Logan provided a new law-office to replace the partnership with Stuart, Sarah Rickard continued to provide a little bewildered emotional stimulus, the wild excitement of a full-fledged temperance movement, then sweeping the country, provided the public activity formerly centered in the legislature, and reminiscences of his trip to Kentucky provided food for thought. It was on the steamer, coming down the Ohio, on his way home from that visit that Abraham had seen a group of slaves, on their way to new owners in the South. He had seen them sit, chained together, being separated from wives, sweethearts, children, days of comparative comfort, going to unknown regions, to new masters and untried

---

* Lincoln to Speed. Feb. 3, 1842. Works, I, 255.

fellow-sufferers. And the thing that he had marvelled at was, as he wrote to Speed's sister, Mary, a slaveholder herself, that they were "the most cheerful people on board. One whose offence for which he had been sold was an overfondness for his wife, played the fiddle almost continually and others danced, sang, cracked jokes, and played various games of cards from day to day. How true it is that 'God tempers the wind to the shorn lamb,' or in other words, that he renders the worst of human conditions tolerable, while he permits the best to be nothing better than tolerable." *

Now, in between fairly happy travels about the circuit over which Lincoln's law firm practised, sitting, talking, arguing, joking with men, the depressed and much humbled young man got an occasional chance to exercise his gift for oratory in behalf of the Washingtonian Society, an organization dedicated to the business of ridding the world of the drunkard through the example of drunkards who had thought better of their habits. In common with most of those who believe that man has an intellectual destiny to fulfill, Abraham did not like to see men debasing themselves in any way. That was the root of his rather apathetic objection both to slavery and to hard liquor. It was also the root of his own sense of shame at not being able to go through with things. That sense of shame was a little assuaged by large draughts of the reformer's zeal, which Abraham took in the form of such forensic pomp as "Happy day," he said, "when—all appetites controlled, all poisons subdued, all matter subjected—mind, all conquering mind, shall live and move, the monarch of the world. Glorious consummation! Hail, fall of fury! Reign of reason, all hail! And when the victory shall be complete,—when there shall be neither a slave nor a drunkard on earth—how

* Lincoln to Mary Speed, Sept. 27, 1841. Works, I, 250-1.

proud the title of that land which may truly claim to be the birthplace and the cradle of both those revolutions that shall have ended in that victory." *

There spoke the amateur of man's perfectability. There spoke the young man who would not go back to what he had outlived. There spoke the pioneer who had seen nine people sleeping on a puncheon floor,—a few cold potatoes in the larder, the rain coming in at the unwalled side of the lean-to, spring water a mile away, the flies and the stench of human filth hanging moistly in the air. There spoke the man who could not bear to believe that the human race was as he had found it, as he himself, in some of his activities, had seemed almost to prove it. "Make drinking unfashionable," he said, as others have said since with no greater effect. But he was not yet quite ready to advocate, openly, making slavery "unfashionable."

All this oratory had a very restorative effect upon Abraham, but even more effective was the news from Louisville that Joshua Speed had survived his wedding night without dying of mortification and that, moreover, the same apprehensive Joshua had managed to find that in marriage there might be true delight. How great a tribute to Fanny Henning that discovery was, in view of the neurotic tendencies of Mr. Speed, perhaps neither Joshua nor Abraham ever realized. It did a great deal to relieve Abraham's mind, to learn that a man like himself could surrender to a woman and yet have enough left to make a man capable of standing up.

The good news from Louisville delighted Lincoln so that he at once sat down and wrote a reply. A little of the crafty politician crept into the closing paragraph:

* Address Before the Springfield Washingtonian Society, Feb. 22, 1842. Works, I, 261 ff.

. . . I tell you, Speed, our forebodings (for which you and I are peculiar) are all the worst sort of nonsense. I fancied from the time I received your letter of Saturday, that the one of Wednesday was never to come, and yet it *did* come, and what is more, it is perfectly clear both from its tone and its handwriting, that you were much happier, or, if you think the term preferable, less miserable, when you wrote it than when you wrote the last one before. You had so obviously improved at the very time I so much fancied you would have grown worse. You say that something indescribably horrible and alarming still haunts you. You will not say that three months from now, I will venture. When your nerves once get steady now, the whole trouble will be over forever. . . . Again you say, you much fear that that Elysium of which you have dreamed so much is never to be realized. Well, if it shall not, I dare swear it will not be the fault of her who is now your wife. I now have no doubt that it is the peculiar misfortune of both you and me to dream dreams of Elysium far exceeding all that anything earthly can realize. . . .

"I write another letter, inclosing this, which you can show her if she desires it. I do this because she would think strangely, perhaps, should you tell her that you received no letters from me, or, telling her you do, refuse to let her see them. I close this, entertaining the confident hope that every successive letter I shall have from you (which I pray may be not few, nor far between) may show you possessing a more steady hand and cheerful heart than the last preceding it. As ever your friend,

LINCOLN.*

* Lincoln to Speed. Feb. 25, 1842. Works, I, 276.

Abraham Lincoln at Home

The House at Eighth and Jackson Streets, Springfield

CHAPTER SEVEN

HUMILIATION AND MARRIAGE

A BRAHAM LINCOLN was a politician and when not engaged in some sort of political activity was pretty certain to be noticeably unhappy. The fact that after 1841 he was no longer a member of the Illinois legislature left him with only law business, for which he did not greatly care, but which at least gave him what he so much needed of contact with human beings to whom his anecdotes and amusing tricks were valuable. Brief as had been his career upon the judicial circuit over which the practice of Judge Logan's firm extended, Abraham had made fast friends and was always glad to return to them. But in spite of this break in the monotony of his no longer official life, he was still troubled and melancholy, worried over the case of Mary Todd.

Mary's and his friends were now divided into two factions. On the one side were the Edwards, who, much as they admired Abraham, rather felt that he did not belong in their sister's world. On the other side were Abraham's devoted admirers and well-wishers, Mr. and Mrs. Simeon Francis, the former the Whig editor of the *Sangamo Journal* who depended on Abraham for help in the shaping of his paper's policies and who could not bear to see his young friend in the doldrums. Mrs. Francis, in addition to her fondness for Abraham, was fond of match-making, and she saw in the healing of the broken fortunes of the two embroiled young people a beautiful chance to give herself some real wholesome enjoyment. She accordingly invited Abraham and Mary to her house without either of them knowing that the other was coming. As Abraham was no great hand at resisting any feminine blandishments when they were offered him, it was not long before he had Mary Todd in his arms again, and when he had her in his arms he could not seem to recall the force of those terrors and misgivings which troubled him so when he was away from the girl. They had kept him from getting a marriage license and appearing at a prearranged ceremony, but, with Mary against his powerful breast, yielding within his amazingly strong long arms, he could not even think what they had been.

Even now, after reconciliation, Mary could not go about constantly with her arms about his neck. Their meetings, because of the humiliation of possible public sarcasm, were clandestine and few. In between them, Abraham tortured himself as only a nature given to moody depression can do. In the midst of his tortures and pleasures he took what comfort he could from the reassuring letters which came from that pleasantly surprised Kentucky bridegroom, Joshua Speed, now no longer a store-keeper in Springfield. And he got a great deal of satisfaction out of a return to his favorite but dangerous sport of writing anonymous letters to the public press. The newspaper, naturally enough, was the obsequious *Sangamo Journal,* but the effect of the letters published in it was far more serious than Abraham had expected it to be. He had merely tried to blow off a little personal and party steam, which had accumulated to a dangerous pressure within him during his political idleness.

It happened, as a natural course of events resulting from the extravagant gusto of its legislators, that the State of Illinois went bankrupt. The dream child of the Springfield Whigs, the State

Bank of Springfield, went to smash. In the spring of 1842 nobody in Illinois could buy or sell anything excepting by exchange of goods. Nobody had anything with which to pay taxes, as their favorite money, the paper of the State Bank, was worthless. In order to keep the state going, and in pursuance of an Illinois law, the Governor and fiscal officials of the state issued a proclamation declaring that after a certain date bills of the State Bank would not be accepted in payment of taxes. The collection of Revenue was stopped until after the legislature had had a chance to meet and decide what to do to get itself out of the hole into which the combination of Whig enthusiasm and universal financial depression had sunk it. There was no question about the legality and the necessity of just such a proclamation as was issued. But it was issued by state officials who were Democrats. Not only were they Democrats but one of them, James Shields, State Auditor, upon whose shoulders fell the burden of sending an explanatory memorandum to the tax collectors, was one of Abraham's particular aversions.

Shields was a very popular and honorable lawyer, who had seen much public service and was so well liked and respected everywhere that he had been able to get himself elected to the state legislature as a Democrat from a Whig district. That made him very dangerous in Lincoln's eyes. And the fact that Shields, an Irishman by birth, was of a pompous and officious disposition and took himself very seriously, made him fair game, in Lincoln's opinion. As State Auditor, this zealous and patriotic public servant had just issued a memorandum of great good sense and considerable tact, designed to show the reasons why the refusal to accept the notes of the defunct Bank had been an action which the state government had to take. But reason and good sense meant nothing to Abraham when a member of the opposite political party could be injured by ignoring those qualities.

Lincoln sat down in the office of the *Sangamo Journal* and wrote a sarcastic letter, signed "Rebecca" containing a lot of clever backwoods burlesque, and insinuating that the only reason why the Governor and Auditor Shields had suspended the collection of taxes in Bank notes, was that they, as public officials, were so greedy that they insisted on having gold poured into the state coffers where they could get at it for themselves. "Rebecca" further stated, in direct opposition to the actual facts, that there was no law justifying the State's position. It seems impossible to believe that Abraham did not know this to be mere quibbling. It is also hard to believe that he would have made the same charges had his own signature appeared below the published letter.* Fortunately for Lincoln at the moment, Mr. Shields ignored the communication.

Abraham was not satisfied. Once more he put the pen in "Rebecca's" hand and wrote a still more abusive burlesque, repeating his first charges and adding some new ones for good measure. Again Shields controlled himself, and again Lincoln, having tasted the delight of being witty without personal risk, returned to scatter his favorite vitriol. Referring, in her third letter, to Shields's circular to the tax collectors, in which the Auditor had explained that the object of the refusal of the State to accept the worthless Bank paper was the suspension of the State's revenue for that year, the unknown "Rebecca" said, "I say it's a lie, and not a well told one at that. It grins out like a copper dollar. Shields is a fool as well as a liar. With him truth is out of the question; and as for getting a good, bright, passable lie out of him, you might as well try to strike fire from a cake

* Works, Vol. I, p. 283.

of tallow." Even after this amazing epistle had appeared Shields made no effort to investigate. Irishman that he was, it took a reflection upon his personal courage to set him going. Just such a reflection appeared in the last "Rebecca" letter which the *Sangamo Journal* printed on September 9, 1842.

But the last "Rebecca" letter was not written by Abraham. It was the product of the pens of Miss Julia Jayne and her cousin Miss Mary Todd, ardent Whig damsels of the town, who had become so interested in Abraham's unfortunate idea of public fun, that they too had begged leave to stick a needle into the bear. It looks very much as if Abraham had been attempting to show Mary what a big man he was politically, by way of making up for what he had shown her of his personal smallness. Perhaps Mary was additionally influenced to believe in her Abraham's importance by a curious document, tied up with pink silk ribbons, which he handed her at this time. This was a carefully prepared and beautifully written list of candidates for the state legislature from 1832 to date, the number of votes each candidate had received being entered opposite his name. Lincoln's name from his first candidacy on, showed a steady increase in votes. In the election of 1840, he had received his greatest vote, clearly proving that he was a rising figure. This unusual document, Abraham had gone to the trouble of having certified by the Clerk of the County Court, and he had tied the certification to the document itself with a ribbon.*

Whatever proof of his political magnificence Abraham was able to adduce for Mary's benefit, his permission for the two girls to write the last letter does much to nullify. For Shields was now aroused. He came to the *Sangamo Journal* and demanded to know the author of the letters. Upon being told, he

* Beveridge, Vol. I, pp. 343-4.

mounted a horse and, with a friend, rode after Lincoln, who was attending court on the circuit. Unfortunately for Abraham some of his friends, who were rather eager to see a duel, saw to it that Shields did not reach him until after they did. Undoubtedly Abraham's direct, face-to-face manner would have disarmed the wrathy Auditor and brought about a reconciliation. But Captain Merryman, who had taken Abraham under his wing as being a chick incapable of handling an affair of honor with the proper firmness and decorum, pushed the situation to a point from which there was no turning back. By juggling the letters which passed between the involved parties Merryman managed to keep up the tension long after Shields's good sense and Abraham's sense of humor would naturally have dissolved it. Abraham as a matter of fact wrote out an apology which would have satisfied Shields had that gentleman been permitted to receive it. Instead, a meeting on the Missouri side of the Mississippi River, at five o'clock in the evening, was arranged, the contestants to fight with cavalry broadswords "of the largest size" over a plank fixed in the ground.

The dueling party arrived at the appointed place at the appointed time. Abraham, although showing a brave face, was very much troubled, and a little puzzled to know exactly how he had contrived to get into such an unsavory mess. He had chosen broadswords because of his lack of the advantage of experience and his possession of the advantage of size, feeling that, as he did not really wish to hurt Shields, the largest weapon, considering his length of arm, would serve the best as a shield. Fortunately for both the foolish Abraham and the nettled State Auditor, reason prevailed, and friends of the two were able to arrange a bloodless reconciliation. Abraham Lincoln walked away from the dueling field that September evening, a changed man. He had written his last anonymous letter, and he had been put through one more hoop by that trainer of sad dogs, humiliation.

He needed something, now, to restore his dignity, and he was close to having made up his mind what that must be. To help him be certain, he wrote to Speed in Louisville, telling of his duel, and ending, ". . . The immense sufferings you endured from the first day of September till the middle of February you never tried to conceal from me, and I well understood. You have now been the husband of a lovely woman nearly eight months. . . . That you are happier now than the day you married her, I well know, for without you could not be living. But I have your word for it, too, and the returning elasticity of spirits which is manifested in your letters. But I want to ask a close question. 'Are you now in feeling as well as judgement glad that you are married as you are?' From anybody but me this would be an impudent question, not to be tolerated; but I know you will pardon it in me. Please answer it quickly, as I am impatient to know. . . . " *

This was early in October. Speed wrote back within a few weeks, explaining in positive terms that this business of living intimately with a woman continued to be all right. On November 4, 1842, hastily and with little preparation that could have temped Abraham to escape, Mary Todd became his wife. If he had believed that his grieving, easily hurt, but tempestuous nature still needed the burnishing of punishment, Abraham had found the place to get it. For Mary Todd was no angel. Charming and appealing as she was in person, she was no Fanny Henning, and she soon contrived to make Abraham understand that life in this world is a business of give and take, no personality

* Works, Vol. I, p. 297 ff.

being free enough nor sufficiently highly sanctioned to disregard the requirements of another.

There was no money in Abraham's pocket. He and his élite bride had no wedding trip other than that slight and muddy journey from the Edwards mansion to Mrs. Beck's Globe Tavern, where they took up their abode without making any attempt at housekeeping. Indeed it was about all Abraham could do to get together the four dollars a week required for the Tavern board, and he had to subtract most of that from what he had been paying intermittently on his outstanding debts. Four dollars, even in the Springfield of 1842, would not, after taking something out for food, supply very much space for two highstrung people to walk about in. Yet Abraham and Mary managed to endure the close quarters for a year. It was not an easy year, and it was a revelation to Lincoln, who had conceived no idea of the nature of a woman, and who found in Mary traits which have contrived to make for more devoted husbands than he wish that they were far, very far away. For Mary had, possibly as a preliminary trace of a mental weakness which came over her in later years, a violent temper which she was not able to control and which when not going in full force, often showed itself merely in the form of mean-spirited carping. Such was the price of Abraham's entrance into the high circle of Springfield's aristocracy, an elevation which did not appear to do his political ambitions much good. If Abraham came to feel that Speed, in telling him of the beauties of married life, had merely been deceiving him, it would indeed not be strange. Certainly, after his marriage he was never so frank and intimate with friend Joshua. In fact, three months before the birth of his first child he wrote Speed, who had heard of the coming event, that no such thing was expected. And this in spite of the fact that Abraham had sworn to his friend that his first child should be Joshua Speed Lincoln.

Perhaps Abraham's disappointment at failing for the second time to receive his party's nomination as a candidate for the national House of Representatives, was as much responsible for the oversight as any domestic infelicity. Certainly, when, although he had felt himself to be the leading Whig possibility, John J. Hardin was nominated in his stead in 1843, and even Edward Baker had beaten him in his own county, Abraham felt that something was wrong. He felt very bitterly about that, but party loyalty made him bow to the inevitable. In 1844, however, when the same thing happened all over again, and the soft soap which Lincoln had applied to the previously successful Hardin, failed to produce the desired effect in the following year, he knew that he was being persecuted. He was hurt, even more than he was surprised. Just when he should have expected to find himself sailing along into national prominence, supported by all the Whigs who had been so loyal to him and so proud of him while he was in the state legislature Abraham found himself being neglected. People that he would have expected to find working ardently for his advancement were working for themselves instead. Even Judge Logan, his law partner, was becoming troubled by Abraham's political ambitions.

Meanwhile, in the little room at the Globe Tavern, into which in their moments of affection as well as those of distress, Abraham and Mary Todd had been wedged, a son was born, but he was not named for Joshua Speed. Mary had, as in other things, asserted herself, and the boy's name was Robert Todd Lincoln. With the advent of this youngster the mad scramble of the tiny tavern room became impossible. The Lincolns moved, at first to South Fourth Street, then to Eighth and Jackson Streets.

CHAPTER EIGHT

THE GENTLEMAN FROM ILLINOIS

ALTHOUGH the election of 1840, coming on the heels of the financial depression for which it was easy to blame the Democratic administrations of Jackson and Van Buren, had brought Abraham Lincoln's party to the presidential chair, a curious trick of fate intervened to unseat it after a month of sovereignty. William Henry Harrison, a gentleman of Virginia, died on the 4th of April, 1840, just thirty days after his inauguration, and the office of chief magistrate came into the hands of John Tyler, also of Virginia, also a gentleman. Tyler, however, upon reaching the pinnacle of office, displeased his followers, by proving that he was not really a Whig at all but a good Southern Democrat. He soon plunged the country into difficulties by advocating, although for honorable reasons, the popular though politically suspect principle of annexation of Texas.

Abraham Lincoln was on the outs as an office holder at this time, but the necessity of getting into office gave him an even keener sense of contact with political issues than he could have taken from the mere holding of an office won. He followed the Texas struggle carefully, in search of new fuel for the Whig wildfire. Texas had originally been a part of Mexico, but had been largely settled by emigrants from the United States. In 1836, although in no sense other than racial a part of the United States, the Texans had rebelled against the sovereignty of Mexico and had, after much reverse and horrible suffering, won a victory at San Jacinto which earned a promise of recognition of the Texan Republic, and a doubtful assurance from General Santa Anna, then the dictator of Mexico, that he would remain on the southern side of the Rio Grande.

It was plain, at this time, that the United States of America was going to grow, and that one of the points of national solidarity was a popular enthusiasm for the ideal of expansion. But behind the popular ideal were other influences which made what appeared on the surface to be a perfectly natural tendency, a dangerous thing to play with.

In the first place, there were among the Texans many who were not averse to a little juggling of land values, gambling as it were upon the turn of American acquisition. And even more important was the fact that the South had begun to realize that economics favored the manner of development which the North had adopted, that the cotton states, if they were to compete with the upper half of the nation, must be strengthened in some way. There was no better way than in the development of Texas, an ideal cotton-growing region. It is not strange that when the presumably Whig president Tyler, advocated a scheme so obviously in the interest of the South, a great hue and cry was raised. With the exception of Daniel Webster, who was in the midst of important negotiations, the entire cabinet resigned. Yet the issue was not even then clearly an alignment of parties. The South was eager, but the Whigs, both North and South, feared to align themselves against slavery. And then too, American blood had been valiantly shed in the liberation of Texas. No political party could afford to stand up and say that that blood was shed in vain. For the popular imagination was printed in many colors with a picture of Travis and Crockett and Bowie, dying in the midst of their massacred men in the ancient shelter

of the Alamo. However unsound the consequences of such heroism might be, its overtones rang louder than public speeches.
Reason, if it would be listened to, must defer to the unreasonable
genius of legend.

In 1844, the Texas-Mexican question actually determined the
successor to the unpleasantly surprising and ineffectual Mr. Tyler.
One of Abraham Lincoln's idols, Henry Clay, was put forward
as the Whig candidate, and an inconspicuous Congressman,
James K. Polk, received the Democratic nomination. The Whigs
made the mistake of allowing their otherwise popular candidate
to declare himself against immediate annexation; the Democratic candidate made no bones about saying that he was very
much in favor of just that thing which Clay opposed. The mass
of voters North and South were interested in nothing else. Those
that did not wish the annexation of Texas on patriotic and
nationalistic grounds, desired it because it meant an addition to
the waning power of the South. Once again the pathetic figure
of the unlucky Henry Clay went down to unquestionable defeat.
In the northeastern states, from Pennsylvania to Maine, the electoral vote was: Polk seventy-seven, Clay thirty-five. It was not,
then, a matter purely between North and South.

President Polk was soon in hot water. Texas was formally
annexed, although the Mexican government, which had not been
consulted, had notified Washington that such an act would be
considered a hostile one. The next step was for the administration to insist upon the boundaries of its new territory. The
Nueces River seemed to be the most logical line, but the administration insisted that it should be the Rio Grande, all the way
to the Gulf, and not only insisted but sent General Taylor to a
point on the Rio Grande opposite the Mexican town of Mata-
moras with instructions to prove that it was right. Upon the

Mexicans crossing the river, to resist what they regarded as an act of aggression, there was a fight, which gave the President his chance to announce to Congress that American blood had been spilled on "American" soil. If the bodies of sixteen American cavalrymen could make Mexican soil American, American it was. Congress did not disagree. All but unanimously it passed resolutions of war.

And in Illinois at this time, Abraham Lincoln, finally successful, after a gap of five years, in getting his party's nomination as a candidate for election to represent in the National Congress the Seventh District of Illinois, was going about on the stump matching his wit and personality against a gruff old preacher named Peter Cartwright. As between Democrats and Whigs at this time, in so far as the State of Illinois was concerned, there was very little difference of opinion to be aired. No candidate for office could oppose the war and hope to live. Neither Lincoln nor Cartwright differed from the mass of Illinoisians on the matter of slavery, both of them believing that it was a bad thing but not a hellish thing. Neither could say anything about it. Neither could afford to be moderate in the matter of the boundary of Oregon Territory, for expansion, not retraction, was the bait that would catch the popular vote.

Abraham had not been idle in the years of disappointment following his marriage, when his chief activity was on the circuit of the Eighth Judicial District of his state as an itinerant lawyer. His temporary absence from public office and the ensuing return to common contact with men and things had done something to dissipate the antipathy which his marriage into Springfield "society" seemed to have aroused in his friends. And in his new law partner, William H. Herndon, an enthusiastic and able young man, passionately devoted to the Whig cause and more earnestly than his senior an opponent of slavery, Abraham had found a lieutenant who could keep the new young Whigs in line behind him. Small wonder then, that Abraham received, in the election of 1846, the largest vote of his career. At last, under the shadow of a cloud of national disgrace brought on by the sultry nature of Mr. Polk's manner of administering the presidency, Abraham Lincoln went to Washington. He had supported the Mexican War and praised its deeds of heroism, finding that easy in view of the fact that they were performed under the command of two Whig Generals. He had promised nothing other than that he would not seek to be a candidate to succeed himself. He had named his second son, Edward Baker, after the Whig Congressman whose trust he had juggled and all but betrayed in attempting to remain in line for the nomination in 1843, after promising his colleague to withdraw.

The outbreak of the Mexican War having called his two energetic fellow-Whigs, Hardin and Baker, to the front, Abraham was left to proceed to Washington in distinct charge of the destiny of the Whig part of Illinois. As far as representation in Congress was concerned that part was only one-seventh. Abraham, after his election, had had a chance to see a city of some size when he went to Chicago as a delegate to the Rivers and Harbors Convention of 1847, a gathering attended by prominent men of both East and West. Abraham was more impressed by the prominent men than he was by Chicago. His position as Congressman-elect—the only Whig Congressman from Illinois— gave him a sense of dignity and importance, a thing which he could always use to advantage. Chicago had importance but no dignity. It was a town, barely a quarter of a century of age, lacking color, lacking an air of permanence, lacking almost everything but bustle and opportunity. Abraham had his eye on

Washington, which he must have conceived to be a far different sort of place, as indeed it was.

There has perhaps never been in the world a city enjoying renown as the seat of a national capital which has done less to repay with distinction, beauty, or any other quality the honor conferred upon it than the city of Washington, D. C., had done up to the time of the Civil War. True, it was the one city in the country which had been laid out according to a carefully and well-drawn up plan, but in 1847 there was very little but mud and pigs to fill up many of the squares and circles which have since become as they were designed to be, the seat of garden plots and monuments, bronze, marble and living bloom. Most of the official boarding houses and other residences were clustered about Capitol Hill, where the unfinished seat of government squatted with its temporary wooden dome like a decapitated sphinx.

Abraham Lincoln brought his wife and oldest child by the longest possible route from Springfield to the national capital, this giving Horace Greeley a chance to rebuke him for collecting from the government almost twice the travel allotment which he should have had. He installed his small family in lodgings on Capitol Hill on the site of the present Library of Congress. After the long and tiring trip, it must have been very terrifying to the simple middle-westerner and his uncertain-tempered wife and their four-year-old child to emerge from an uncomfortable train in a kind of ramshackle barn full of all sorts of unkempt and dirty loafers and to be confronted by a roaring, gesticulating, threatening horde of mad-hearted cab drivers. Whatever Mary and the little boy felt, Abraham could afford to be amused. He was, he thought, on the threshold of national prominence. Washington would have to recognize him as a political figure of no mean degree, elected, though a Whig, from a Democratic state by an all but overwhelming vote. There was personality in that. The fact stood in the back of Abraham's once harassed and troubled mind as the solvent of his sense of doom, his feeling that secret things were lying in ambush waiting to thwart him. He felt that he stood upon his own feet, that he had reached this point in his career by virtue of his own indomitable effort. He was glad to have arrived at his destination and felt that he could now afford to forget that he had lived for years in terror of deceit and treachery on the part of his friends, in suspicion of hostility, and in bitterness at thought of the humiliations to which he had been subjected. Well, at last these elements of personal discord had been overridden. Abraham Lincoln had reached Washington.

Before the end of the Congressional session he was able to write home to his law partner Herndon, in Springfield:

. . . "I suppose I am now one of the old men; and I declare on my veracity, which I think is good with you, that nothing could afford me more satisfaction than to learn that you and others of my young friends at home were doing battle in the contest and endearing themselves to the people and taking a stand far above any I have ever been able to reach in their admiration. I cannot conceive that other men feel differently. Of course I cannot demonstrate what I say; but I was young once, and I am sure I was never ungenerously thrust back. I hardly know what to say. The way for a young man to rise is to improve himself every way he can, never suspecting that anybody wishes to hinder him. . . ." *

If Mary Lincoln had looked forward to her life in Washington as a partial reward for the pride she felt in having her

* Works.

ungainly husband elected to the halls of the mighty, she must have been somewhat disappointed. She did not appear to be popular in Washington, kept to herself in Mrs. Sprigg's boarding house, appearing only at meal times, and left the city for the West again after a scant three months. Abraham had decided that she interfered with his business. Her life could not have been a very pleasant one, for new members are not apt to be prominent socially in the life of the capital even though they possess far greater store of graces than Mary Lincoln's husband boasted. Washington was a sorry place, too, to get about in. There was no means of transportation other than that provided by the violent and exorbitant hacks which rushed up and down the streets splashing everyone with mud. There were as many backyard privies, pigpens, stables and dung heaps as there were houses in the city of thirty thousand, and the small center of public buildings was, during the sessions, crowded with haranguing politicians, many of them seldom sober. None of the dwellings of the city had running water, there being no public water supply. There were practically no sidewalks, and only two streets with any pretense of pavement.

The uncouth city was more appealing to Abraham than it had been to his wife. His fellow legislators soon became attached to him because of his simple humanity and his ability to make life seem as true and real and close at hand as the eye saw it and the ear heard it. Time went by, but Abraham's way of seeing and reproducing things in simple conversation, narrative and reference, preserved unbroken the unity of the moment. He would sit by the fireplace in the post office of the House of Representatives and draw to him men who would have sat through ten sessions in the House without ever knowing that he was there.

Meanwhile, twenty-seven thousand American soldiers were

falling of wounds and disease in Mexico in furtherance of the
evident wishes of their masters, the people of the sovereign states
of the Union. The war itself had been popular, but Abraham
thought he detected an opportunity to prove that those responsible for it were not. He had supported the war and now, in the
Thirtieth Congress, was voting supplies and equipment to keep
it going, but the executive head of the nation was a Democrat,
while Zachary Taylor, the military hero of the hour, was a
Whig. Abraham knew what you could do with a set of circumstances like that. Not for nothing had he come in contact with
powerful Whigs in Washington who knew more about the shaping of the party's destiny than you could learn in Illinois in a
dozen years. Before coming to Congress Abraham had not only
supported the war, but in the *Sangamo Journal* he had even
seen to it that President Polk was bludgeoned for being too easy
with Mexico. Now things were different. The Whig leaders had
concluded that the Democratic President could be made very
uncomfortable by merely raising the question of whether or not
the war was a just one. Mexico was pretty well subjugated by
this time and no one could accuse the carping Whigs of undermining the unanimity with which the administration must face
a National danger.

Abraham sat in his seat, in the crowded House of Representatives, the worst seat in the entire hall, and bided his time.
All about him were lawyers, like himself and yet unlike himself. They were chiefly skilled exponents of the ungentle art of
getting what they wanted under the guise of serving the public.
Among them were men like John Quincy Adams, John Gorham
Palfrey, Robert C. Winthrop and George Ashmun of Massachusetts, Alexander H. Stephens and Robert Toombs of Georgia,
Joshua Giddings of Ohio, Williamson Cobb of Alabama, James

Dixon of Connecticut, David Wilmot of Pennsylvania, Caleb Smith of Indiana, and, in his own delegation from Illinois, Orlando B. Ficklin, John A. McClernand, and Robert Smith. The things they wanted were not always the same. Many were interested only in the development of the West and the possibilities of profit arising therefrom in railroads and increased markets; others were interested chiefly in putting down slavery, either on moral or economic grounds; others, like Abraham himself, had little heed for anything but the aggrandizement of party influence. Robert Winthrop, gentleman, scholar, and devotee of the curiously single interests of industrial Massachusetts, was the Speaker of the house, and in his choice, the body of which Abraham was now a member definitely lined itself up with a majority against the President and hence against the Mexican War. But it is notable that this political alignment was not focussed against slavery, for the Southern Whigs, later supporters of the Confederacy, like Alexander Stephens and Robert Toombs, voted for Winthrop as speaker, although John Gorham Palfrey of Winthrop's own state, a minister, and an ardent anti-slavery moralist, failed to do so. If Abraham considered the matter of slavery as an issue of importance at this time he did very little about it. The Mexican question was the burning issue of the moment, the solidarity of parties being dependent on it. Opposition to it was, as we have seen, not a matter of section so much as of party.

Before coming to Washington, before his election, in fact, Abraham with that eagerness of his to put himself right in the eyes of those whose support he expected, whether or not he was in entire agreement with them, had written to a friend who was an abolitionist, ". . . I never was much interested in the Texas question. I never could see much good to come of annexation, inasmuch as they were already a free republican people on our own model. On the other hand I never could very clearly see how the annexation would augment the evil of slavery. . . . I hold it to be a paramount duty of us in the free states, due to the Union of the States, and perhaps to liberty itself (paradox though it may seem), to let the slavery of the other states alone; while on the other hand, I hold it to be equally clear that we should never knowingly lend ourselves, directly or indirectly, to prevent that slavery from dying a natural death—to find new places for it to live in when it can no longer exist in the old. Of course, I am not considering what would be our duty in cases of insurrection among the slaves. To recur to the Texas question, I understand the Liberty men (abolitionists) to have viewed annexation as a much greater evil than ever I did; and I would like to convince you if I could, that they could have prevented it if they had chosen. . . ." *

Now, sitting in the National House of Representatives, with the eyes of the nation, if not actually upon him, at least perfectly willing and apt to look his way, the gentleman from Illinois, putting slavery rather out of his mind as a rather distressing question, saw the opportunity to strike a blow for consolidation of the Whig party, which the abolitionist agitation in parts of the North had already threatened with schism. Slavery was not pleasant to think about. Abraham had, just before coming to his post in Washington, rather half-heartedly acted as counsel for a slaveholder named Matson, whose slaves had sued for liberty on account of residence in Illinois. As was natural in a state like Illinois, Matson, in spite of Lincoln's support, had lost his case and, under indictment for a statutory offense, had fled the State without paying Lincoln his fee. Just at the moment, therefore,

* Works, Vol. II, p. 10.

slavery was an unpleasant subject. But here was the matter of Texas coming to a head.

On the twenty-second of December, 1847, Abraham introduced into the house a series of resolutions which were the beginning of the end of another phase of his political career. He put his head into the lion's mouth, and although the lion did not bite, neither did the audience applaud the stunt. In these very pointed resolutions Abraham questioned the statements made by President Polk in his message to Congress proclaiming a state of war with Mexico, May 11, 1846, and in subsequent messages. Furthermore, the young congressman from the Sangamon demanded to be informed authoritatively, for the benefit of a curious House of Representatives, whether or not the spot on which the blood of American citizens had been overtly shed was or was not American territory in any sense, however remote. He also, very acidly, asked if it were not true that those very American citizens whose blood was shed were members of the armed forces of the United States of America sent into a Mexican settlement in spite of the fact that their commanding General, a Whig, had stated that no such step was necessary for the defense of American interests.

These resolutions were not adopted by the House and no one paid any special attention to them. They were merely a part of the campaign of the Whig leaders, of whom Lincoln was an instrument, against President Polk and the Democratic party. As a further part of this same scheme of attack, Abraham voted, to his everlasting loss, for resolutions introduced by Mr. Ashmun of Massachusetts, in which the war with Mexico was described as having been begun by the President "unnecessarily and unconstitutionally." Without Lincoln's vote the resolution would not have been adopted, as the vote was 82 to 81. Abraham followed this excited and enthusiastic Whig sniping with a long address which he delivered before the House on January 12, 1848. In this address, aside from the fact that he called the President all kinds of unpleasant things, "a bewildered, confounded, and miserably perplexed man," Abraham did little but repeat the well-tried Whig arguments against the Administration's action. He spoke as if from a sense of duty to his party, not with that tremendous personal force which had many times before enabled him to hold his hearers spellbound. As in the case of Robert Matson and his slaves, Abraham lost the verdict. No one commented on what he had said. No one seemed to think it extraordinary that he had said anything. Except in Abraham's home district in Illinois, the speech was forgotten, until its *obiter dicta* on the subject of the right of revolt could be used against him. This was a section of his speech in which he said, ". . . Any people anywhere being inclined and having the power have the right to rise up and shake off the existing government, and form a new one that suits them better. This is a most valuable, a most sacred right—a right which we hope and believe is to liberate the world. . . ." *

But that unusual remark was not what troubled the people of Illinois, nor the fact that their Sangamon County representative had called the President's remarks upon his Mexican policy the "half-insane mumbling of a fever dream." What troubled them was that their representative, in whom they had placed confidence, and who had waved his hat and given godspeed to the sons of Illinois, six thousand strong, departing for the front to defend their country's interests (as they supposed), had stood up in Congress and called the self-sacrifice of those heroes a campaign of robbery and dishonor, rapine and murder.

* Works, Vol. II, p. 37.

When Abraham learned through his faithful young partner, Billy Herndon, how his constituents were interpreting his attitude in Congress it bothered him a good deal. No one likes to be misunderstood and to have his idea set at naught because he has failed to take into consideration the inequalities of human judgment. Abraham felt that the fact that he was vigorously opposing what many good Americans believed to be an unjust war should have earned him praise rather than blame. He did not realize that what to one man may be a passionate moral issue, to another may be villainy and betrayal. The young men at home were more radical than Abraham had ever been. They would have been glad to see Whig interests advanced, but they wished to have their interests made Whig interests. Abraham was a little different. He took the party as it was and asked no questions.

In his unattractive and lonely room at Mrs. Sprigg's, Abraham sat when he had nothing else to do, checking over lists of people back home who must have Whig literature sent to them. He was unofficially helping the Whig National Committee. Now that Mary and little Bob had gone away he felt often out of sorts, perhaps wanting, more than he disliked the tricks which his wife's incalculable personality played with his environment, the solace of someone to praise him. For he got no praise and little attention of any kind in the serious conduct of his business at the Capitol. When he was particularly lonely he would visit the library of the Supreme Court, digging out sources and special cases, or go wandering among the pathetic shops of the strange city, looking for little things for his children, or carrying out commissions for Mary, reminding himself thereby of the life which he could neither quite do without nor quite be happy in. Sometimes he wrote to the two little boys, whom he regarded with devoted and wondering pride. But when Mary hinted that she would like to take a trip to New York or Boston during the early summer, Abraham paid no attention. He was too much absorbed with the political difficulties of the hour. It was fairly plain to him that he had lost all chance of being asked to reconsider his political promise not to run for Congress in the following year. But here was a presidential election at hand and the Whigs were on the point of choosing a candidate.

Abraham had joined with a number of Southern Whigs and one member of Congress from Connecticut to form a society called the Young Indians, and it was Alexander H. Stephens of Georgia, one of the leaders of this group and one of Abraham's few Congressional intimates, who had put forward the idea that General Zachary Taylor was the man for the Whig Party to nominate. And Zachary certainly was, in everything but fitness for the office of President. In the first place, he was well known as a Whig. In the second place, he was a Southerner and a slaveholder and could thus command respect and votes in the South. In the third place, he had just won the Mexican War, in spite of being hampered by the jealousy of a Democratic president. He was a popular idol. And most important of all, his candidacy would help to dispel the unfortunate feeling which the Whig condemnation of the war had bred in the heart of the nation. These considerations, in the minds of Abraham and the Whig leaders, outweighed the fact that the hearty old General could scarcely either read or write and had never been known to have any idea on any national subject.

Although Abraham must have known how unfitted "Old Rough and Ready" Taylor was for the office once held by Washington and Thomas Jefferson, he was perfectly willing to throw over his ancient idol, Henry Clay, and fight hard for the General's nomination. For with Abraham at this time, a weak and ignorant Whig who could win was better than a high-principled statesman, Whig though he might be, who had the habit of losing. So the young politician from Illinois went to the Philadelphia Convention in June, 1848, and spent considerable time trying to keep alternate Whig delegates from Illinois, who were known to favor Henry Clay, from getting their seats.

He need not have troubled, for in spite of the outraged feelings of the old warriors of the Whig party, General Taylor was easily nominated, although for the sake of caution the convention which did the trick was careful to avoid any statement of principles. There were, in fact, no principles other than the principles underlying a panic-struck desire to put down the incipient revolt within the ranks of the Whig party which had arisen out of the development of new interests in the northeastern states. Abraham knew little or nothing of these interests, but he could not help seeing the ominous signs of internal disruption in his party. He supposed that the abolitionists were at the bottom of the trouble, and he accordingly made a fairly careful study of the slavery question and came out of the study with the conclusion that he was right in thinking, as he always had thought, that slavery could never be a national political problem. The thing to do, therefore, was to strengthen and solidify the Whig Party, and give the country the benefit of its leadership.

With these problems in mind, Abraham, unofficially a representative of the Whig National Committee, and personally an eager and ambitious young politician who thought he saw a chance to make himself useful to the cause, set out in the summer of 1848 upon a trip through the unknown territory of New England, the seat of the rebellion among what had once been Whig numbers. To the stronghold of Calvinistic industrialism,

came Abraham Lincoln, of the heterogeneous but aggressive
West, carrying, in his bag of tricks, the support and approval of
the leaders of Southern Whigdom, men who twelve years later
were to be leaders of a greater and more ominous revolt against
not a mere political party but the very existence of the United
States of America. And Abraham's listeners in the North, what
there were of them, were to be men of the stamp of James
Russell Lowell, whose anonymous "Biglow Papers" had been for
two years appearing in the *Boston Courier* and the *Boston Standard* and, almost simultaneously with Abraham's visit, appeared in
book form. The sarcastic remarks of Mr. Birdofreedom Sawin,
veteran of the Mexican War, who had lost a leg, an arm, an eye,
and four fingers in that sorry struggle, in deciding to support
Mr. Lincoln's candidate, old Rough and Ready, are worth listening to. Mr. Sawin had thought that his physical sacrifices might
have qualified him to run for the presidency himself, but he
apparently decided that as he had not lost his head Zachary
Taylor would be the better man. After explaining this fact the
rhyming hero said:

"Next thing you'll want to know, I s'pose, wut arguments I seem
"To see that makes me think this 'ere'll make the strongest team;
"Fust place, I've been consid'ble round in bar-rooms and saloons
"Agetherin' public sentiment, 'mongst Demmercrats and Coons,
"And 't aint ve'y offen thet I meet a chap but wut goes in
"Fer Rough an' Ready, fair and square, hufs, taller, horns and skin."

This was the attitude to General Taylor, whom Abraham
Lincoln supported, of an intelligent portion of the New England
public. But Abraham was not dismayed, he went about the northeastern states, speaking where and when he could, avoiding all
mention of slavery and pleading with all the power of his amaz-

ing personality for the safety and success of the Whig party.
Those who heard him were delighted with his presence and his
manner, but the newspapers did not often record what he said.
And yet he was relatively happy, because he was doing something, although he did not quite know what it was that he was
doing. For the moment, he was contributing to the eleventh hour
triumph of the party which he loved, not so much with tenderness as with dogged and insistent pertinacity. In reality he was
riding for a fall, into the brambles of neglect and bitterness. His
efforts and his beliefs, his sacrifice of the fine, honest sweetness
of his inner nature, were all to be in vain and to earn him nothing
but the depressing realization that he had been barking up the
wrong tree.

Back in Illinois, in Lincoln's own excessively Whig district,
where Billy Herndon had been whipping the young men into
line, Judge Logan, Abraham's former law partner and fellow-
Whig, had been decisively defeated as a candidate to succeed
Abraham in Congress. And in Massachusetts the Calvinistic intellectuals, with a stern if limited moral sense, and little patience
with the slow accomplishments of economic determination, were
forming a new party, in the interests of New England thought,
New England society, and New England business, all of which
were definitely against the existence of slavery as a background
for the cotton business, in the upper reaches of which was situated
not only their prosperity, but even the seed of their apparent
moral sublimity. Abraham would not talk about the Whig
troubles in his own state, preferring to believe that everything
was as it should be, but he strenuously attacked the new Free
Soil party. And it was perhaps this very attack, this panic of
defense which his Whig loyalty imposed upon him, that led him

into the position from which that same Free Soil movement was
to pluck him, some years later, for its leader under the banner
and title of Republican. For in the course of his New England
campaign on the heels of the high-minded and astute Senator
William H. Seward of New York, Abraham came to realize that
there was more to the Whig problem than the mere creation of
an illusion favorable to its candidate. Seward, though a loyal
Northern Whig, was a practical humanitarian, who had some
of that Calvinistic sense of moral urgency which was quite foreign to Abraham, but which made the experienced and dignified
Senator almost a Free Soiler in his hatred of slavery. The power
of the speeches which Lincoln heard Seward deliver in the early
autumn of 1848 brought the young politician from Sangamon to
a place from which he might eventually save himself, though
nearly lost. Although his conclusion had no immediate effect
upon his method of campaigning, and remained in him merely
as food for thought, he said to Seward, ". . . You are right. We
have got to deal with this slavery question, and got to give much
more attention to it hereafter than we have been doing." *

After a trip through the near Northwest and a call at Niagara
Falls, where he had been joined by his wife, Abraham returned
home to a changed public opinion, to the bosom of a state which
now distrusted and all but disowned him because of his, to it,
inexplicable attitude toward the late war. He knew now that he
was politically dead, and, although he hoped for a resurrection in
the wake of a triumphant Zachary Taylor who surely would
reward his henchman's faithfulness, Abraham could see little to
be happy about. He was still in debt; his living expenses were
increasing, and his salary as a legislator would soon cease; his
law business was not prosperous. His father, always shiftless and

* Seward. Works, Memoirs, 19.

improvident, was troubling him for help; Mary had domestic troubles and could not keep servants in her employ; those friends who had meant much to Lincoln had, many of them, been estranged through the taking of different political paths; everything seemed to cry out for readjustment and new consideration; the face to face contacts which gave him his spark seemed disconnected and confused; his life in Springfield was not what it had been; it was not the free, popular, vital thing of his early days; but jealousy, suspicion, distrust, and plain dislike had entered into it to confuse it more. With these things in his mind Lincoln returned to Washington for the final session of Congress knowing that even though Taylor was made President there would be no Whig in Congress from Illinois and no Lincoln in any office whatsoever. All Abraham could do in this final session was to record through frequent support of the Wilmot Proviso, which carried with it the declaration that slavery should not be extended to any territories carved out of the spoils of the Mexican War, his new belief that slavery was really a political issue. And in addition to recording this change in his state of mind the extraordinary excitement over slavery which had found its way into a Congress that supposed the thing permanently dormant, gave him, through speeches and debates, a new conception of what the North believed slavery to be—a crime greater than robbery or piracy, a thing which befouled the very Constitution which fostered it.

Abraham, in this session, even went so far as to propose a measure for the gradual emancipation of slaves in the District of Columbia, but he kept his old feeling about the subject alive in this proposal, by adding a provision for the giving over to their masters by the District authorities of any fugitive slaves. He was willing to admit that slavery was a problem, but he was still unwilling to go the absolute lengths of the Free Soilers, and the Free Soilers noticed his delinquency and later let him hear of it. So Abraham fell between two fires, his District of Columbia bill arousing the extreme Southerners to anxious protest under John C. Calhoun, and the lukewarmness of it infuriating the anti-slavery men of the North. This was an important if unhappy point in Abraham's career, for it saw the apprehensible beginning of the oft-forgotten Southern belief that it was the North which was undermining and threatening the Union, and the beginning of that disciplinary anger at his attitude which at once showed the power of the Free Soilers and the necessity of adjusting himself to their point of view.

Lincoln's District of Columbia bill was never introduced. The last session of the Thirtieth Congress ended in a dark blaze of bitterness under an ominous cloud. Retreating from the acerbity of his personal disaster Abraham took refuge in plans for the distribution of that party patronage which the hollow triumph of Zachary Taylor, and indeed of all the Whigs but Lincoln, had led him to expect might come his way. But there was bitterness here too, for the office which he most desired—that of Commissioner of the General Land Office—was given to another, in a manner which made it plain to Lincoln that the men who had promised and claimed to support him had been very lukewarm in the act. Even his second choice, the Governorship of Oregon, was not offered to him, and to make matters worse, he was offered the secretaryship of that territory, a minor and humiliating position for the man who had given everything to save his party. He had given everything but his true self which still lay in the darkness of his heart, waiting to be discovered. And it had some time to wait, while James Shields, Abraham's pet aversion and his opponent in that half-comic near duel of 1841, was moving up through the Senate to higher things, and that other enemy, the brilliant Stephen A. Douglas, was mounting toward impressive leadership in the Democratic party.

A hurt and chastened man, creeping out of the shed husk of the arrogant politician, returned to the no longer genial town of Springfield, and once more took up the healing course of personal contact among the men in whose supposed interests their actual living beings had been lost.

CHAPTER NINE

A CIRCUIT LAWYER ON THE STUMP

CRUSHED and again bewildered Abraham Lincoln the unsuccessful politician shrank back into Abraham Lincoln the
successful human being. The body which carried both of these
potentialities about in its enormous frame was seen chiefly in
court rooms, in taverns on the Eighth Judicial Circuit, in the
all-too-short beds under the insufficient lamps and candles of
small-town inns. The business of Lincoln and Herndon as a law
firm kept the senior partner chiefly on the road, and a gay,
adventurous, genial, human road it was. It ran through the counties of central Illinois, through the lives of Illinois shopkeepers,
farmers, pioneering settlers, lawyers, bartenders, light women,
miscreants, doctors, loafers and bankers. It wound about the heart
of the new West, and its people were in the very act of creating
a new personality destined to find its way into and to enrich the
eventual figure of the typical American. It was its own food. It
took little or no color or substance from other times or other
places. It had in it little of the South, little of the North, little of
the East, although its components had come from all of those
regions.

To Abraham Lincoln, smarting under the rebuke which the
national capital appeared to have given him, it was home. Its
friendly tenderness met and clasped the tenderness of his own
life. He lived in it. Elsewhere he merely strove, struck out with
his hands like a drowning man. The little squares of Illinois

towns with their alternate mud and dust, their frame hotels, post offices, court rooms, and schools and churches, were each of them home to him. From long familiarity, their citizens knew and acclaimed him. They saw in him the culmination not of sophistication and scheming, but of their own simplicity. They never saw, and would not have understood if they had seen, the dark chambers of horror and despair which a larger world set roaring in him with winds that were cold and impenetrable.

On a court day in any one of these towns, there would be in some tavern of an evening a congregation of lawyers, judges and court attendants, plaintiffs, defendants, and onlookers. There would be a great roaring of voices unrestrained and exuberant. There would be lulls and gusts of laughter, the clatter of glasses, the scrape of boots, the creaking of chairs and the thunder of nudged tables. There would be a smell of rum and whisky on the air, penetrating the floating levels of tobacco smoke. Abraham Lincoln, who would not have been responsible for either the smell of liquor or the fumes of tobacco, but who liked to be where they were, would have been sitting somewhere in the midst of this uproar with his head and shoulders as far down in his chair as he could possibly get them and his feet raised and resting on the highest possible ledge, the mantelpiece if there were one. At such times, and they were times which Abraham sought to make as numerous as possible now—he did not even go home to Springfield for the week-end when he could help it—the tall, hollow-cheeked lawyer smiled. His eyes lighted up with the enjoyment of his sense of being centered in humanity, of being where voices spoke to a man and not to an idea. These evenings, perhaps the happiest of Abraham's life, came at the end of days in court rooms under the eyes of judges, juries, prose-cutors, and litigants all of whom knew and liked Abraham Lin-

coln the lawyer and neither knew nor cared about Abraham
Lincoln the politician. That was why Lincoln was happy in this
life as he had never been able to be happy in the public life to
which his strange ambition to have place and distinction as a
politician had too often compelled him. Here on the circuit,
hidden by the thickets and groves of interior Illinois, Abraham
had escaped from himself into himself. That greedy, hurtful self
which conspired with the worldly appurtenances of political life
to shame and humiliate the tender, humane, genial and lively
self of the country lawyer was far away from him now. The years
he spent in this happy personalized seclusion taught him a great
deal about himself and above all revealed to him the fine triumph
which came with development of his ability to influence men by
force of living talk. In this development was the gem of that
creative gift which distinguished the last few years of his life.
Perhaps the gift had a better birth that it was conceived in the
peaceful refuge of the friendly provinces out of the way of the
shadow of fear which lay over the sophisticated world. Abraham
was so certain that he must now keep away from that world that
he even refused a highly advantageous offer to join a firm of
Chicago lawyers. He would remain hidden in the bush of the
Eighth Judicial Circuit where good fellowship and plain talk
could be his meat and drink, and where the disdainful finger of
polished sophistication could not find him.

Abraham remained then, for five years, making himself over.
But he never completely forgot his ambition, nor the sting of his
repeated failures in the face of it. During these five years, he
must have thought a great deal about the why and wherefor of
political occasions, but he saw little of national life and, though
an eager reader of the papers, read them in the light of an
Illinois sun. He had begun to understand his gifts of speech and

to make the most of them. His oration on the death of Henry Clay was the first achievement in his career of real literary distinction.*

But in spite of this development, his opinion on national political issues remained a little hazy. He still, in spite of the moribund state of that organization, believed in the Whig party and thought, nationally, chiefly in terms of its advantage. But he had begun to realize that the life of the nation was changing. That commercial supremacy was completely displacing, as a national interest, the earlier triumphs of what many had believed to be pure philosophical democracy. As a matter of fact, it was merely a change of distribution, not a change in supremacy. The country had grown, and so had the interests of its financiers. Where once there had been only the lords of the plantation and the lords of the counting house, now there had appeared the lords of development. And as the West was the great center of development and as such, important alike to North and South, Abraham Lincoln could not, as a Westerner, neglect consideration of the conflicting powers eager for control of its development. These powers were centered in the South which wanted slavery extended wherever American territory was extended, in pursuance of the tacit understanding that part of the United States should be free and part slave, in the North which wished to extend the region of its manufacturing and trading influence and which could do so more readily under an industrial as opposed to a plantation civilization, and in the greater centers of the New West where many an alert investor and seeker after power sat like a spider in his web watching for the speculative fly to come and feed him. Even at this early date in American national history, the chief sources of wealth were, control of

---

* Eulogy on Henry Clay, July 16, 1852. Works, Vol. II, p. 155.

money, control of transportation, control of raw materials, control of manufactures, and, as human life has ever been a commodity, control of labor. The North and East, in the decade before the Civil War, with the exception of the raw material cotton, and the slave form of labor, held the whip hand over all of these. In the West, looking toward the Pacific Coast, only recently added to the American nation, lay the potential wealth of railroads, and the consequent development of possible manufacturing and distributing centers along their routes. Thus the control of the rising West was a matter of prime importance to the commercial interests of both North and South. For if the North got that control, the South, competing with free labor and manufactures, would have little or no chance of extending the institution by which it maintained its existence, the growing of cotton by slave labor.

Lincoln had long since seen that money was the governing force of his nation, and he had very shrewdly allied himself with what he believed to be the side most likely to take and retain control of the source of the national wealth. No one familiar with the facts could believe that his naturally humane feelings against slavery had anything to do with this allegiance. He did not believe in abolition and was, even in 1854, a supporter of the Fugitive Slave Law, that bane of the Calvinistic Northerner. He believed, as he was willing to admit, that slavery was an evil and should not be kept from dying a natural death. But he did not believe that any active steps should be taken against it. As property he felt a distaste for the idea of meddling with slaves.

In 1854, although his views on slavery did not change, a political occurrence of great importance served very radically to change Abraham's use of the views he held. In January of that year Stephen A. Douglas, United States Senator from Illinois, Lincoln's arch-enemy and the most powerful of the Democrats, although the one least liked by the South, presented to the Senate a report on the subject of the Territory of Nebraska, looking toward its admission into the union. It is not necessary to go into this report in detail, although its consequences were storm and fury in a nation which had for four years thought itself free from volcanic disturbance. Senator Douglas's report suggested that the Territory of Nebraska in coming into the Union, had the right to decide whether or not it would permit slavery within its boundaries. The Missouri Compromise, which in 1820 had calmed the unrest of the nation and laid the matter of slavery away from public view, had affirmed and been nationally recognized to affirm that there should never be slavery in the Territory now called Nebraska. Douglas's report was therefore, in a general sense, a suggestion implying the repeal of that Compromise. Perhaps never in American history has any man been more abused and maligned than Douglas was, as a result of this radical bombshell thrust into a Senate given to calling a spade anything but a spade. Yet it is now plain to us that the Senator from Illinois, ambitious as he was, was not guided solely by his desire to obtain the nomination for the presidency in making his pronouncement. It is true that he was not popular with the Southern Democrats, but it is also true that his Nebraska scheme did not immediately nor permanently make him so, and it is hard to understand how he could have believed that it would. It is much more probable that he had in mind the interests of his native state and particularly of Chicago, in planning an organized government for a part of the Union essential to the successful completion of an Atlantic-Pacific railway. It has for far too long been supposed that slavery was the cause of the Kansas-Nebraska controversy, and not merely, as in truth it was, a ramification of it.*

It should be borne in mind that in 1854 the Whig party, the party of Lincoln, was practically dead, though Abraham still believed that he could detect signs of life in it. The Free Soilers of the North had become a powerful faction and had all but formed a new party, the Republican party of to-day. The nation was in the throes of political schism. All parties needed an issue, and all possible issues were concerned with the economic consequences of national expansion. Nebraska Territory was the logical region of immediate national expansion. Its social structure would determine the nature of its industrial development as a state. The slave power, recognizing that a failure to get a fair share in new territory for its peculiar institution would mean danger to itself, sought to affirm its right to expand equally as the "free-labor" wage-slavery of the North sent out new shoots. The North recognized that it must capture the West or its hungry industrial life would soon have no fields upon which to feed. The Democratic party, powerful as it was, could not mean the same thing to a Northerner that it did to a Southerner. The Whig party could no longer mean anything to anybody, and could not, therefore, provide a horse to which the industrial interests of the North could attach their wagon. Two things were therefore necessary—to strengthen party organization along the Free Soil lines, using the wreckage of the Whig party where possible, and to weaken the Democratic party, destroying Douglas and assimilating in the new Republican-Free Soil party those who chose to follow the Northern idea.

When Abraham Lincoln, therefore, still reluctant to call himself anything but a Whig, in spite of the fact that the Repub-

* Cf. Watkins, Albert. Lincoln, Douglas and the Nebraska Bill.

licans were using him, was put forward by his friends as a likely stump speaker in the current Illinois campaign, there fell upon him unwittingly the task of inventing party doctrine by the simple expedient of negativing everything Douglas stood for. Douglas was entirely indifferent about slavery, and not much concerned whether it spread or not. He certainly did not openly favor it. He was a liberal, progressive-minded man, well-disposed toward Catholics, foreigners and other things antipathetic to the then one hundred per cent American. After the stormy passage of the bill which allowed the division of Nebraska Territory into two territories, each to choose by popular referendum whether or not it should have slavery, Senator Douglas, braving the storm of abuse which the fiercely partisan North was heaping upon him for his "traitorous" hostility to the time-sanctioned Missouri Compromise, returned to Illinois to try to secure the nomination for Senator for Abraham's arch-enemy, the Democrat James Shields, thus making an Illinois victory for his Nebraska bill. In this campaign, Douglas met Lincoln. And in Lincoln he met a bitter, determined fighter, who by reason of his own mistakes had twice gone down for the count and was reaching out for the ropes again, supported by his anti-Nebraska friends who needed his personal power as a stump speaker, who knew that no one else could nullify the effect of the great intellectual powers of the "Little Giant."

Lincoln spoke in answer to Douglas on a number of occasions during 1854, making what was his most dignified and most important public speech up to that time at Springfield on October fourth. In this carefully considered argument against the repeal of the Missouri Compromise Abraham showed a grasp of the facts of history which would not have been possible for him to exhibit five years earlier. He made some mistakes, one of them a serious error of fact which he later had to admit was an error, but on the whole his argument was clear, logical, and certainly not ineffectual. But even this effort was, it now seems, a political one. It was delivered, in the presence of Senator Douglas, for the purpose of making the Senator's motives appear base. For Abraham was determined to be a candidate for State Senator, and the belief which the people of Illinois were allowed to retain in him would be the index of his success when the state legislature met in December to elect. Abraham was still insisting that he was not an abolitionist and was undoubtedly sincere in his protestations that all he cared about was not letting slavery be extended. Much as he hated the Democratic candidate he could not bring himself to be, in this speech, as vituperative and absurdly sarcastic as he often had been, in the unfortunate and ill-considered past which had held so many snakes in its grass. Much as Abraham wished to be Senator himself, he was, for almost the first time, fair-minded and generous in what he said. And his fair-mindedness and generosity received as unpleasant a reward as could possibly have been arranged for them.

In order to prevent the nomination of not Shields, whom the Democrats discovered to be a hopeless standard-bearer, but ex-Governor Matteson, whom they put forward as a likely Nebraska man, it was necessary for Abraham to take the few votes left to him on a late ballot and with bitterness in his heart beg their sponsors to go for Lyman Trumbull. Abraham's ambition was a personal one, but his loyalty to the party which served that ambition, like the truly conservative state of mind that it was, was stronger than his sense of duty to himself. This particular instance of party loyalty was a bitter pill for Abraham to swallow, much as he was pleased that his action had brought about the defeat of the Douglas candidate. The adroit politician that he was, the skillful jury lawyer, realized that negatives would not, by themselves, make a true victory. A temporary victory had been gained in the defeat of the Nebraska candidate on the heels of the passage of the bill to organize that territory, but there were issues which the struggling politicians themselves could not reckon with.

Stephen A. Douglas was undoubtedly sincere in his explanation of the reasons why he did not think it a "crime" to organize two new territories out of one which lay in a region supposedly under a mandate against slavery and to allow those territories to choose whether or not they would permit slavery within their borders. The Senator believed, very reasonably, as it now appears, that there could never be profitable exploitation of slave labor either in Kansas or Nebraska, the two states which comprise the then disputed territories. There is to this day no cotton-growing enterprise of any importance in either of those states and there never has been. And slavery in the United States was never profitable on a large scale in the production of any other raw material or any other form of manufacture. There seems little doubt that no matter whether Kansas had voted slavery up or down there would still have been no marked extension of slavery in actual fact.

But slavery had in 1854 and 1855 become something more than a question for logical determination. It had become the mechanical advantage by which a large portion of the population of the United States was to lift itself into political power. By the late summer of 1855, the astute Lincoln, who a decade and a half before had been mildly curious about the emotions of slaves bound together and headed "down the river," had become highly excited about the matter. He now found that slavery made him miserable all of the time. He felt that something must

be done about it, and he was sure now that nothing peaceful
could be done about it. Slavery had become a political issue for
good and all and as such had finally approached close to Abraham Lincoln's heart.

And on the newly organized territory of Kansas, a region
of rolling plains and watercourses studded with cottonwoods, of
buffaloes and antelopes, of fertile soil and immense agricultural
possibilities, the political wit and wisdom of the nation was focus-
sing the burning glass which it was accustomed to use in ex-
amining the problem of Negro slavery. Kansas was being settled,
but it had gotten off to a very bad start. Its first governor was
slow in getting to the scene of his official activities, having indulged himself in a preliminary tour of inspection of his new
domain, and having taken the occasion to invest heavily and
questionably in the most likely looking real estate of the territory. Long after the northerly territory, which retained the name
of Nebraska, had been organized and started on a peaceful if
uninspiring career as a tangible part of the United States, Kansas
was in the grip of a furious domestic conflict which we are in
the habit, now, of referring to in terms of Lawrence, border
ruffians, James H. Lane, John Brown, Sharps rifles, and slavery. *
One of the first causes of the bitter strife has been for the most
part neglected. Lawrence was the center in Kansas of those
forces interested in making the Territory into a slaveless region
open to the exploitation of Northern industrial power. After
much ill-feeling it was sacked in 1856 by the forces of the pro-
slavery Kansas. Border ruffians were those gentlemen who believed that the Kansas-Nebraska Bill had intended to make of
the erstwhile territory of Nebraska, two territories, one slave
and one free, and that any attempt to make the one called Kansas

* Isely, W. H. The Sharps Rifle Episode in Kansas History. See Bibliography.

a free territory was against the principles of the bill adopted by the Congress of the United States and hence a kind of treason. James H. Lane and John Brown were two eager champions of the Northern cause, who did not hesitate in the course of their activities against the crime of slavery to indulge themselves freely in mayhem and murder, arson and pillage. Sharps rifles, known as Beecher's bibles after the well-known preacher, who recommended the settlement of Kansas by Northern men equipped with the best firearms then obtainable, were provided for many companies organized to emigrate to Kansas and paid for by popular subscription, largely from the purses of New England manufacturers and financiers interested in the possibility of the construction of a transcontinental railroad. And slavery was the supposed cause of all the trouble in Kansas.

But it should be remembered that the first serious trouble in that troubled territory was due to the murder of one settler by another over a matter of property that had nothing whatever to do with slavery. It merely happened that the murderer was a pro-slavery man and the victim a free soiler. The incident was used to arouse the feeling already existing between the two parties struggling for control of Kansas. Here were representatives of the civilization of South and North aligned against one another, recognizing a difference in interest and point of view which was fundamental and which made it at the time, as it had been for two generations, impossible for the two to agree. It has been too often assumed that the only difference between the North and the South was centered in the institution of Negro slavery, but such is certainly not the case. The culture of the South was based upon a sense of society essentially feudal, carrying with it for those who entertained it a quality of mind entirely unable to see life in the terms familiar to the bustling

business man and shrewd small farmer of the North, who had
no upper layer of gilded folk to look up to for the pleasures
of admiration and respect. The agricultural limitations of the
South did certainly impose upon the dwellers in that part of the
United States a certain type of production, a certain source of
wealth and it is true that that system made it possible for the
once universal institution of slavery to survive beyond its reasonable time. But slavery did not, as many have chosen to assert,
create the life of the South. Slavery itself took color and plausi-
bility from the social arrangement which fostered it. In 1860,
when the slave system reached its culminating point, the population of the slave-holding communities of the United States was
about twelve and a half millions and the number of slaveholders
was three hundred and eighty-four thousand. But nearly three
hundred thousand slave owners owned less than ten slaves and
could not therefore be considered to have been slave capitalists.
If we are to consider the struggle between North and South in
its true light, it is necessary to recognize that slave capital was
centered in the hands of a comparatively small group of powerful
plantation owners, just as in the North the wealth has always
been centered in the hands of a few who have used that wealth
to their own advantage in the exploitation of their less fortunate
fellow-citizens. It therefore might be said that the converse of
De Tocqueville's statement about the South, to the effect that it
was just like the North except for slavery, was true. The chief
resemblance between the North and the South was in slavery,
or rather in the concentration of its wealth in the hands of a
few powerful individuals. It was these individuals who were
running the South, and it was these individuals who were running the North. It was these very men, North and South, who
for their own interests and because a new land undeveloped is

so much raw, uncaptured wealth, were sending their fellow-citizens with arms and slogans, politicians and lawyers to preëmpt the choicest spots. It was these same leaders of American life in the 1850's who were providing Abraham Lincoln, little as he then realized it, with something to follow, and something to fight.

When Abraham met Stephen A. Douglas on the stump in 1854 and again in a later campaign, he did not realize, so forceful and convincing was his own presentation of what he believed to be the facts in the case, that Douglas, in claiming that Kansas could never be a slave state even though the people voted for slavery, had more right on his side than was vouchsafed to the Lincolnian denials of the assertion. Neither did Douglas know exactly why that was so. Perhaps he only hoped that it was and said it anyway. But there was a very good reason why it should prove true. In 1856 the price of slaves in the slave-selling states had risen to between fifteen hundred and two thousand dollars. As it was conservatively estimated that one slave was required for the cultivation of every twenty acres of new land, and as no plantation could be profitable that did not till many times that area, it will be seen what an enormous outlay of capital would be required to maintain slave labor in a vast territory like Kansas. And capital was the one thing which the South could not readily get hold of. The commercial activities of the North during the first seventy-five years of American national life had seen to that. There could be no way of utilizing slave labor in the West without a drastic reduction in the price of slaves. This was not possible, for the South, economically speaking, was not a unit. Those states which could not successfully produce cotton could produce Negroes for sale to the cotton states. As these Negroes were their chief article of trade the border states would not consider any measures looking to a reduction in the price of slaves for the benefit of their neighbor Southern states.

All of these extremely theoretical but very sound explanations would have been at the time very dry food for the active comprehension of Abraham Lincoln. He preferred to find out what his opponent was going to say and either to prove him wrong or make him appear ridiculous. After the campaign of 1854 Abraham's opponent was a composite personage, chiefly Douglas, but otherwise anyone who favored the Nebraska Bill. Abraham had now made the extension of slavery his chief *bête noir,* but it was seconded in disgrace in his mind by the extension of intolerant ideas, such as those represented by the strange offshoot of the old Whig Party which was known as the Knownothings. The Knownothings were the current hundred per cent Americans, avowing hostility to all foreigners and non-Protestants. As the Knownothings, however, were an essential part of any possible organization of political activity which might become able to combat the influence of the slave power, although there were differing opinions at large as to whether or not the strange secret party favored slavery or not, it was rather awkward for Abraham to dislike them so. But he did detest them and what they stood for, for, whatever his shortcomings, he was a human being as honest as they make them, with an unquenchable distaste for any and all forms of hypocrisy. In August of 1855 he wrote to his old friend Joshua Speed, who had not followed him politically at a very close distance: "I now do no more than oppose the extension of slavery. I am not a Knownothing, that is certain. How could I be? How can anyone who abhors the oppression of the Negroes be in favor of degrading classes of white people? Our progress in degeneracy appears to me to be pretty rapid. As a nation we began by declaring that 'all men are created equal!' We now practically read it, 'all men are created equal, except Negroes.' When the Knownothings get control, it will read, 'all men are created equal except Negroes and foreigners and Catholics.' When it comes to this I shall prefer emigrating to some country where they make no pretence of loving liberty,—to Russia, for instance, where despotism can be taken pure, and without the base alloy of hypocrisy." *

In 1856 Abraham Lincoln, the slow-moving conservative, was still trying to believe that he was a Whig, although, as others told him, there no longer was any such thing as a Whig. He must have known that he could not keep out of the new movement which was aligning the newly conceived Republican party against the Knownothings for control of Northern political power. It was a safe bet that some months after the rest of the North and West had admitted the coming ascendency of the Republicans Abraham would climb upon the bandwagon. For the Republican party's first platform was chiefly concerned with the question of Kansas and its possibilities as a slave or free region. Early in 1856 Abraham took time from his pleasant legal duties along the circuit to attend a convention at Decatur, Illinois, which aimed to organize for the campaign of the summer. Lincoln's radical Republican, abolitionist law partner, William H. Herndon, really precipitated Abraham's entry into the ranks of the Republicans by signing his name to a call for a meeting which was unmistakably abolitionist. Herndon managed to get Lincoln's approval of the liberty he had taken and the game was on. Abraham entered the party on the understanding that it was to be kept very, very conservative. His first active service as a member of the Republican party was his appointment as a

* Beveridge. Lincoln, Vol. II, p. 354.

presidential elector at the Bloomington convention of May and June, 1856.

At this time the country was in a highly excited state. Lincoln, called upon as the great inspirational speaker, made an address before the Bloomington convention—an address which he was rather anxious to have listened to but equally anxious to keep out of print. He made no notes and no one took it down at the time. Our knowledge of it comes from a friend's account, delivered long afterward and probably accurate enough in substance.*

Abraham reviewed in this speech the troubled state of the nation. He told, in his high-pitched, emotional voice, with all the mastery of an actor, of the horrible violence reigning in Kansas, trying to saddle upon that unwilling territory the curse of extended slavery, of the attack of Preston Brooks upon Charles Sumner in the Senate, taking care to say nothing of Sumner's violent and abusive speech which had brought on the attack, and also exaggerating its effects by saying that the gentleman from Massachusetts was slowly dying; telling of the attack upon Lawrence, Kansas, of the unjustifiable and bloody ways of the border ruffians who had by trickery threatened to make slavery legal in Kansas against the manifest wishes of the state, of the intention of the Republicans not to interfere with slavery in the slave states, and of the party's recognition of the justification of the Fugitive Slave Law as a safeguard to legitimate Southern interests. He told how slavery, being sanctioned by the Constitution, bad as it was, must be temporized with for the time being; he said that Senator Douglas was the fiend behind the Kansas outrages, behind the attack upon Senator Sumner; he explained

---

* Whitney, Henry Clay, author of Life of Lincoln, 1908, and Life on the Circuit with Lincoln, 1892.

how the arrogant champions of the South must be met and overcome; how the Union must be kept together, by a reasonable appeal to public opinion if possible, but by force if necessary

That was a speech, delivered in Lincoln's own personal heart-to-heart style, with all the weight of his hope of himself and his tenderness for humanity behind it, which none could listen to and remain unaffected, especially as it was carefully designed to contain only the exhortations and strictures which those who were present wished to hear and to believe in. Not only did it make Lincoln one of the most important men in his party, considering that he was not seeking any office at the moment, but it attracted attention to him, by hearsay, all over the country, the Republican sections of it at any rate. But at the same time Lincoln was estranging, by his apparent readiness to serve the new masters, who had shown him in the last senatorial election that if he did not serve them they would crush him, some very close friends among the old line Whigs who were destined to give him much trouble and unhappiness before his tragic career was ended.

When the presidential nominations for the 1856 election were made the country was divided into three political sections of importance; the Democrats, with James Buchanan as their candidate, the Americans (known as "Knownothings") with Millard Fillmore as their candidate, supported also by the remains of the old Whig party, and the new Republican party, with the adventurous John C. Frémont as their leader. The Democrats, like the Knownothings and Republicans, protested that their wish was to preserve the Union, but they contended that anti-slavery agitation was the thing which most greatly endangered it. The Knownothings, chiefly concerned with their antipathy to foreigners and non-Protestants, had attracted to their ranks many old Whigs who saw plainly the danger to the nation of any such opportunism as the Republicans had been displaying. The Republicans were the representatives of the new capitalism of the North and West, which feared the slave capital of the South as a dog fears a sharer of his bone.

Abraham Lincoln, the mouthpiece, the oratorical ace of the "Black Republicans," was in his element in the campaign of 1856. Everywhere were great meetings to be addressed, crowds about the platforms in squares and parks, bands playing, processions by day and by torchlight, excitement, with no damping sense of definite meaning, enthusiasm, at having something to shout about and an excuse for shouting. Abraham felt fairly certain of his party, quite naturally, as he never failed to hold his audiences spellbound. It was, indeed, the spell which guided his outpourings, rather than the reasoning behind them. He was disappointed at having failed to receive the Republican nomination for the vice-presidency, for which he had been suggested, but he was once more facing a relatively hopeful future. Even the harassed home life, with the uncertain tempered Mrs. Lincoln, who did not like Abraham's simple and homely household manners, and who quarrelled with all her servants as well as with her husband, was easier and of a different atmosphere when there was prospect of good connections ahead. And Abraham's increasing value to the Republican party was certain to lead to something. Both Abraham and Mary Lincoln understood, though they may not have spoken much of what might be in store, that after all the years of defeat and humiliation for the erstwhile politician of the Sangamon, he was now on his way to the front. Although he had lost the nomination for Vice-President, he had received a hundred and ten votes on the first ballot, so many more than he had expected that it must have given him the idea that, with a little care during the next four years, those hundred and ten might be multiplied and transformed into a nomination for the presidency itself.

But in 1856 Abraham had the job of selling to the country an alarm over conditions in Kansas, conditions, not exaggerated it is true, but caused by factors which the Republicans did not admit, and whose responsibility was shared by North and South alike. It was the Republican newspapers of the North that saw to it that feeling over Kansas was kept high, and that the apparent conflict between the interests of slave and free in that territory was not allowed to slacken. But in spite of Abraham's eloquence and his value to his party as a vote-getter for other candidates, the election of 1856, which set the Springfield lawyer toward the culmination of his career, saw a complete and fairly convincing triumph for the Democrats, James Buchanan, that mild and unpretentious bachelor, being elected with more than a score of electoral votes to spare.

The die was cast, and the party of Lincoln was on the outs, determined to fight, determined to resist any compromise which would result in the salvation of the Union by giving equal consideration both to South and North.

CHAPTER TEN

THE TOP OF THE LADDER

ALTHOUGH the nation-wide fear of the "blackness" of the Black Republicans had asserted itself in the form of a Democratic triumph in 1856, it was soon apparent that the forces which had been unable to agree in their opposition to the political power of the South and the Democrats of the North were going to find a way of working together. Abraham Lincoln watched the operation of these forces with keen and calculating judgment as he went about his happy duties as a circuit lawyer, duties which were rapidly becoming closely bound up with the advancing interests of Northern and Western industrialism. He had become counsel for the Illinois Central Railroad Company and served them well, in return for which services the company forced him to go to law in order to collect his fee of five thousand dollars, a large one for the time, but certainly not excessive. He had been invited to act as local counsel for the firm of John H. Manny, reaper manufacturer, in a suit brought by Cyrus McCormick for infringement of patents. When Lincoln, whose reputation as a legal spell-binder and inspirational jury speaker, was well-known to the Western bar, was asked to be of counsel in this case it was assumed that the hearings would be in the State of Illinois. The skillful and thoroughly trained lawyers from the East who were managing the defense for Manny, wanted to get local sympathy and they soon learned that Lincoln was considered to have the key to the storehouse of that commodity. Accordingly one of the defense lawyers was sent to Springfield to have a look at the prize package of the Illinois bar. He found Abraham putting up a bed in one of the simple rooms of the frame house at Eighth and Jackson Streets. The lawyer was not impressed with Lincoln's qualifications as a lawyer. He lacked, as always, the marks and manners of cultured dignity. He answered the door in his shirt sleeves and was over-cordial with the visitor when his errand had become apparent. But he soon convinced the gentleman from the East that whether or not he, Abraham, was a good court lawyer, he was at least a human being who could make the sound of the human voice a thing of importance beyond the mere meaning of its words. A strange thing coming from a tall, gawky, yellow-faced, shock-haired, shrill-voiced small-town home-owner. The Eastern law-yer was impressed with the possibilities of that anomaly, and went away leaving hard cash and a definite engagement of Lincoln's services behind him.

Perhaps coming on top of his popular success on the stump, the acclaim which he received after his first campaigning against the Douglas idea, his new interest in political possibilities, the apparent sincerity of the Republican party's successful overtures in his direction, this new distinction gave added impetus to his imagination. If it did, he was, as was not uncommon in his experience, soon to receive a blow. For the reaper case was not heard in Illinois at all but in Cincinnati, Ohio, whither Lincoln duly journeyed in high excitement, with a speech already in mind, and a very clear idea of how he was going to impress the court. He was full of glee and boyish exuberance. He cracked jokes with his brother counsel, one of whom was Edwin Stanton, who was later to give Abraham a great deal of trouble as a cabinet officer under him. But the eminent Eastern counsel, having engaged Lincoln purely as an inspirational bait for Illinois opinion, now that the case was to be heard in Ohio, had no use for their curious acquisition. They shunned him when they could, snubbed him constantly, and in court, for the sake of legal expediency, ignored him entirely.

Abraham was something more than hurt. He felt that he had been truly insulted, insulted because he was a lower order of being who had presumed to walk with the chosen, the elegant who had earned their eminence by diligent application to the opportunities and demand of civilized education. He left Cincinnati, resolved to improve both his mind and manner, to become something more than the large frog in the little puddle of Illinois which his experience convinced him was what he had been up to this time. He went home feeling that he would prefer never to see Cincinnati again, but realizing that he could not any longer use his beloved Springfield, the confined domesticities of his home, as sand in which to hide his head. Thus it was that during the several years following the great reaper case fiasco, Abraham Lincoln applied himself more carefully than ever to the unpleasant task of learning what it was that made a finished and polished product of a truly cultured and sophisticated man. During these years he wavered a great deal, between unbounded and sometimes unwarranted belief in himself and absolute and humiliating disbelief.

In 1858 he gave himself, the state of Illinois, and the nation at large an extremely good time by flinging himself furiously but unsuccessfully into a state-wide speaking campaign, which, because it attracted the most attention of any of Abraham's struggles with Stephen A. Douglas has become known as the Lincoln-Douglas debates. Up and down the state of Illinois went the two candidates for Senator, Douglas in a private car, with hosts of shouting advocates, a cannon for salutes, a beautiful wife, a great voice, a quick wit, and a powerful confident ambition. Lincoln generally followed alone in a common coach, often on the same train, with few followers, not much noise and little pomp. The Republican candidate and his friendly press seldom failed to mention the inequality between the two modes of travel. That was rather in the spirit of the entire campaign. No more than any campaign ever seen in this country was it a campaign of real political issues. People will not attend political meetings in tens of thousands merely to hear an abstract principle expounded. Few of Senator Douglas's enthusiastic Democratic supporters cared, in reality, whether "popular sovereignty" as a means of determining the law of a state or territory was a good thing or a bad one. Few of Lincoln's admiring retainers cared whether or not the Dred Scott decision was the slave-power plot which their candidate declared it. What the crowds turned out for, what the thugs fought for inside and outside of the halls, what the cannon roared for, what the fireworks were lit for, was the special performance of the two candidates, the element of personality and battle which invested the campaign. When Douglas made a telling point, as he seldom failed to do, it was accepted by the crowd as a right or left to the jaw might have been and it had its effect not in the mind but in the emotions of the crowd. So with Lincoln, too, who had the better of many of the exchanges, having a better sense of what the crowd wanted to hear and a better sense of humor. When the last joint debate closed at Alton, Illinois, in October, 1858, not one person who had listened to the series, not one person in the United States was any nearer to a clear understanding of the issues involved, but the country was stirred to a pitch of excitement which, under the circumstances, was not a healthy state. Abraham had managed to put Senator Douglas in an awkward position by an extremely clever ruse, suggested to him by the ardent Republican, Henry Asbury, of Quincy. He knew that Douglas was not at heart a slavery man; he knew that if put in a position where he would have to state his choice between the favor of Administration at Washington, and the favor of the constituents in Illinois who were considering his reëlection, the enemy would be in a bad predicament. In other words, Abraham saw that, while it was necessary for Douglas to support his reiterated doctrine of popular sovereignty, it was also necessary for him to support the Dred Scott decision, which had affirmed, from the mouth of the United States Supreme Court, that a slave taken by his master from a slave state to a free state did not thereby become a free man. Lincoln saw, with some pain to himself, that if Douglas as a Democrat were to support this decision it would be difficult for him, as an advocate of popular sovereignty in Kansas to say that a people could keep slaves out of their territory if they wished to do so. For they could not very well keep all Southerners out, and they could not well forbid Southerners from taking their slaves with them either singly or in quantity.

Douglas very cleverly tried to get out of the position into which Lincoln forced him, and he so far succeeded as to win the senatorial election and return to Congress as a Senator from Illinois. But as Lincoln had foreseen, his opponent's inability to come out firmly for acceptance of the Dred Scott decision, greatly weakened the Senator's position in the Democratic party. Therefore, although the world in which Abraham's embarrassing question belonged was an artificial world created purely by his own imagination, that inspired politician succeeded by asking it, in paving the way for the defeat of the Democratic party in 1860,

The Lincoln Who Faced Douglas

possibly the most important election ever held in the United States.

When the election of 1858 was over and Douglas's victory was assured, Abraham realized what he had done. That he had strengthened his party in the same old way, by sacrificing himself. But this time his ambition could not keep him from realizing that the sacrifice might not be permanent. It is very much to be doubted that he actually thought when he was arranging his trap for Douglas that the rebound from its spring would send poor defeated Abraham along to triumph in 1860. Ambition or no, his sense of uncertainty, his feeling of inferiority would have prevented his being very sure of that. But it may have let him hope. And the hope was buoyed up by the increasing national interest in his great talents, which the almost comic sequence of debates with Douglas had created in him. But ambitious and hopeful as he may have been, he still did not believe in himself thoroughly. He had no focussed thought that could enable him to say to himself, "This is what I think and therefore I have power." He knew how to fight with that marvelous personality of his, but he did not, even in 1859, know what he thought. He merely knew what he did not like others to think, and only that when for party reasons he confronted others where there were people gathered to listen.

Now, on the ascent toward his greatest height, when something in the country other than the man's own determination was helping to sweep him along, Abraham was in one of his unaccountable moods of depression and could not see the brightness of his own particular sky. The grave echoes of his earliest days were sounding in him. He went about his business in Springfield and on the circuit, hailed by his friends as a coming power, but in his heart there was something that made him disbelieve

in it. The self-defeating vacillations of his father cropping up in
his own nature made him feel that there was no use trying,
that he, being what he was, could not have the thing he desired,
the "place and distinction as a politician" so long coveted, which
the presidential nomination would have assured him. In a curious
effort to resist the apparently inevitable onrush of his success,
he remained very obstinate, halting like a stubborn mule at
barriers his advocates wished him to take with a showy leap. It
was almost as if he were setting traps for himself trying to make
people disappointed in him, as he was now disappointed in
himself.

At home in the story and a half house in Springfield, from the
yard of which Mary had had most of the trees cut away and
which was entirely unrelieved by any grace of planting, past
which the bustled and wide-skirted gossips of the town went
on their way to market, picking their way gingerly among the
stones and caked mud ruts of the streets, Abraham sat in his
shirt sleeves with his back leaning against an overturned chair
back, his feet in the air, alternately staring at the stove and reading a newspaper full of comment on the prospects of himself
and his party. He tried not to think of the issues, the labors
involved. He looked back into his memory, rather, at the filth
and squalor of his parental homes, in Kentucky, Indiana, and
Illinois, at the village of New Salem, now a village no more, at
the hills he had traversed surveying with John Calhoun, at the
towns of the circuit where, more than anywhere else, he had
of late found a perfectly equipped theater for the dear simple
figures of his sense of life. He thought of his market basket,
and the market to which he always carried it on week-days
when he was at home. He would do that again to-morrow.
Meat, green-truck, bags and packages, and the pleasant smell

of vapors from pickle barrels, whisky barrels, and great cheeses.

Out in the world, built high over even the vapors of such simple things as these, was a movement which was without his help or approval carrying Abraham to a position in which he would find it impossible to cover himself with the bushel of his humility. Things were happening, the kind of things of which he knew little or nothing, things which his jovial cracker-barrel humor, and ready story-teller's wit, kept out of the gatherings he attended and in which they might have been discussed. But these things were pointing at Lincoln and calling out his name. For Lincoln had proved himself a great stump speaker, an inspirational crowd swayer, and he had great personal popularity in his own state, partly due to the settled conviction which his public behavior had established, that he was as honest as the day is long, and partly due to the mellow human geniality which his nature exuded whenever he was not suffering from his besetting melancholy. Furthermore, Abraham Lincoln had no personal enemies. There were men he hated and feared, like Shields and Douglas, but even these men did not hate him, for they did not fear him. Some did consider him a yokel, a clumsy country lout, but then, there were times when he considered himself in no better light. And in the ranks of his own party he was, where not invested with the bright aura of mystery, universally liked and trusted. And where the mystery was, there was also a certain charm. The other powerful Republicans, William H. Seaward of New York, Charles Sumner of Massachusetts, and Salmon P. Chase of Ohio, were either out and out abolitionists or otherwise tainted by extremism. What the party wanted was a conservative, tender-minded man who could influence the man in the street and yet be influenced by the party managers, who stood

for nothing positive. More and more did Abraham's re-
luctance to side with the more radical measures of his party,
especially with regard to slavery, make it seem that he was the
man.

The East, at any rate, wanted to have a look at him, and
accordingly invited him to New York to address a meeting at
Cooper Union in February, 1860. Abraham accepted a little
timidly but went boldly. He spoke, and spoke as if he were
Abraham Lincoln, not merely a Republican politician. But it was
not a very good speech and it added little to the strength of the
Republican party. Its most significant feature was Lincoln's very
timely condemnation of the raid of John Brown on Harper's
Ferry, a thing which, inasmuch as all of those who were praising
the perpetrator were Republicans, needed some definite disavow-
ing. Lincoln spent most of his time discussing the attitude of the
signers of the Constitution as to slavery, a laboriously contrived
syllogistic arrangement calculated to prove that the framers of
our august charter intended to say things about slavery which
they did not say. Abraham had before this had an opportunity
of studying the *Federalist* and other propaganda issued in support of the Constitution but he had unquestionably not gone into
the background and origins of that document as thoroughly as
many a school child of to-day has done. Indeed it would have
been very difficult for him to have done so. The papers of James
Madison which show so clearly the state of mind of the framers,
had been discovered following Madison's death, but were not in
Lincoln's day very easily accessible. The carefully edited records
of the Debates in the illegal Federal Convention which drafted
the Constitution and in the various State Conventions had not
been issued. Abraham would undoubtedly have been unpleasantly surprised, though he might not have changed his argument,

had he read the following paragraph from the work of an able modern historian:

"To sum. up: the organic law of this nation was formulated in secret session by a body called into existence through a conspiratory trick, and was forced upon a disfranchised people by means of a dishonest apportionment in order that the interests of a small body of wealthy rulers might be served. This should not blind us to the fact that this small ruling class really represented progress, that a unified government was essential to that industrial and social growth which has made this country possible. It also should not blind us to the fact that there was nothing particularly sacred about the origin of this government which should render any attempt to change it sacrilegious." *

In other words, what the framers thought about slavery was very much beside the point. Abraham's Cooper Union speech was notable chiefly in that it showed how staunch a Republican he was, and that it at the same time sounded an extremely conservative keynote for the coming party campaign. For Lincoln made it plain that he did not countenance any attitude toward slavery which would give the lie to his repeated statements of intentions pacific toward the South, pacific not unfortunately in the sense of avoiding conflict, but of insisting that if conflict came it would be the South's fault, exactly what the South was at the same time saying of the North. At any rate Abraham was still not going to have it said that he wanted to interfere with the time-sanctioned institutions of the South. He was not going to shoot the neighbor's cow, but he was going to see that it got no fresh pasture.

After the Cooper Union speech Lincoln went through New England and made several speeches all similar in tone, on his way to visit his son Robert, who, at Phillips-Exeter Academy,

* Simons, A. M. Social Forces in American History. New York, 1926.

was getting the polish and suavity which his father had so often suffered for the lack of. On the fourteenth of March Abraham was back in Springfield, two hundred dollars richer for his Cooper Union speech and politically a great deal stronger. His chance of getting the presidential nomination was greatly increased by the fact that although Seward of New York was the most likely candidate, Horace Greeley, that tough-witted politician who was the *New York Tribune,* and at the time one of the most powerful influences in the East, would not have allowed Seward to be nominated for the postmastership of Painted Post if he could have helped it. And Greeley like all the others knew that the West must be served.

While this set of circumstances did not necessarily point to Lincoln, it pointed, for his followers, a way into the divine fracas of Chicago. And although Abraham would have preferred to have had it come about otherwise, a little fancy bargaining in the more secluded conclaves of the Chicago convention secured the votes of the Pennsylvania delegation, which were necessary for a nomination. Abraham would have preferred not to have been tied down by any convention promises, because he would have preferred a free hand, not essentially because he was averse to the doubtful ethics involved in political trading. Indeed he had himself agreed to pay the expenses to the amount of one hundred dollars of a delegate from Kansas who was, he knew, very much in his favor. This fortunate fellow was Mark W. Delahay,* an unscrupulous, wild-cat juggler of frontier interests who had secretly kept Abraham informed of what was going on all through the troubles in Kansas several years before. Furthermore, during the previous year when Lincoln had ranged the state with Senator Douglas trying to defeat the "Little Giant" and to get the

* Works, Vol. V, 178.

senatorial nomination for himself, Abraham, in need of the support of the large German population, and realizing that the important *Chicago Staats Zeitung* supported Senator Seward, bought up the impoverished owner-editor of the *Springfield Staats Anzeiger* and made a contract calling for the decisive support of the Republican party so long as Lincoln had an interest in the paper. The editor was Theodore Canisius, who lived up to his bargain and was later rewarded by Abraham with a comfortable place in the United States Consular Service. *

While Abraham's sense of personal honesty was extremely high, there was nothing formal about it. More than an ethical standard it was merely the natural product of a nature extremely just and tender. It never allowed its possessor to impose upon others, except upon the stump, when he considered that all bets were off, but neither did it hinder him from indulging in profitable practices which, if formally incorrect, were not positively injurious to any individual. A realization of this characteristic makes it unnecessary to decide whether or not Abraham knew of the more or less corrupt political bargains which gained him the votes of Indiana and Pennsylvania in the Republican convention of 1860. Nor is it necessary to know whether or not he knew of the action of his friend Ward Lamon, who issued, with the help of some enthusiastic young Republicans, a great quantity of bogus tickets to the convention hall and saw that they all got into the hands of Lincoln admirers with good lungs who managed to get into the hall in time to leave few seats for the Seward *claque* and its legitimate tickets. Probably Abraham Lincoln did know of these things, afterwards. Certainly he knew and was bound by the compact with the Pennsylvania delegates, which provided for the giving of a cabinet position to the very questionable Simon

* Barton, Wm. E. Life of Abraham Lincoln, Vol. I, p. 422.

Cameron. Lincoln was not likely to have instigated such procedure but it is fairly certain that, in spite of his definite request that he be committed by no promises, he did little to prevent their being made or to discount any profit taken from the making.

While, in Chicago, Horace Greeley, the implacable foe of his former law partner Seward, was bending every effort to keep that able and intelligent man from getting the nomination, Abraham remained in Springfield, dividing his time between the dusty law office of Lincoln and Herndon, the office of the *Journal,* and a handball court near the *Journal* office. Here he waved his great palms about and disported himself like a boy in an effort to conquer the chill of misgiving which kept coming over him. While the great figure of the country lawyer was bending to thrash a little ball against a brick wall, getting up a grateful bodily warmth there at the heart of a fine spring day, full of the smells of earth, dusty clothing, and bright air, the mouth moist with living juices, the hair waving in the wind, the long legs shifting and leaping, the face set in attitudes of tension and of kindly laughter when a point was missed, the breath coming with difficulty, and now and then gasping a loud joke to the boys who watched while Abraham Lincoln was being Abraham Lincoln, Horace Greeley, who had not at first been overly interested in Lincoln, was coming to the conclusion that the lanky son of Illinois was the only man who could be used as a focus for enough balloting strength to keep Seward out. That was enough, combined with the astuteness of the Lincoln faction, who had been busy turning their irons in the fire and were now ready to strike. On the second·ballot Seward had slipped back a little and for the first time in more than twenty years the ambitious Abraham Lincoln began to come forward. On the third ballot the results of the faction bargaining were apparent. Abraham had three hundred and sixty-four out of four hundred and sixty-six votes and thus became the Republican party's nominee in the most important election ever held in the United States. Who knows what state of mind that awkward body was carrying about the handball court in Springfield between the messages that came from Chicago. Belief and disbelief, pride and fear, hope and despair were all there, mingling with the grimaces and lights which showed in the lines of the gaunt, hurt face.

Abraham was in the *Journal* Office when he received the news of his nomination. Although he had not felt able to remain in the high tension atmosphere of his home while the anxiety of waiting was upon him, his first thought was to go home and tell Mrs. Lincoln, who, if we are to judge from her later performance, must have been thinking of the nomination in terms of a trip to New York for shopping and a fine array of new and dazzling clothes which, though she seemed to care little, would be difficult to pay for. Yet there is little doubt that she was genuinely glad of Abraham's final success. She did not share his fear and foreboding. It was the moment for which she had hoped but of which she had long despaired.

Abraham was not yet elected, but the summer of 1860 was not in very heavy leaf before it became apparent that his nomination was almost as good as his election. For that fierce warrior, Stephen A. Douglas, handicapped alike by his own inflexible determination and by the popular recollection of Abraham's fancy bulldogging of the 1858 campaign, had lost the Southern half of his own party. The Democratic convention in Charleston, South Carolina, full of the increasing spirit of resentment which the quite arbitrary attitude of the entire North had instilled into the cotton states, had been unable to agree upon a candidate. Douglas was after all a Northerner, and the North was ruining the South. The protective tariff, which enabled the North to get a high price for its manufactured products throughout the country, in the South as well as in the North, failed to protect the South at all. It meant that the cotton states were forced to pay more for the manufactured and other articles which they had to purchase from the North, but were not enabled to get any higher price for their cotton. That was the beginning of economic ruin, and the high-handed Northern disregard of the fact was at this time more responsible than the issue of slavery for the irreconcilable differences between North and South which had arisen in 1860. Southern planters, who could get capital for their enterprises nowhere but from Northern capitalists, and who were now indebted to individuals in the North to the extent of hundreds of millions of dollars, were being forced into a position in which they could have no hope of shaking off this Northern grip upon their system of life. It was obvious to the most heavily involved that the North would soon hold a mortgage on the entire South. Small wonder then that, although Southerners of the slave power class had of late been Democrats, they could not support Douglas, who was, though a Democrat, a Northerner, and one who had shown that his loyalty was to the North. The Democratic convention moved to Baltimore and tried again. Its proximity to the Senate, where Douglas was conducting a bitter campaign against Jefferson Davis, that able and devoted Mississippian, was enough to split the gathering. It split, and one faction nominated Douglas; the slave-holding faction nominated John C. Breckinridge of Kentucky, Lincoln's own now estranged state. From the moment of this rift in the Democratic party which Abraham Lincoln had helped to bring about, there was never any chance that that shrewd politician, Stephen A. Douglas, would be elected.

There were not a few in the Republican party who did not care for Lincoln as a candidate and regarded him merely as a figurehead. Many indeed were afraid that he would make a mess of the campaign and accordingly saw to it that he was not allowed to take any part in it. It was the party, not the man, that commanded strength at the polls in 1860. And the party won, carrying Abraham, against his belief, and even against the wish of that simple reserved part of him which belonged in Springfield, into the presidency. Although he received little more than one-third of the popular vote cast Abraham was in, and the Republican party was so pleased that it was for the time being to pat its overgrown candidate on the back, and make him feel that he was the apple of its eye. But not for long.

PART TWO

THE BIRTH OF A MAN

CHAPTER ONE

THE CUTTING OF THE CORD

THE extravagant protests which the North was making, to the effect that the South was crying before it was hurt, to everyone's professed astonishment, though to no one's real surprise, resulted in desperate action on the part of the South. The leaders of opinion, at least of that opinion which found its way into expression, in the cotton states, had quite rightly, considering the fact that Abraham and his backers had said that continued division of the Nation on the matter of slavery would inevitably result in trouble, interpreted the election of Lincoln as a final statement on the part of the North that it did not care what a powerful group of Southerners thought and that it would pay no attention to the accusations of that group to the effect that it was not getting fair play. Whatever the logic of the Southern position, it is hard to see how they could have felt any other way.

The election of November, 1860, though a triumph for the Republican party in the sense that through the division of their chief opponent they had come into power, was not to all appearances a triumph for the nation. President Buchanan, vaguely sensing the weight of the difficulties in which his administration was to close, sat back and did nothing while his cabinet divided its allegiance between the "conspirators" of the North and the "plotters" of the South. Certain members of the cabinet went so far as to strengthen with military resources the states which would be likely to side with the South in the event of conflict. Senators began to resign and go home. Senator Crittenden, of Kentucky, an honorable and patriotic gentleman who had offended Lincoln shortly before by urging the people of Illinois to prefer Douglas as their Senator, proposed a compromise with a view to relieving the frightful and ominous tension which hung over the Congress. It was Senator Crittenden's hope that he might save the Nation, as it had been saved in 1820, and again in 1850. Crittenden proposed that the Missouri Compromise line of 36′ 30″, North of which slavery had presumably not been permitted, be restored and extended all the way to the Pacific Coast, slavery being recognized South of the line and not recognized above it, but any state could be admitted either north or south of the line with or without slavery if the matter was provided for in the state constitutions. Crittenden's proposals also contained articles affirming that Congress had no power to abolish slavery in places under its exclusive jurisdiction and situated within the limits of states that permit the holding of slaves; that congress should not be allowed power to abolish slavery in the District of Columbia without permission of the two states from which the District had been taken. That Congress should not be permitted to interfere with the transportation of slaves from one slave-holding state or territory to another and that Congress should indemnify the owners of fugitive slaves which were rescued and consequently kept from their owners in spite of the national Fugitive Slave Law.

These compromise suggestions contained nothing more drastic than had been contained in the earlier Compromises on the subject of slavery and merely demanded recognition of the fact that the nation was in danger, that it had no power short of war to wipe out slavery, and that it was better to resort to the time-honored national custom of compromise out of which the Constitution itself had been formed, than to lose the benefit and dignity of that position to which union had brought the unreconciled and widely differing people of the United States. Such a yielding, to anyone who seriously believed that slavery was a civilized anomaly existing by virtue of special conditions certain to change of their own momentum in good time, need not have been unacceptable. The differences between North and South were serious. The South, as Jefferson Davis well said, believed that the trouble was in the fact that, through the election of the Republican Party, "a sectional hostility has been substituted for a general fraternity." In so far as there had never been previous to the election of 1860 a party alignment on purely Northern and Southern lines, he was certainly right. But there were those in the North, far removed from actual contact with the people, the culture, the life and labor of the South, who believed, not unnaturally, that their abhorrence of slavery was a divinely inspired state of mind marking them different from and morally better than the misguided people of the cotton states. Abraham Lincoln was against the spread of slavery, but he did not share with the great number of members of his own party, this purely "holier than thou" attitude. He was still concerned with the political aspects. It was a question of control. Almost at the very moment when the legislature of the State of South Carolina was cutting the cord which bound it to the Union, Abraham, in Springfield, from which he too was soon to sever himself, was telling the party representatives who came to see him, that he would not come out for the Crittenden compromise. He gave no reasons, and consequently left it for posterity to form its own. They can hardly be woven into one statement of fact. There were many influences. First, there was the leaning of the compromise toward

Douglas's old principle of popular sovereignty. That in itself was something which Douglas's opponent in that curious campaign of 1858 could never give assent to. There was Senator Crittenden's action in throwing the weight of his support to Douglas, the wrong man, as Abraham thought, in that same campaign. And, perhaps strongest of all, was Abraham's belief, as yet unjustified, as yet vague and vacillating, that he was on the right side, politically, though he was not perfectly sure why and though he had to do much arguing with himself to maintain the belief. Added to all these was a false notion of the sublimity of the Constitution and an unwarranted assumption of insight into the motives of its framers.

These elements combined to draw the curious picture of the same man who had gone stumping through New England to support the Southerner Zachary Taylor against the abolitionists and mildly anti-slave natives of that canny region, now favoring the biases and judgments of those very citizens by supporting, whatever might be the differences between his reasons and theirs, the principles of sectional hostility. Perhaps the spectacle of the defeated Douglas, running out his term in the Senate by serving on the Committee of Thirteen appointed to consider the differences between North and South, yielding his political beliefs in an effort to find some way of saving the Union, meant nothing to Abraham, even if he watched it. It is hard to believe that that is the case and it is hard to believe that his decision on the matter of the Crittenden compromise, which even Republicans like Seward might have been willing to accept, did not cause the Republican party's new leader many qualms and misgivings before the summer of 1862.

Whatever it caused him then or after, his answer was given. Two days after he had given it the Committee of Thirteen voted on the compromise, the Republican members voting against it, the party dictum having gone out. Seward, a member of the Committee, who had leaned toward compromise, could not now entertain the idea. His leader, who had offered him the post of Secretary of State, had vetoed it. The chance for Seward to be another Clay was gone. With Seward's vote in Committee went all the other Republican votes. In the larger sense that was the end. There were further attempts to reconcile the differences between North and South, but the South had given up hope and even Alexander H. Stephens found it impossible to have any faith in Lincoln's remarks that he intended no harm to the South. Lincoln's suggestion that he would be interested in appointing a few opposing Southerners to his cabinet met with no response.

South Carolina had gone, and was feeling out the sentiment of the other cotton states, who at first replied guardedly. As each day passed and no rays of light were seen, other states began to lean towards secession. In January, a conference of representatives of these states met at Montgomery, Alabama, to set up a new government. In the meantime the Federal garrisons of the forts in Charleston harbor were left in a ticklish position, South Carolina professing no longer to recognize the authority of the Federal government and the Federal government, under the wobbly James Buchanan, being unable to make up its mind whether or not it wished to be aggressive as General Jackson once had been, or pacificatory and weak. No steps were taken one way or the other, the South Carolinians being unwilling to do anything that appeared actively belligerent and the national government trying hard to keep its eyes shut and see nothing. The stock exchange in New York, like a thermometer in the mouth of an infected patient, was indicative of serious ill.

And when the stock exchange looks bad, look for blood-shed.

Meanwhile, the little village of Springfield, Illinois, was still Springfield, and the problems of North and South were merely newspaper issues there. On the day after the election of Jefferson Davis to the Presidency of the Confederate States of America, then in process of formation at Montgomery, two men to whom Montgomery and its life was as remote as Constantinople, sat in a little back room of a three story brick house facing the main square of Springfield.

The trees of the square were sharp against a sad gray sky. Under their branches stood saddle ponies hitched to iron posts, carts with wheels like great bony haunches raising above their bodies, their horses unhitched and tied to the axles, great-topped buggies like enormous beetles. The vehicles looked lifeless and old, the horses stood staring dejectedly at the ground. The chill of a raw February afternoon was a little softened by the smell of woodsmoke from the chimneys of the town.

In the little room up one flight of stairs beyond the rust-streaked sign reading: Lincoln and Herndon, the two law partners were talking over old times. The younger of the two men, a stocky rather leonine personage of perhaps forty years, sat with his feet on a long T-shaped table which was covered with un-brushed green baize. On this table, scattered among the feet of the lawyers, were several untidy bundles of legal looking papers. Occasionally the junior partner aimed a jet of tobacco juice at a cuspidor between two windows which looked out into a yard full of outhouses, piles of crates and boxes, old stove-pipe, discarded shoes and other rubbish.

Lincoln, the senior partner, wore a shabby, shapeless suit of black wool. There was still no gray in the great mass of his

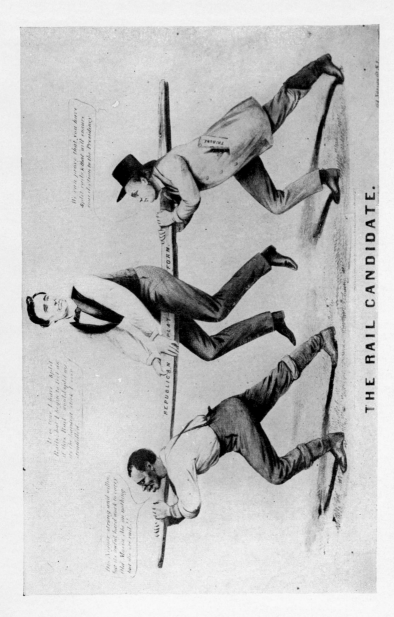

THE RAIL CANDIDATE.

What the Press Thought of Abraham's Candidacy

almost black hair, but the narrow face under the broad low forehead was now so deeply lined that it seemed almost to be covered with scars. The small gray eyes seemed dimmed; they wandered about and would not rest upon Herndon's. The small chin was covered by a new growth of slight black beard. In spite of the sadness of the eyes above it, the beard, as its owner lay back full length upon the black horsehair sofa along the wall farthest from the windows, bobbed up and down to the time of a shrill laughter.

The long black slab of Abraham Lincoln, weary of imperfect and unsatisfying judgments and decisions, of the struggle with office seekers, of the importunities of Mrs. Lincoln, who wanted this and that place for relatives of hers who because of Southern sympathies needed protection, had been relaxing by recalling to his partner's mind the pleasant days of riding the circuit as a traveling lawyer in the eighth Judicial district of Central Illinois. Those days were gone, with their simplicity and their single kindly demand. Abraham had not thought of them merely as days of earning a living, that living which the extravagant and unwise ways of his wife, combined with constant payments on old debts, had made so hard to accumulate. And his flier in Congress in 1848 and 1849 had not swelled the depleted pocketbook to any noticeable extent. Furthermore his stepbrother and father out in Coles County seemed always in need of help. He was a little disgusted with their shiftlessness but he could not always refuse them. Even this background of financial importunity had not been able to make his circuit days seem days of drudgery. The contact with simple, plain-spoken, plain-minded people which they had given was worth more than anything else to him.

Those days were over now, and letting them go from him was to Abraham a little like an unpracticed swimmer letting go of a boat for the first time. Now, in his last days of the old life in Springfield, he clung by means of anecdotes and reminiscence to the fringes of the system of ordinary behavior and ordinary thinking which the political accidents of national life had determined that he should leave. Now he remembered a story he had told to the landlady of a bawdyhouse whom he was defending. He had managed to get a change of venue for the lady and had driven her and some of her girls across the prairie to the next town. On the way they had sung songs and told stories to one another. He repeated some of them now, for his junior partner's adoring benefit.

The junior partner had heard it all before, but he laughed as heartily as the narrator. He spat again and told a story of his own. The senior partner lay back on the sofa for a while, with his feet stretched out full length before him and his arms, which were folded behind his great head of hair, making him look a full foot larger than the actual six feet four which intervened between his shoe soles and his scalp. Finally he flung himself into a sitting posture with a jerk, slapped his knees and stood up, his baggy coat falling clumsily down about his hips. He turned to his companion and looked at him solemnly. The younger man leaned back in his chair, his head outlined against the afternoon light which came in through the two rain-splotched windows that looked out upon the rubbish of the yard. There was not much to say, and Lincoln said no more. The two exchanged confidences. Lincoln insisted that his departure should make no difference in the firm, and Herndon denied that he cared to use his relationship to Lincoln as an excuse to get a soft political job. *

Herndon looked up into his partner's face. He knew how

* Herndon, Wm. H. and Weik, Jesse W. Abraham Lincoln, 1888.

much his own ardent activity and his political ideas had helped to stimulate the naturally sluggish flow of Lincoln's own. He knew how much the side of the Republican party which he represented and which Lincoln had always been a little shy of, was responsible for the political forces which were now taking the better half of his firm away from him. That, and the ambitious little woman in the strange cheerless house at Eighth and Jackson Streets, the once sparkling and socially distinguished Mary Todd.

The two men stood for a moment, the taller looking over Herndon's head, his glance going slowly about the old dusty office in a sort of ocular farewell. Then they turned away and clattered down the narrow wooden stairs, Lincoln talking in a tone of disgusted depreciation of the exalted office of President of the United States of America. So far it had been no fun at all, he said, and he was afraid it would only get worse. After all, there had been some people who couldn't conveniently get to Springfield to make him miserable. They probably would all be in Washington, never doubt it. He was sick of office holding already and the inauguration was still a month away.

As the two men stepped into the street, an old wind-blown piece of the *Illinois State Journal* in a changing wind, ranged back up the square and scuttled away from Lincoln and Herndon, carrying its depressing news of coming darkness. Abraham and his partner walked on. Lincoln talking of the unpleasantness of giving up a sheltered personal life, of which a man could know the worst, and of surrendering to public service, out in the unprotected open, where every passerby could stick his finger into you until you got as bruised as a grocer's apple.

Every time an enthusiastic citizen would stop the two men to shake hands with the newly bearded giant or to call out, with that excited effort of linking himself with someone marked out for distinction, "Good luck!" or "Hello, Abe!" or "When do you leave?", Lincoln would give Herndon a tragic, despairing look. He would have liked to gather all that came to him and thump them down on cracker-barrels in a circle about him, to stop the march of their inquisitory fawning with a "Listen, did you ever hear this one?" That would stop them. He was afraid of them when he couldn't do that. Afraid they might be saying under their breaths that Lincoln was not man enough for the job. He was man enough to make them laugh, at any rate, and he hankered to be able to prove that, if nothing else.

At the corner of Eighth Street Abraham turned and grasped Herndon's hand, saying an affectionate good-bye. Herndon stood watching him as he strode down the street. Although the junior partner did not then know it, and it is very doubtful that Lincoln thought of it, these two were never again to walk over that same ground together.

The home on Eighth and Jackson Streets had been rented, not without considerable misgiving and more difficulty. Lincoln believed that the tenants would "use it all up" before he ever got back to it.

During the winter the family had moved downtown to the Chenery House to board. The Chenery House was not a home. There wasn't room enough in it to get away when you wanted to, and six feet four of nervous, unhappy Lincoln could no longer walk the streets of Springfield with his own child's heart-load of oppression. Nor could he walk into a store and tell the boys what such and such a thing reminded him of. The boys had a feeling that the high and mighty politicians had now automatically become Abraham's intimates, that the America of which their fellow townsman had been elected Chief Magistrate, was something which did not extend to Illinois. They treated him as if he had changed, when he knew that he had not, even feared that he had not. They deprived him, thus, of the only way he knew how to make contact with life.

It was a bad winter, and the worst hour of its worst day was the hour before eight o'clock on the morning of February eleventh, 1861, the day before Abraham's fifty-second birthday. In the Chenery house, on that eventful morning, there were too many people doing too many things in too small a space. The family was in an uproar as all families, and particularly nervous ones, must be when they move, bag and baggage, even though the move be merely to the seashore. And the Lincoln family, mother and father and three sons, to say nothing of two recently acquired young secretaries, was moving from the peaceful, friendly town of Springfield to what many agreed was the only genuine hell-on-earth then in existence, the terrified, uncertain, arrogant, filthy, half-completed city of Washington.

And the nervous strain of the past year, crowning the power of other years of apprehension and bitterness, had told upon that family. Upon the lax and genial master of it, who through-out its days had struggled for the place which his desire to avenge himself for past humiliations told him he must fill, in a world in which he really believed that he did not belong. Upon the mother of the family, ambitious, arrogant, who had had to urge her difficult husband always to the point of energy, and who had, on the side, had to use her position to secure fat places for the husbands of her relatives and friends. And upon the children, least of all perhaps upon Robert, the oldest, who had been away at school in New Hampshire imbibing through contact with its sons the culture of the plutocratic North.

On the morning of February eleventh, Mrs. Lincoln, capable

and energetic, although rather high-strung, busied herself with the children, only Robert who was seventeen being old enough to be personally responsible for his conduct in time of stress. Willie was only ten and Thomas but seven.

The gigantic shallow-chested figure of Abraham himself stalked nervously about the narrow confines of the coarsely furnished suite at the Chenery House, seeing that everything was ready. The trunks which he had roped and marked with his own hands, had been piled into a cart and driven to the station under the supervision of Nicolay and Hay, the two young secretaries. There was an air of finality about it all. It seemed to Abraham a little as if he were being dispossessed.

He never quite knew how everyone got out of that madhouse of a hotel and into the carriages which were to carry the company through the streets of Springfield. He did not know how they ever got started on that dank and chilly morning, past the Square, past the State House, the office of Lincoln and Herndon, Chatterton's jewelry store, where he had bought Mary's wedding ring with its inscription "Love is Eternal," past the Globe Tavern where he had begun married life, past the friendly shops, the homes of friends, and finally into the dismal yard of the Great Western Railway Station.

That journey, with its smell of stale livery hacks, horses and damp leather, its grind of iron-shod carriage wheels through the sticky winter mud of the streets, the intermittent hollow, headachy rumble of the vehicle and hoofs over the wooden sidewalk crossings, and the soggy penetrating chill of the overcast sunless air, was not a pleasant journey for Abraham Lincoln. This was being President, was it, to go cooped up in a black box of a stinking, swaying hack, all folded up like a jackknife, feeling the horror of too close confinement, the old inescapable claustropho-

bia? Was this the womb from which a man must issue into
the terrifying world of power and distinction, terrifying but
coveted?

Long before eight o'clock, the scheduled hour of departure,
a crowd had begun to gather in the tiny waiting-room of the
station and to overflow into the muddy cinder-black yard between
the low flat-roofed brick building and the high-swung, hump-
backed train of cars, at the end of which a crushed looking locomotive with a funnel like a great black turnip was standing
belching acrid smoke. That smoke seemed to give to each drop
of moisture in the saturated air just enough weight of soot to
make it fall. Little grimy grains descended again and again upon
the heads and shoulders of the increasing crowd.

At five minutes past eight Abraham had to leave the handshaking bee that was going on inside the station. The train with
a shriek of mislaced whistle and a clanging of bell, rolled forward a little into place. Abraham, holding fast to a little black
satchel, and with a great gray rope of shawl knotted like a hawser
about the capstain of his head, his rumpled stovepipe beaver
resting on his ears, followed the railroad official to the back platform of the last car of the train. There he stood, pulled up to his
full height, looking as an untrained actor looks at his audience,
at the crowd below him, while Mrs. Lincoln, with the help of
her brother-in-law and the two young secretaries, loaded the
excited children on board.

Abraham stared at the crowd and took off his hat. His adam's
apple moved convulsively under the shawl. The whole party
was on board now. The Governor of the State, ex-Governor
Moore, Lockwood Todd, Orville H. Browning, Colonel E. V.
Sumner, Captain John Pope, and a few other officers, Judge David
Davis, of the Circuit Court, Norman Judd, Elmer Ellsworth,

Ward Hill Lamon, Lincoln's personal friend and bodyguard, and a number of others. Just as Mr. Wood, who represented the railroad was about to reach up proudly and pull the communication cord to start the ship of state on its way toward the high seas of administration, Lincoln leaned forward, resting his hands upon the rail of the platform.

The crowd stood in silence waiting. Here and there someone coughed. Most of the thousand or so citizens who had come to say good-bye to Springfield's favored son, stood with their hats off in the mist, waiting for some sign to prove that it was a greater thing to watch a President of the United States, whom many men thought would be the last, standing on the rear platform of a very unbeautiful railroad car, than to pass a longlegged melancholy awkward giant on the street in Springfield and say to him, "Hello, Abe!"

People were talking about the probability of there being a revolution in the country. What would a revolution be like anyway? Wonder if Old Abe knows anything about revolutions? What does he think, anyway? Maybe he'll say. Maybe someone'll ride up to him the way they did one day when he was speaking in the Square uptown and shout out, "Say, how would you like to sleep with a nigger?"

One or two in the crowd, a little bothered by the unwonted silence of the reputed backwoods comedian, noting perhaps, the look of sadness in his face and the beginning of a tear in his eye, could be heard whispering, "He needn't take on so!" or "Thinks he's God Almighty!"

As roots go into the earth, the little fibers of the gray breaths of that gray thousand Americans went into the lusterless, lifeless air of that Illinois morning.

Then there was a general shifting of position, a more intent staring of the upturned faces. Lincoln was speaking. His shrill, high-pitched, tight-throated voice sounded through the mist above the rhythmic "pssst-pssst" from the steam dome of the engine up forward.

"My friends," he said: "no one not in my situation can appreciate my feeling of sadness at this parting. To this place, and the kindness of these people, I owe everything. Here I have lived a quarter of a century, and have passed from a young to an old man. Here my children have been born, and one is buried. I now leave, not knowing when or whether ever I may return, with a task before me greater than that which rested upon Washington. Without the assistance of that Divine Being who ever attended him, I cannot succeed. With that assistance, I cannot fail. Trusting in Him, who can go with me, and remain with you, and be everywhere for good, let us confidently hope that all will yet be well. To His care commending you, as I hope in your prayers you will commend me, I bid you an affectionate farewell." *

Lincoln's face was drawn with that dry melancholy which in emotional people who are able to command their emotions, often takes the place of actual tears. The group of men standing behind him said nothing. The crowd about the car was silent for a moment. The drizzle had changed to thin gray snow.

The conductor of the train pulled the signal cord. The locomotive rang its bell and blew a damp white cloud from its shrill whistle. The crowd, now waving and speaking collectively, uttered a murmur of farewell which gradually mounted into a shout of cheering.

The loose-jointed train humped itself and clanked slowly away out of the damp cavern of the station yard, leaving the

* Nicolay and Hay, Abraham Lincoln: A History.

fellow-townsmen of Abe Lincoln to the simple daily rounds of
their mid-western life. That little train of a locomotive and two
cars carried Abraham Lincoln the plain country lawyer, the
cracker-barrel fun-maker, the politician, the maker of phrases,
out of the protective womb of his province into the whirlpool
world in which the broken pieces of the United States of America
were being ground to new shape.

As the train puffed swayingly along the uneven rails through
the snow-spotted prairies of Sangamon County, past wagons,
saddle-horses, and people on foot, all drawn to the tracks by the
hope of seeing the President-elect go by, Abraham Lincoln,
shocked into reaction by his own emotion, sat in the stuffy car
and operated with the keen knife of his wit upon the cancer of
sadness and nervous premonition which grew in his heart. He
called his friends Hill Lamon, Judge Judd, and Orville Browning to his seat and looked at them solemnly.

The children were staring out the windows in pleased excitement, Mrs. Lincoln was brushing the wrinkles from her
fine new traveling dress and folding and putting away in the
rack the appurtenances which she had made a special trip to
New York to buy. Colonel Sumner and the other officers with
several others of the party were talking to Mr. Wood of the
railroad company about the itinerary and the probable time of
reaching one place or another, of the frequency of railroad
wrecks and the causes of them.

There was a general atmosphere of uncertain danger in the
stuffy, creaky little car that smelled of smoke and coal oil. Aside
from the prevalence of wrecks on the railroads of those days,
newspapers everywhere had for some time been printing vague
news of plots to keep the new President from being inaugurated.

Whether these stories were based on fact or were not, the editors knew that the average American would think them better reading than the complicated and mysterious deficiencies of old Mr. Buchanan in the White House, or the obscure intentions of those Southern gentlemen who, at Montgomery, Alabama, on February eighth, had set up a government called the Confederate States of America, and announced the severance of the ties which bound the cotton states to the remaining states of the Union established in 1787 by the Constitution.

Most members of the little retinue of the Honorable Abraham Lincoln, en route for the chief magistracy of a Republic of eighty-five years, which at the same time showed signs of going the way all other republics had gone, believed that their friend's enemies were bent upon his destruction. It is probable that some of them—there was no great mind among them—believed that the conference at Montgomery was convened for no other purpose than that of devising ways to do away with Mr. Lincoln and seize the government at Washington, for use as the capital of the new Confederacy.

As Lincoln sat, looking up from his swaying jiggling chair at Judd and Lamon, there was a twinkle in his gray eyes. He wasn't going to make a hectic railroad trip any worse by thinking about people chaining trees to the railroad track or burning bridges to wreck his train. Moreover, the railroad official on board had assured him that there was a pilot engine not far ahead and an extra signal man at every curve. It was not fear that was bothering Abraham, at least not fear of physical harm. He merely felt that there was something conspicuously off about him which the people whom he was going to rule would notice and deride. It was as if he had forgotten to button himself up, or, as he did when a sculptor had been doing a bust of him a few months before, forgotten to put his undershirt back on. Combined with the personal anxiety, was a dreadful worry lest he should lose the little black bag in which he was carrying the galley proofs of his as yet secret inaugural address. But these troubles did not beset him continuously. They even suggested anecdotes to him. One of these he told now, beckoning the men closer to him.

When the story was finished, those who had listened to it burst into violently subdued laughter and turned to cast an ashamed eye at Mrs. Lincoln, who in her place at the other end of the car could scarcely have heard them. Several of the men who had been standing near-by and who had overheard the high humor of the relation smiled deferentially but a little nervously, looking at one another in surprise. Then some one asked Lincoln a question, hoping to change the subject. But he would not bother about politics. He waved them aside shaking his head in objection. Then he lay back in his seat, with his shawl spread over him, and tried to sleep. It would not work. His mind looked too much upon himself. Sleep had no chance of taking him unawares. He kept thinking of the strange illusion of the two faces, both Lincoln, but one pale and dim, which he had seen in a mirror when lying down in his room not many days before. He had believed that vision to be a mere illusion, in spite of the fact that he had seen it more than once. He did not realize how susceptible his type of emotional system was to hallucinations and unreal perceptions. He had always been a little superstitious, even having taken his son to see the possessor of a toad-stone in the hope of curing some minor trouble. He believed, rather more actively than is generally considered healthy, in a definite and presumably malign fate. So the vision worried him. His ambitious but not too wise wife had thought it an omen, signifying that he was to serve two terms as President, perhaps unconsciously indulging her own hope. An illusion, Abraham concluded that it was, but he could not quite rid himself of the sense of it. It was a trifle ominous.

And surely it seemed that he was plunging into the course of a very fateful series of events. God knows what kind of kettle of fish that old doddering Buchanan would have cooked up by the time March fourth came round. And what did those Southern fellows want anyway? Did they really want to go against the men who had made the Union? Why should they? Well, it seemed as if some of them did. Queer people.

Lincoln sat up and rubbed his hand over his chin. The young beard which he had grown during the preceding month felt strange and pleasant to the touch. Perhaps he felt that it stood between the naked, bewildered suffering of his heart and the outer world of suave and polished men which he disliked, almost feared, to face.

If I'm as ugly as they make out, he thought, this ought to be a help.

When the train rattled into the station at Indianapolis, late that afternoon, the cheers of a great crowd and the booming of cannon roused the tender-minded Westerner to a sense of his national prominence. The welcome made him, for a little, forget the seeming incongruity of his position. He forgot that he was merely an uneducated, matter-of-fact, small-town lawyer and stump speaker, and remembered that he had at least been chosen by his party to lead the nation.

True, in the election which had made him President-elect his opponents had received from the sovereign people a million more votes than he had, but still no one man had received as many as he did. He might as well pretend that there was no worm of uncertainty in his heart.

He stood on the back platform of the car and made a very dignified speech in which he declared, without specifying what liberty other than the liberty of holding slaves as property, had been assailed, that . . . "not with politicians, not with Presidents, not with office seekers, but with you, is the question: shall the Union and shall the liberties of this country be preserved to the latest generations?"

In the evening of the same day, feeling very awkward, but glad to be away from the confining, sickening motion of the crazy train, Lincoln fell a little below the dignity of his afternoon address. Misgivings were coming into his mind again. What right has Lincoln to be headed for Washington? There must be a mistake. He could not, he thought, be wrong about himself. His feelings were too simple to be wrong. It must be that the people who had pushed him up and onto this fateful train—Billy Herndon, Mary Todd, the party leaders,—it must be they that were in error about him. All this in the back of his head while he talked to the Indiana legislators, painfully conscious that he could not be at his best so long as his ability as a catchword orator must be restrained by his sense of what was owing the few days of presidential life left to old gray-headed James Buchanan.

It was too much. Lincoln began to kick himself back into flippancy to prevent himself from thinking too much about his grievances.

He spoke to his audience of those who professed devotion to the Union with the same voice by means of which they declared that they would resist Federal coercion. What is coercion? What is force? Do they love the Union? And yet they would resist it! . . . ". . . In their view," he said, "the Union as a family relation would seem to be no regular marriage, but rather a sort of 'free-love' arrangement, to be maintained only on 'passional attraction.' "

And next morning, when Abraham Lincoln woke up in his hotel bed in Indianapolis, the Eastern papers, that had stood with their mouths open, waiting for such crumbs of wisdom as a famished and torn nation desired, made wry faces over the mouthful their doubtful champion had dropped them. They confessed the taste of gall.

All along the route thereafter the progress of Lincoln's badly-balanced, jerky little train, which grew grimier every minute, the impolitic angels of perversity and uncertainty galloped from cow-catcher to tail lantern, seldom missing the great skull of the President-elect.

At Cincinnati the six feet four of provincial lawyer, the big man of Springfield, could not forget the unhappiness of his earlier visit during which, because of having been ignored by senior counsel in a law case in which he had been retained, he had felt that sophistication in the person of an attorney with a better education and a more polished manner had set its heel upon him.

Even as President-elect of the nation, the site of that energetic city on the Ohio River meant to Lincoln the sense of lost confidence in himself, of sinking of the heart. He now addressed two gatherings here, not in his happiest mood. He addressed his first remarks across the river toward Covington, Kentucky, his native state where dwelt many inclined to be Democrats and to lean upon slavery with a moderately fraternal arm. To these fellow-Americans, citizens to whose service he knew that he was devoted, but who were not of his political faith, he still spoke as an outsider rather than as a national figure. He quoted from his Cincinnati speech of 1859 and remarked that even in his new position he saw no reason to retract a word of it. "'We mean,'" he quoted, '"to treat you as near as we possibly can, as Washington, Jefferson, and Madison treated you. We mean to leave you alone, and in no way to interfere with your institutions; to abide by all and every compromise of the Constitution, and, in a word, coming back to the original proposition, to treat you so far as degenerate men, if we have degenerated, may, according to the example of those noble fathers, Washington, Jefferson, and Madison.'"

This was neither clever nor wise nor kind. It was a little spiteful. The Kentuckians felt it and the hearts of those among them who did not wish their economic reliance upon slavery to dismember the Union, sank, for the time, out of reach of any more words from Lincoln. They would have liked to know what the new President meant when he said he would in no way interfere with their institutions. Many of them felt that slavery being their institution, had the same right to expand with the new territory of their nation as did the more northern institution of wholesale merchandising. The North regarded the former as the South did the latter, as eminently distasteful. Those Kentuckians, nor any other Southerners, were ever able to learn what Mr. Lincoln had in mind.

To the German citizens of Cincinnati, in the same chill mood unable to shake off the distaste for the city which had hurt him and no longer needing votes, Lincoln said a few half-hearted words, remarking that he could not tell at the moment what he was going to do, that he did not, in fact, know. He referred to "foreigners" and said that he saw no reason for keeping them out of the country if they had any reason for wanting to come in.

The Germans were disappointed. To the last man, believing him their friend, not merely thier acquaintance, they had voted for him. The nation, when it read of what he was saying and how sadly and weakly he was saying it, was equally disappointed. Those who praised him, praised him because they believed he was showing himself to be a weak though honest man who would make the better tool for their purposes.

But whatever Lincoln said, however it saddened him to find no higher words upon his tongue, however it made him convinced that he was not the man for the job, there were thousands upon thousands who wanted to see the rail-splitter, the backwoodsman, the gawky giant who was going toward the crystal chandeliers of the White House.

Everywhere that the little toy train went, it found curious gazing crowds, some shouting, some silent, all unruly and eager to get a look at the new President of whom such queer, chuckling, behind-the-palm things were told. As the cars clattered along, that unhappy man himself told stories to his friends, played with the children, stared at his wife, lay back in his chair and slept, and walked to the platform to wave his hand and say, as he did at Steubenville, Ohio, and many other places, that the confidence which people seemed to be placing in him was unfounded.

Sometimes, sick of the motion of the train and unhappy at the direction it was taking, it would seem to him that he could not go on. Then his speech would all but fail him and that happy circumlocution about the nakedness of an idea, which is the orator's very breath, would be beyond his power to command.

Then he would merely state solemn platitudes. He would say, "We should all be bound by the majority of the American people," knowing that the office toward which he was headed had been secured to him by the vote of not more than one-third of the adult males of his country. Sometimes, with a feeling of tragic horror in his heart, he would find his mouth saying, "The crisis, as it is called, is altogether an artificial crisis."

Occasionally, however, shaken into himself again by some commonplace human incident of life on the way, he would recover his wit a little, without recovering the sanity which usually balanced it. At such times he would, while the crowds waited for him to open his mouth, call for a little girl, for whom he said he had grown his new beard, and ask her how she liked it, or, as at Utica, New York, on the eighteenth of February, "I appear before you that I may see you, and that you may see me, and I am willing to admit that so far as the ladies are concerned I have the best of the bargain, though I wish it to be understood that I do not make the same acknowledgment concerning the men."

By the time the exhausted party of pompous politicians, vainglorious military men, fidgety and scantily sympathetic children and wife, obsequious secretaries, had reached the city of New York, Lincoln was calmer, though perhaps not happier, than any of them. Such worries as he had felt for the effect of his reticence on national subjects were lessened with each crowd at each wayside platform. He noticed that nobody really listened, that no one ever seemed to know when he repeated at one halt the words he had used at the previous one. He began to appreciate, not without slight increase of inner sadness, that no one except the politicians, the men whom he knew so well, cared what he said, and then only that he said not too much. He felt something like a "Wild Man of Borneo" being exhibited from a circus car.

And Lincoln would have felt much better about it all if the terrible droning chorus of his heart had not, despite the government of his wit and his ready ability to assemble common things into uncommon meanings, cried out, unquieted, "Lincoln's not the man! Lincoln's only a child, base as a child, awkward as a child! He doesn't know anything really!"

As the black turnip of a locomotive, mounted on its squat trucks, belching forth fire and smoke, waddling its clanking drivers like a cat in agony, pulled its two frail cars into the depot at Philadelphia on the afternoon of February twenty-first, 1861, Lincoln felt that the inevitable horror was drawing very close to him. Like an ambitious child bent upon being a champion swimmer, he none the less did not want the water to be cold. And the nearer he got to the great iron dome at Washington which was the very vortex of his whirlpool waters, the colder did their current seem to be.

Philadelphia, as it jerked backwards past him, while he stood half dazed in the triumphal carriage which bore him from the depot to the Continental Hotel, seemed to be all elbows and hands, hats and beards, voices, bunting, motion and cold. At the hotel he thanked the crowd for whatever it was that it had shown him and repeated his earlier remarks as to the artificial nature of the supposed national crisis.

"It is true, as your worthy Mayor has said," remarked Lincoln, "that there is a great anxiety amongst the citizens of the United States at this time. I deem it a happy circumstance that this dissatisfied portion of our fellow-citizens does not point us to anything in which they are being injured or about to be injured; for which reason I have felt all the while justified in concluding that the crisis, the panic, the anxiety of the country at this time is artificial."

If he had seen into the heart of many an honest Southerner, a thing which he had not yet done, the honest Abraham Lincoln would, politics or no politics, never have lent his tongue to the

uses of such quibbling as that; nor would he have believed that
his "political warfare" and no other man's was "in favor of
the teachings that come forth" from the sacred walls of the
Hall of Independence.

If by his repetition of the statement that there was nothing
really wrong with the country, Lincoln was trying to whistle
himself into the bravery of believing that the route he had to
walk was neither dark nor lonely, there were earnest, bustling
friends who were soon to shake him out of that bravery.

Abraham was sitting in his room at the Continental Hotel
in Philadelphia on the evening of February twenty-first taking
off his shoes. He thought he saw that in thirty seconds he would
be, with free toes, lying on his back in the middle of the floor
with a bed-pillow under his head, enjoying himself hugely. Five
minutes without being molested had warmed him a little and
made him feel that he might, given time, be himself again, like
a fish thrown back into water after a bad time among the rocks.
At the end of the five minutes, however, he was lost.

A knock on the door and a question and answer brought into
the room Lincoln's friend Norman B. Judd, of Chicago, one of
the heavyweights of his entourage, who was followed by a
stately flash of man named Pinkerton.

Lincoln welcomed these two solemn gentlemen, who looked
as if they had been caught in a raid, with a pleasant story about
the men whose pigpen fence was so crooked that the pigs escaped into it every time they thought they were escaping out of
it. Meaning to say that the shoe laces, with which he was busy
were a bit like that fence.

When the President-elect had heard Judd's story and seen the
hopefully acquiescent nods of Mr. Pinkerton, he forgot his shoes.
These fellows were telling him that there was a plot against his

life and that he must, without anyone's knowledge, give up the rest of his tour and take the eleven o'clock train for Washington that very night, passing through Baltimore without stopping, unexpected, unheralded and unrecognized. It appeared that Baltimore was the scene of the proposed plot.

Lincoln was genuinely troubled by this news. He remembered now that Baltimore was the only city, Maryland the only state, through which his way to the capital must lie, which had sent him no official invitation and no greeting. That looked bad. And yet, he thought, why should anyone plot against him? But it did look rather bad. He saw what it would mean to his enemies to have him sneak into Washington like that. They would call him yellow-livered or worse.

He pondered a moment, thinking with something of a shudder of the jostling, damp-handed crowds that had swelled about him everywhere. He began to see danger in their midst. Yet he had planned to penetrate one to raise a flag over Independence Hall on the following morning and to proceed into another one at Harrisburg to deliver a speech.

He decided that whatever danger there might be he would keep to this schedule, and if nothing went wrong, continue as planned.

In the morning, tired and haggard, but perhaps a little sharpened by the new brooding of his fear and anxiety, he went through the flag-raising ceremonies and made a speech in which he indirectly referred to the possibility of assassination. He was a romantic soul and, although he could keep his mind from the threatened danger, he felt that he must use it as a means of drawing his audience closer to him. In doing so he unconsciously drew the danger closer to his own heart.

Just when he was ready to leave Philadelphia he received word from Senator Seward in Washington that the supposed plot had carried its noise to that place also. That confirmation, sketchy as it was, settled Lincoln's mind. He thereupon decided to let his managing friends arrange for a secret trip back to Philadelphia from Harrisburg that night, and for an even more secret one from Philadelphia direct to Washington via Baltimore before daylight. With that decision, unpleasant though it was, Lincoln's spirits began to rise.

That evening, when Harrisburg had had its fill of speech-making, handshaking and cannon-firing, Lincoln retired to his room in the Jones House and summoned the members of his retinue to his side. Mr. Judd explained the situation and told of the plan for getting Lincoln through to Washington in secret. Lincoln sat looking from face to face among his friends, trying to make out what they thought of his decision. He paid little attention to Colonel Sumner's soldierly remark that such a procedure as was proposed was nothing more or less than cowardice. He had made his decision and he would stick to it. He now believed, at least partially, in his danger, and he determined to go ahead and avoid it.

When that solemn meeting had disbanded with phrases and grunts representing various gradations of opinion, Lincoln, with only Lamon at his side, slipped from the hotel by a side door and into a shuttered carriage in the dark. The two men were driven hurriedly to a deserted railroad crossing outside of the town, where stood unlighted, a single day coach hitched to an engine panting under full steam.

The two left the carriage and climbed into the empty car, fumbling about in it in the dark until they found and were identified by the nervous railroad official who had the trip in charge. This gentleman immediately pulled the signal for the train to start.

Lincoln rather enjoyed the excitement. He sat in the dark car and stretched his ungainly legs. The railroad official, who had never heard any of his stories, and Lamon who had heard them all, laughed equally at the diversion which he offered them.

At ten o'clock the train reached West Philadelphia. Here there was another mysterious, melodramatic shift. Lincoln and Lamon got out of the train and sat in a tightly sealed carriage, almost suffocated by the odor of livery stable broadcloth steeped in horse. Finally the carriage began to move. Lincoln had no idea of its direction. For all he knew the driver might have been the wrong man.

For nearly an hour the dizzy carriage rumbled in unmapped circles through the City of Brotherly Love. Finally, when the cramped position of the President-elect had begun to make him feel a little tenderly about the idea of assassination, the carriage creaked and growled its way into the shadow of the Baltimore depot.

A long train made up with sleepers and day coaches and lighted dimly by oil lamps stood like a dead whale upon the nearest track. The end door of the last car stood open and a man leaned in its shadow. Lamon walked up to the man and whispered in his ear. He then turned and beckoned to Lincoln, who was bashfully standing there, gaunt as a lamppost, with a flat soft hat on his massive head, his shawl wrapped in a rope about his neck, and his short overcoat making his legs look like the side posts of a ladder.

Lincoln climbed the high car steps, strode into the dimly-lighted cavern above and quickly plunged between the curtains of the berth which was hastily pointed out to him. He lay back at full length, or as near it as a railroad berth of 1861 would allow a man of six feet four to do so, and drew a deep breath. Outside, in the aisle, Lamon, with the necessary tickets, was telling the conductor that his traveling companion was sick and could not be disturbed.

The sick man lay folded like a camp-stool in his bunk, now and then poking his watchful companion outside and whispering through the curtains whatever his present situation reminded him of. In a bunk adjoining an enthusiastic detective lay with his eyes open.

At half-past three on the morning of February twenty-third, Lincoln, tossing in his berth, his head already troubled by misgivings as to the justice and wisdom of his manner of fooling the people who had chosen him presumably to lead them, heard the grind of brakes and the slow buckling into a full stop of the loose-jointed line of cars. He looked out the window with one eye. The detective was already on the platform looking about. It was Baltimore.

Somewhere in the barn of a station an early passenger was thumping cavernously on an empty booth, trying to interest someone in selling him a ticket. There was a sound of steam, a clink of couplings, the swing of a lantern. The car moved a little. No one was in sight. The creosoty smell of engine smoke drifted through the car. Occasionally a passenger snored.

Lincoln lay still, his heart beating very fast. Slowly the car wheels ground the rails. The car moved ahead. It was off on its journey through the supposedly malicious streets of Baltimore, bound for the Washington depot.

The streets, lighted here and there with gas lamps, were empty, as all streets, guilty or innocent, are likely to be at that hour. Scarcely a man or beast saw the passage of that car along the track, over the cobbles of the Maryland city. But Lamon and the detective and Lincoln himself breathed more easily as the car, hitched to another train, picked up speed and headed for open country toward the Potomac.

At six o'clock the unfinished dome of the capitol stood up against the dawn. Lincoln, sitting behind drawn curtains, saw it with a sense both of relief and of regret. There was no way out of it now, not even a fatal way. He would have to go through the fog, cold as it was.

He was so tired, so sick at heart when he reached the station at Washington that he scarcely cared for the excited caution of Lamon and the detective. In the crowd getting from the train, with his face partly muffled in his shawl, he walked like a man in a daze.

Outside the station Senator Seward was waiting with a cab. Everyone piled in and they drove unrecognized through the early streets to the side door of Willard's Hotel, where the party waited while Seward went around to the front door to get Willard himself and sent him to meet his distinguished and secret guest.

Lincoln had gone strangely silent. He looked very pale and worn. He asked, almost tearfully, to be shown to his room and left alone. When the door closed upon him he flung himself down on the bed and lay as if exhausted, with his long black forearm pressed upon his eyes.

CHAPTER TWO

A NATION AND ITS LEADER

FROM the adoption of the Federal Constitution until the election of Abraham Lincoln under its provisions, no decade showed more material progress than the decade immediately preceding the latter event, the decade which provided the occasion for Lincoln's rise to national prominence. The mind of the American people, during this era, was turned very largely in the direction of that material progress. Its frenzy, its peace, its hope, its despair, its faith, its very activity, depended upon prosperity. The Southern slaveholder's concern for his peculiar institution was for the most part a concern for the sources of his wealth, as the Northerner's concern with anti-slavery ideas was a concern for its own fiscal potentialities. During this decade, moral and ethical position was not given exclusively to either North or South. The very party which advocated the retention and fostering of slavery, advocated also the freedom of the seas, the freedom of trade for the benefit not of nations and parties, but of the whole civilized world.* The very party which professed to regard slavery with horror, at the same time believed in such doubtful business as the paying of a guaranteed subsidy of almost a million dollars to a private steamship owner, and was willing to consider the granting of franchises to New York street railways if thereby it could get its coffers enriched by some hundreds of thousands of dollars. No, there was no one

* Stanwood. History of Presidential Elections, p. 203.

seat of morality, nor of reason nor of justice. There was a little in all sections and in all sections much that was corrupt and horrible. The unpleasant thing to contemplate is the fact that men of all parties had then, as always, in order to keep the machinery of the American political system in motion, to sub-scribe to or wink at things which no truly unhampered man of character could have countenanced privately.

It was this money-grubbing world, harassed by conflicting notions about slavery and by incomplete recovery from the financial stringency of 1857 and 1858, over which the simple honesty of Abraham Lincoln was called to rule. And Abraham had, and continued to have, a conceived duty to wink at things with the best of them, to countenance unholy things for the sake of the power without which no party can run the government of the United States, a government which by virtue of its very Constitution is dedicated to the interests of those who have or covet the power which comes from wealth. Unfortunately for Abraham's peace of mind and for the peace of the country for the next few years, the details of economic issues, of material circumstance, were and always had been since his first financial failure, since his strangely ill-chosen advocacy of the Internal Improvement Acts of Illinois, impossible for him to master. He could master men, fortunately, and he learned to master himself, thereby ultimately preserving the Union which the indecisive and partisan activities of himself, his friends, and his enemies had, up to 1861, done so much to undermine.

Abraham came to Washington under very depressing circumstances. For days he felt scared and strange, harassed by the thought that everything he did must receive criticism that would hurt him or praise that could not satisfy him. His cabinet appointments worried him terribly, and, even more terribly, the importunities of the press and public that wanted to know what they were. His inaugural address, which Senator Seward, designated to be Abraham's Secretary of State, did not like and wished to modify, also worried him. He submitted to some of Seward's modification of language with a little quiet hurt, perhaps feeling in his subordinate's suggestions a touch of humiliating criticism. But Seward had threatened to kick over the traces and cause hostility from the start of the administration by refusing to serve as Secretary of State even though he had previously accepted the offer of that post. The gentleman from New York must be placated, everybody must be placated.

Washington was full of wild talk. The Confederate States had got under way, and were something to be reckoned with even if not recognized. It was all a misunderstanding. People should not look at things as they did. The trouble looked serious, but was it? Old Buchanan was not doing anything. The "Peace Conference" had accomplished nothing but a suggestion of constitutional amendment that looked a good deal like an offspring of the Crittenden compromise, dressed up in a plainer suit of clothes. And Congress in the fine frenzy of its last days had, unfortunately for the Republican party, adopted and prepared for ratification by the states, an amendment based upon the suggestion of the Peace Conference. It was an amendment from which the South hoped little but from which the North hoped much. It made things a little difficult for Abraham, who had been so definite in his rejection of the Crittenden compromise and who now was faced with a constitutional amendment, almost, you might say, a part of the nation's law already—for there was little doubt that sufficient states would ratify it—an amendment which read: "No amendment shall be made to the Constitution which will authorize or give to Congress the power

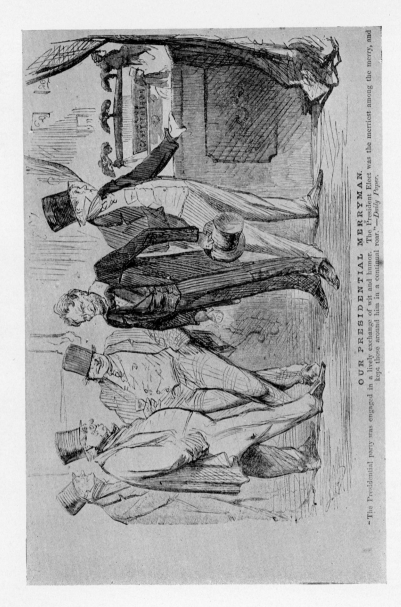

OUR PRESIDENTIAL MERRYMAN.

"The Presidential party was engaged in a lively exchange of wit and humor. The President Elect was the merriest among the merry, and kept those around him in a continual roar."—*Daily Paper.*

From Leslie's Weekly

to abolish or interfere, within any state, with the domestic institutions thereof, including that of persons held to labor service by the laws of said State."

This was unlike the Crittenden Compromise, to which as a matter of policy Abraham objected, and which the Congress had just refused to submit to a vote of the people, in that it did not say anything about the extension of slavery. As an amendment it did not please Abraham, however, nor did it please the South as a whole. Abraham felt that it was none the less a part of the law of the nation, there being no doubt that sufficient states would ratify it. He did not oppose it by any word of his. But as a conciliatory measure it could not stem the tide of secession which the election of "Black Republican" Lincoln had loosed in the South.

By the fourth of March, South Carolina, Georgia, Mississippi, Florida, Louisiana, Alabama, and Texas had left the Union as formally as failure of the Union to recognize the fact permitted. It was a raw and blustery day that dawned upon the District of Columbia, a little piece of Federal soil sandwiched in between two still openly loyal but very doubtful states. And, nervous, harassed, solemn and scared, six feet four of Abraham Lincoln lay in Willard's Hotel wondering how he was ever going to summon up, in that chill wind, sufficient warmth to make his lined face, his taut, pained lips, move in appealing speech up there on the great platform before the unfinished Capitol. There was little reassurance for him in the atmosphere of the official life of the city, now concerning itself, miraculously enough, chiefly with him. Everyone was apprehensive. Those who were not openly frightened appeared secretive and sullen. Where was the light of genial, careless humanity? Everyone seemed to be listening for a noise. Perhaps it was the boom of the artillery, which the officious if capable General Scott had placed at favorable points to serve in case of riot, that people listened for. Perhaps it was the wild throaty tumult of a mob, storming the inaugural pavilion. Whatever it was, there was no sound but the horrible rumble of carriage wheels, the clatter of hoofs, through the dismal streets. And there was the beating of Abraham Lincoln's heart, higher and more rapid than usual.

He never knew how he got through his Inaugural Address,. nor what effect it had upon those who heard it. Everyone heard the string-tight silence of political and human tension and few the shrill, quivering voice of the new President. Everywhere in the crowd, as in Abraham's. voice, there was real emotion. The Chief Justice who administered the oath was the same who had just after the last inauguration delivered the opinion of his court in the Dred Scott case. Now he was crowning the man who had most bitterly assailed his expressed opinion, whose hostility had triumphed in the nation, whose activities could not but alienate the already exasperated South. But Roger Taney loved his nation. So did Stephen A. Douglas, another of Abraham's bitter enemies, who as the gaunt man from the Sangamon spoke his concluding words, stood behind him holding his hat as if in sign that he would serve. "In your hands, my dissatisfied fellow countrymen," said Lincoln, "and not in mine, is the momentous issue of civil war. The government will not assail you. You can have no conflict without yourselves being the aggressors. You have no oath registered in Heaven to destroy the government, while I shall have the most solemn one to preserve, protect and defend it. . . . We are not enemies but friends. Though passion may have strained, it must not break our bonds of affection. The mystic cords of memory stretching from every battlefield and patriot grave, to every living heart and hearthstone all over this broad land, will yet swell the chorus of the Union when again touched, as surely they will be, by the better angels of our nature." There spoke both Seward and Lincoln, the words Lincoln's, the emotion his, the conciliatory idea Seward's. The speech, so great was the occasion, had little intrinsic value. The awe and solemnity of the occasion had much. Men remembered the occasion who had not caught a word of the speech. When printed in the papers it. did. not look like very much. It merely said, in rather half-hearted words that the South should not make such a row, because it could not point to any Constitutional guarantee of which it had been denied the full protection. That of course was quibbling, because, whether just or not in the eyes of Northern Calvinists, the South believed that it had a grievance. It was not just, though it may have been logical, to stand before something to which a friend was pointing in objection and say, "I see nothing." The address went on to say that as the Constitution said nothing about the ability of any state or group of states to get out of the Union it was impossible to get out. This, of course, neglected to consider the fact that Union could in no case ever be anything but a voluntary arrangement no matter what the Constitution might say. If anyone wanted to get out badly enough to risk everything in the act, could anything but violence stop it? But there was violence in the air, how great and how horrible no one saw. Yet, said the address, ". . . The Union . . . *will* constitutionally defend and maintain itself. . . . In doing this there need be no bloodshed or violence; and there shall be none unless it be forced upon the national authority." That was that. "All the vital rights of minorities and of individuals are so plainly assured to them by affirmations and negations, guarantees and prohibitions in the Constitution, that controversies never arise concerning them." Therefore, said the address, the question of the prohibition or protection of slavery in the territories, not being mentioned in the Constitution, that question should not be allowed to be a troublesome one. If a minority believed that it was a troublesome question and demanded a settlement of it, they should submit to the fact that the majority thought it otherwise. That was logical, but the South could not be expected to delight in the logic of it.

The cold March wind blew through these words and made their edges sharp. The new President stepped down from the platform, and after the ceremonies drove with old Mr. Buchanan, as nervous as a rabbit in a dog kennel, through scattered platoons of champing cavalry up the ugly length of Pennsylvania Avenue to the White House. Nowhere was there any trace of the rebellion and riot which so many, anxious for excitement, had involuntarily feared.

Abraham and his buxom consort, he in enormous white kid gloves, and she with red face and a great blue feather in her hair, drove in the evening to the Inaugural Ball, a festivity but thinly attended by the socially prominent of the city, a tawdry, bitter entertainment, in which no one but Mrs. Lincoln took any interest. It was her event and, like a horse in a race from which all others are scratched, she made the most of it. But for Abraham it was a torture. He did not like his gloves, he did not like the formal atmosphere of the ball. He wished he were back in Springfield. He began to realize the task ahead of him, and to understand that introduction to it through the medium of an unaccustomed social event, was the surest way of emphasizing his unfitness of it. That day and that night, Abraham Lincoln was not the only man in Washington who thought he was unfitted for his office.

That first night in the White House, whatever it was for the gratified Mary Todd, was not a happy one for Abraham. He climbed out of it as early as he could and bearded the terrors of his office, which, with a sinking of the heart he soon understood to be no mere ghosts. If the new President had any hope of temporizing with the fearful problems facing the national government, his hope was soon dispelled, for one of the first things he learned on March 5, 1861, was that the Federal garrison at Fort Sumter in Charleston Harbor, South Carolina, was running short of provisions. Furthermore, it was the opinion of the general commanding the armies of the United States, that Major Anderson's garrison should be reinforced, if the post were to be held, and immediately abandoned if it were not. This grave problem, involving as it did the question of the government's policy toward the seceded states, took Abraham's mind away from the sordid and depressing business of dealing with the hordes of office seekers who were besieging the White House, while two little Lincolns looked out of an upper window and wondered what it was all about.

The President was a little timid about asserting an opinion of his own in such a matter as this, and yet he was perplexed because his time honored system of understanding men by facing them and getting down to good human talk with them was impossible in Washington on account of the lack of time, the necessary enforcement of a certain constraining presidential dignity, and the fact that there were entirely too many people to be dealt with. The result was a terrible state of mind which left him not knowing whom he could trust, and that very state of mind made him occasionally take advice when it would have been better to reject it, and occasionally reject advice which would have been better taken. It sapped his already weakened confidence in himself and left him unable to make up his mind as he was constitutionally unable to let it be made up for him.

President Lincoln had spent months in his little Springfield home worrying over his cabinet appointments. When he announced them, after his arrival in Washington, it certainly looked to the public as if he were trying to punish himself by giving himself the most uncongenial and internally hostile set of advisers a man could possibly have picked. Not one of them either sympathized with or understood the man under whom they were to serve. Each had his own ambitions, at least one was positively corrupt. With all, possibly excepting Seward, self-interest was the prime consideration. The first question which Abraham Lincoln submitted to his advisers, was that of the course to be pursued in South Carolina. As usual, Abraham himself was a needle indicating the fluctuation of popular opinion. The country itself, at least that part of it which was left after the estrangement of the several Southern states did not know where it stood nor what it wished. New York did not want war, much as it wanted Northern supremacy. War was bad for business. But the financial interests as well as the popular emotional interest of the North did not want their section to appear frightened by the attitude of South Carolina. Withdrawal of the Union forces from Fort Sumter, Abraham thought, might be misconstrued by the country, South as well as North. Reinforcement might lead to war. And, after all, had not the Republican party been faced for some time with the idea of violence? Curiously enough, Seward, the author of the "irrepressible conflict" idea, was the one member of the cabinet who at the moment wished to avoid stirring up the jingoes in either North or South. Abraham would have liked to have his cabinet say that Sumter should be relieved, but when first asked they said the opposite by a margin of five to two. So, not feeling ready to make up his mind in the way he wished not to, the President did nothing. He refused to meet Commissioners sent from the South to discuss the question of Fort Sumter and went on pretending to himself and everyone else that the situation was not so serious as it was made out to be. He knew what he would have liked to think and do, but he lacked initiative and could not act. Again after several weeks he consulted the cabinet. Again the cabinet voted five to two, but this time in the opposite direction, indicating that the disputed fort should be relieved. That was apparently what Abraham wanted, but still he was unable to assert himself and take the necessary action. He gave orders to have a relief expedition prepared but nullified the orders by allowing it to be understood that it was not contemplated to use it.

When the first of April came around and it appeared beyond question that the President was unable to force himself to take a definite step, the honest, if misguided, Secretary of State, who had never seen such a man as Lincoln before and could not believe that he was anything but a kind of occasionally inspired simpleton, came to the conclusion that the government must have a head and that he was the man. Accordingly, the Secretary, with the best will in the world, but with an arrogant assumption that in the light of our more favorable opportunity for judging Abraham seems foolhardy, sent to Mr. Lincoln a private letter long unknown to the public. It was entitled "Some thoughts for the President's Consideration." This is what it said. It was dated April first, 1861.

First: We are at the end of a month's administration, and yet without a policy, either domestic or foreign.

Second: This, however, is not culpable, and it has even been unavoidable. The presence of the Senate, with the need to meet applications for patronage, have prevented attention to other and more grave matters.

Third: But further delay to adopt and prosecute our policies for both domestic and foreign affairs would not only bring scandal on the administration, but danger upon the country.

Fourth: To do this we must dismiss the applicants for office. But how? I suggest that we make the local appointments forthwith, leaving foreign or general ones for ulterior and occasional action.

Fifth: The policy at home. I am aware that my views are singular, and perhaps not sufficiently explained. My system is built upon this idea as a ruling one, namely, that we must

Change the question before the public from one upon slavery, or about slavery, for a question upon *union or disunion:*

In other words, from what would be regarded as a party question, to one of patriotism or union.

The occupation or evacuation of Fort Sumter, although not in fact a slavery or party question, is so regarded. Witness the temper manifested by the Republicans in the free states, and even by the Union men in the South.

I would therefore terminate it as a safe means for changing the issue. I deem it fortunate that the last administration created the necessity.

For the rest, I would simultaneously defend and reënforce all the ports in the Gulf, and have the navy recalled from foreign stations to be prepared for a blockade. Put the island of Key West under martial law.

This will raise distinctly the question of union or disunion. I would maintain every fort and possession in the South.

(It should be borne in mind in reading the extraordinarily belligerent and spread-eagle second section of Secretary Seward's quaint letter, that Seward wished, as Lincoln did, to placate the South if possible and conceived that one way of doing it would be to show signs of national excursions and acquisitions in the black belt of the West Indies. Mexico, for instance, had always been close to the slave power's dreams of expansion and here at the very moment, was Napoleon III of France sticking his finger into the Mexican pie. Cuba and the other islands near it were also dream children of the Southern mind. And here at this very moment was Spain, watching like a hawk, the domestic strife of the Santo Domingans, waiting, supposedly to seize the island. Why should not the United States object to that, growling so hard that the hawk would drop Cuba as it fled? Seward thought that nothing filled people's minds like a good noisy war. Hence:)

For Foreign Nations

I would demand explanations from Spain and France, categorically, at once.

I would seek explanations from Great Britain and Russia and send agents into Canada, Mexico and Central America to rouse a vigorous continental spirit of independence on this continent against European intervention.

And if satisfactory explanations are not received from Spain and France,

Would convene Congress and declare war against them.

But whatever policy we adopt, there must be an energetic prosecution of it.

For this purpose it must be somebody's business to pursue and direct it incessantly.

Either the President must do it himself, and be all the while active in it, or

Devolve it upon some member of his cabinet. Once adopted, debate on it must end, and all agree and abide.

It is not my especial province;

But I neither seek to evade nor assume responsibility.*

* Works (Lincoln), Vol. V, p. 280.

But the Secretary was so sure that responsibility would be thrust upon him in the form of a grateful answer from his chief that he began immediately to pull the wires. Under the name of the President, he sent a dispatch to the Brooklyn Navy Yard, ordering an expedition to prepare to go to the relief of Fort Pickens off the coast of Florida. "I would maintain every fort and possession in the South," he had said. But he had also said that the evacuation of Sumter would be desirable and he did not wish any disturbance to be caused in the sensitive harbor of Charleston, by the possible dispatch of the expedition which was being held in readiness, pending the President's word "go," for the relief or strengthening of Fort Sumter. Because of this, Seward, in the dispatch over the President's name, directed that the most powerful warship allotted to the Sumter expedition should be transferred to the Fort Pickens expedition. Mr. Gideon Welles, Connecticut editor, serving, as querulously as the rest of Abraham's amazing cabinet, as Secretary of the Navy, got word that someone was tampering with his department. As he hated Seward more than any other current cabinet officer he naturally suspected that suave statesman, and he was furious.

The Secretary of State was dumbfounded at the reply he received from the supposedly simple-minded and frightened Abraham. For Lincoln, who had not the slightest doubt of what he wanted to do, nor of the essential wisdom of what he had stowed away in the inner recesses of his mind, merely lacked the ability to see how things might be done. He had been going about his business as if in a stupor, and it was no wonder that Seward thought him incompetent. But Seward did not realize that the Chief Executive was a splendid instinctive cook who merely had an aversion to breaking eggs. In the present case, the eggs from which a palatable omelet might have been made were growing older without a crack in the shell while the sense of a perfect dish lay closed within the fastnesses of Abraham's strange nature. Seward's unbelievable communication came to him in the midst of the turmoil of the White House, the two little children running about underfoot, Mary fussing over state dinners which he thought she should not give, the secretaries, Nicolay and Hay, pestering him to have some order and system about his official business, office seekers streaming in and hiding behind the portières to catch their game unawares, all the chairs in his private apartments conspiring by their size and shape to keep him from getting a comfortable five minutes sitting, servants puttering about, possibly laughing at him.

And here was this thing from Seward, not laughing at him, but telling him plainly that he was dumb and incompetent and had better hand over the reins to a real man. That was enough. The shock of it broke the eggs and the omelet began to cook. Someone had opposed him. He was furious, he was hurt, but he was calm, and he would be magnanimous. As if he believed that his presence where he was was a bitter and irrevocable mistake, he resolved to crucify himself upon the long, cruel arms of public error. He would not lose his temper. Knowing humanity, he would blame no one for anything. He himself was strong. He knew, he felt, more about everything than any two of anyone else. He could afford to be generous in spirit. He could even afford that difficult performance of turning the other cheek. And this because, deep down inside, he knew, he felt, he was.

He did not wait long after receiving his Secretary's letter. Putting on his strangely minute glasses and crossing his great legs, his lips showing taut, he wrote:

Executive Mansion, April 1, 1861.

Hon. W. H. Seward.

My dear Sir:—Since parting with you I have been considering your paper dated this day, and entitled "Some Thoughts for the President's Consideration." The first proposition in it is, "First, We are at the end of a month's administration, and yet without a policy either domestic or foreign."

At the beginning of that month, in the inaugural, I said: "The power confided in me will be used to hold, occupy, and possess the property and places belonging to the Government, and to collect the duties and imposts." This had your distinct approval at the time; and, taken in connection with the order I immediately gave General Scott, directing him to employ every means in his power to strengthen and hold the forts, comprises the exact domestic policy you now urge, with the single exception that it does not propose to abandon Fort Sumter.

Again, I do not perceive how the reinforcement of Fort Sumter would be done on a slavery or a party issue, while that of Fort Pickens would be on a more national and patriotic one.

The news received yesterday in regard to St. Domingo certainly brings a new item within the range of our foreign policy; but up to that time we have been preparing circulars and instructions to ministers and the like, all in perfect harmony, without even a suggestion that we had no foreign policy.

Upon your closing propositions—that "whatever policy we adopt, there must be an energetic prosecution of it.

"For this purpose it must be somebody's business to pursue and direct it incessantly.

"Either the President must do it himself, and be all the while active in it, or

"Devolve it upon some member of his Cabinet. Once adopted, debates on it must end, and all agree and abide"—I remark that if this must be done, I must do it. When a general line of policy is adopted, I apprehend there is no danger of its being changed without good reason, or continuing to be a subject of unnecessary debate; still, upon points arising in its progress I wish, and I suppose I am entitled to have, the advice of all the Cabinet.

Your obedient Servant

A. LINCOLN.*

The self-confident and for the moment stupid Seward, must have been very much pained to receive that gentle and truly considerate letter. For it left him in a curiously equivocal position, the position of a man who has spent his money before it was in the bank and is suddenly brought to the realization that it is never going to reach the bank. He had sent orders to Brooklyn in the President's name. Now the President, in justice to his Secretary of the Navy, desired to have those orders countermanded. Furthermore, the Secretary of State, either taking too literally something which he had heard the President say or assuming that he could make up Abraham's mind for him and so direct indirectly the policy of the government, had let it be understood even as far as the Southern commissioners who were hoping to settle the Charleston harbor problem, that Fort Sumter would be evacuated. It is true that Lincoln, as early as March fifteenth, had said that although he had not fully determined to withdraw Major Anderson and his command from Sumter, he thought that that is what would be done in the end.† Now, the unhappy Seward was confronted with the realization that although the President still gave no positive signs of activity, he did intend to keep the reins of government in his hands, and to make decisions for himself. That was very aggravating. For Seward did not believe his chief capable of making decisions in

* Works, Vol. V, p. 280.
† Crawford, Samuel W. The Genesis of the Civil War, p. 364.

such a crisis. And it is not, all things considered, strange that Seward should have held such an opinion. It is surprising that he should have acted upon it as he did, but Abraham had certainly been indulging in some curious temporizing for a man who had at heart so clear a sense of the right and wrong of issues. It was unfortunate for his associates that that clarity did not send up shoots nearer to the surface, where they might be seen and hoped for. It was unfortunate for the nation as well. For Seward's unwarranted assumption of power led to a confusion of orders covering the two expeditions to Fort Sumter and to Florida, with the result that both of them were failures. And these failures, combined with President Lincoln's unfortunate habit of human friendship for incompetent and unscrupulous men which had permitted him to send Ward Lamon to South Carolina as a kind of roving commissioner who committed himself far too deeply, made a situation which only needed added to it the impetuosity of a few South Carolinians in order to produce war.

When Abraham found out that the Fort Pickens expedition had been a misfire, he actually concluded that something must be done, and having been forced by Seward into a position from which he could not but admit that he must be the doer, made April sixth, 1861, the day of his resolve to send the expedition for the relief of Fort Sumter, which Seward had allowed the South to believe would never be decided upon. And Charleston, learning through private channels of the President's decision, conceived that the North had acted with duplicity, and had merely pretended that Sumter was to be evacuated in order to gain time for military preparation. The South now presented an ultimatum to Major Anderson, and that intelligent and patriotic officer promised to evacuate the fort by April fifteenth,

Abraham Lincoln Under the Strain of War

if not relieved before then. The South wanted the prestige of the possession of the chief fort in one of its chief harbors, but was very anxious to avoid responsibility for what appeared to be inevitable war. President Davis, of the new Southern Confederacy, was anxious and careful. It was accident that produced the overt act which began one of the most terrible wars of all times, though no accident that the ground had been prepared for such a conflict.

The accident was made up of several elements. One of these was the fact that Seward's meddling had made it impossible for the Sumter relief expedition to succeed, the Navy having confused orders and assigned its most powerful vessel to the Florida squadron. Another was in the impatience of the gentlemen who in Charleston were charged with the matter of direct negotiation between Major Anderson and the Southern government at Montgomery. These gentlemen did not wait for final orders from Jefferson Davis, but themselves assumed the responsibility of deciding that Anderson's reply to their terms was not satisfactory and of giving the order to fire upon the disputed fort. After that, events controlled themselves and the men who had hoped they would be otherwise. The first shell from Fort Johnson rose into the air above the still dark harbor of Charleston at half past four in the morning of April twelfth. It burst directly over the astonished but resigned command of Major Anderson. It was bad luck for the Major, but for the tall sad man in Washington it was the best luck in the world. For the South, by mere chance, had put itself in the wrong.

The State of Virginia had long looked with equal dismay upon what it considered the unwarranted attempt of the Federal Government to coerce the cotton states and upon the action of these states in breaking the bonds which for three-quarters of a century had held them in Union. It had long and earnestly attempted to find some way of satisfying its feeling for state sovereignty and of at the same time stemming the tide of secession. As a result of a convention held with these objects in view a resolution was presented to President Lincoln, to which, on the day following the bombardment of Fort Sumter, the President made answer as follows:

Hon. William Ballard Preston, Alexander H. H. Stuart, George W. Randolph, Esq.

Gentlemen:—As a committee of the Virginia Convention now in session you present me a preamble and resolution in these words:

"Whereas, in the opinion of this Convention, the uncertainty which prevails in the public mind as to the policy which the Federal Executive intends to pursue toward the seceded States is extremely injurious to the industrial and commercial interests of the country, tends to keep up an excitement which is unfavorable to the adjustment of pending difficulties, and threatens a disturbance of the public peace: therefore

"Resolved, that a committee of three delegates be appointed by this Convention to wait upon the President of the United States, present to him this preamble and resolution, and respectfully ask him to communicate to this Convention the policy which the Federal Executive intends to pursue in regard to the Confederate States.

"Adopted by the Convention of the State of Virginia, Richmond, April 8, 1861."

In answer I have to say that, having at the beginning of my official term expressed my intended policy as plainly as I was able, it is with deep regret and some mortification I now learn that there is great and injurious uncertainty in the public mind as to what that policy is, and what course I intend to pursue. Not having as yet seen the occasion to change, it is now my purpose to pursue the course marked out in the inaugural address. I commend a careful consideration of the whole document as the best expression I can give of my purposes.

As I then and therein said, I now repeat: "The power confided in me will be used to hold, occupy, and possess the property and places belonging to the Government and to collect the duties and imposts; but beyond what is necessary for these objects, there will be no invasion, no using of force against or among people anywhere." By the words "property and places belonging to the Government," I chiefly allude to the military posts and property which were in the possession of the Government when it came to my hands.

But if, as now appears to be true, in pursuit of a purpose to drive the United States authority from these places, an unprovoked assault has been made upon Fort Sumter, I shall hold myself at liberty to repossess if I can, like places which had been seized before the Government was devolved upon me. And in every event I shall, to the extent of my ability, repel force by force. In case it proves true that Fort Sumter has been assaulted, as is reported, I shall perhaps cause the United States mails to be withdrawn from all the States which claim to have seceded, believing that the commencement of actual war against the Government justifies and possibly demands this.

I scarcely need to say that I consider the military posts and property situated within the States which claim to have seceded as yet belonging to the Government of the United States as much as they did before the supposed secession.

Whatever else I may do for the purpose, I shall not attempt to collect the duties and imposts by any armed invasion of any part of the country; not meaning by this, however, that I may not land a force deemed necessary to relieve a fort upon a border of the country.

From the fact that I have quoted a part of the inaugural address it must not be inferred that I repudiate any other part, the whole of which I reaffirm, except so far as what I now say of the mails may be regarded as a modification.*

Here again, so sure was Abraham that there could be no two ways of considering the difficulties which had arisen within

* Works, Vol. V, p. 282.

the Union, he considered it sufficient merely to reaffirm what he had already said and which he hoped would have seemed explicit to the people of the nation. It was not explicit, and it did not explain why, if Fort Sumter was not to be relieved, it had not been abandoned, nor why, if it were not to be abandoned it had not been relieved before this. Nor did it explain to a people who had supposed that there had been a promise to abandon the fort, why an expedition had sailed with what appeared to be war-like intent. Abraham was in a ticklish position. There was nothing he could do but maintain the dignity of his position. And such a course, with its official evasions, was certain to lose him what he had hoped to save, but which he was now reconciled to, the loss of the peace of the land.

The President's reception of the Virginia commissioners must have left these gentlemen with little hope of reconciliation, little hope of maintaining the Union which they preferred to dis-Union. If they needed anything more to convince them, they got it on the fifteenth of April when Mr. Lincoln issued a proclamation calling out seventy-five thousand militia troops for the purpose of suppressing the opposition to the administration of the laws of the United States which had sprung up in some of the states, and which had proved too powerful for the ordinary course of judicial procedure. Ominously enough, the President also called for an emergency session of Congress to consider measures for the public safety. He had learned the fact, though not the truth of the bombardment of Fort Sumter, and he could not now recede from the position which he had taken. He must meet force with force. He did not then believe, nor did many others, that the South could long resist. He did not believe that non-resistance could have accomplished anything but loss of prestige to the Federal government. Perhaps he realized that his delay in coming to a decision not as to what should be done but as to the fact of the doing, his hugging the maternal breast of safe and nutritious silence unable to tear himself from his own inner calm and to face the outer world which worked by decision and command, had precipitated action which he would have chosen to avoid.

Whatever he thought, the fat was in the fire. On April seventeenth, Virginia seceded from the Union of which it had been the parent acre. Washington was suddenly confronted with an enemy, directly across the Potomac, fortified by another potential enemy to the North. For on the nineteenth of April, the Sixth Massachusetts Regiment, answering the President's call, passed through Baltimore, Maryland, on its way to the defense of the capital. And Baltimore resisted its passage. Four of the soldiers and a number of those who had tried to stop them were left dead in the streets, a prominent citizen of the city among them, a mere bystander. But the Regiment did succeed in getting to Washington with their disquieting story. They were not immediately followed by others. For bridges and railroad tracks had been destroyed, as a result of the Baltimore riot, and the Maryland legislature was meeting. The governor begged Abraham not to send any more troops through Maryland. Abraham was worried and felt that, while the troops must come and Maryland offered the only route, none the less that State must be placated or it would soon be with the others aligned against him. He arranged a compromise which would send troops to Annapolis instead of through Baltimore, but, again growing timid, and hearing that the Maryland legislature was to assemble at Annapolis on the 25th, he ordered General Scott to watch what the legislature did and if it showed any sign of opposing the United States government and its laws, to go as far as he liked as soon as he could. Bombardment was not forbidden. Fortunately for the State of Maryland, and for that particular legislature, learning that Annapolis was full of Federal troops, the legislators assembled at Frederick on the twenty-sixth. On the twenty-ninth, both branches of the legislature voted against secession.

But there were other states to worry about, particularly Missouri, which required a considerable amount of jockeying before being definitely assured to the side of the North. Meanwhile, a goodly number of soldiers having reached Washington and eased Abraham's distracted mind, the public press of the North was beginning to grow bloodthirsty. It howled for action, for a concentrated blow to be struck at Richmond where, after the secession of Virginia had been confirmed by the vote of its people, it had been decided to locate the Confederate capital. But Abraham could not yet be sure that this violence and brutality apparently coming from the mouth of his people really did represent the sentiment of that people's heart. As always, he wandered about the White House, the War Department, his own office, the streets at night, and the dark quivering alleys of his memory as well, waiting for some voice to speak to him and make him certain. He was still the conservative, cautious mirror for mankind. He was not happier personally in his elevation to high office, nor more able to seize and direct as a perfect administrator might be expected to do. One half of him felt calm and serene, certain that there was good reason in his enduringly careful and deep-principled temper why he had been chosen for the place he held. The other half of him was a kind of unhappy legal blur poured over him, filling the moments of activity which joined him to his task keeping out the sharp sense of touch which could have made him a leader. A leader at this crucial moment of the war he was not. Only in the sense that his deeper self could rise up and say no to anyone else's effort to take the reins was he even the ghost of a leader. And yet his later actions make it certain that, underneath, he had a more perfect equipment for balancing the right and wrong of things, for guiding the nation through its evil time, than anyone else then in public life. But in 1861 and most of 1862, no one and no thing was able to tear away the veil and let that equipment use itself, least of all Abraham himself. Although his great instinctive intelligence, that finest manifestation of human mind, made him vastly the superior to all those about him, the superstructure of timidity and fear which made him over-humble left him, even three months after his inauguration, in the position of an apprentice, going to school to the politicians and backers who guided, not the nation, but the party.

Although what he had said in some of his pre-inaugural speeches made it seem otherwise, it is probable that he was not unmindful of the fact that he had been elected by a very distinct minority of the people whom he was called upon to govern. He did not know how much support he could count on. And he did know that a large number of those who had voted for him did not sympathize with his conservative and pacific ideas. This state of affairs made him feel that he must pursue two courses: that he must learn what was expected of him, and that he must gain the favor of at least a majority in the states still remaining in the Union.

It was hard, in the early summer of 1861, to know just how things stood. The North wanted to believe that its power was irresistible and consequently could easily believe that it had a huge trained army where it had, in reality, nothing but a horde of doubtful volunteers built upon a nucleus of some few thousand regulars. It was not positively known, but it was widely suspected

that the Confederate armies under General Beauregard, the hero
of Fort Sumter, were large and well trained and well equipped.
What should be done? Abraham was afraid both to be aggressive
and to disregard the cries of those who bid him be so. He was
not yet sure of himself. He yielded. It seemed that the fear
which was to govern him at that crucial moment was the fear
that the North, in its jingoistic desire for activity, would get out
of hand and simply override him. Certainly the people of the
North were being well supported by their representatives in Congress. Senators and members of the House alike, were, with
comparatively few exceptions, shouting for a quick and decisive
stroke. The only men in the nation who raised their voices
against such manifest foolishness were, unfortunately, the military men, the experienced campaigners. They knew that you
could not raise an army of volunteers, equip it, officer it, train
and get it ready for the field in a few months. General Scott,
the Commanding General, knew this. Colonel William T. Sherman, who disapproved of Mr. Lincoln, but knew his military
matters, knew the same thing. He in fact refused a proffered
position in the War Department.*

The officers were overruled. General Irwin McDowell was
given orders, the Cabinet having said that it wanted action, to
attack the Confederate army which was operating in Virginia,
and which everyone supposed to be preparing for an advance
on Washington. A grand review of the greater part of Mc-
Dowell's force was held in Washington. Twenty-five thousand
men lined up for the President's inspection. Few men had ever
seen such an imposing military gathering. Small wonder that
there was a further violent outpouring of spread-eagle patriotism.
A man who has never seen a horse will think a pony he has

* Memoirs of Wm. T. Sherman, 1886, p. 199.

seen the greatest of its kind in the world. Whisky and banners, music and high talk, made the occasion of that review a memorable one. High indeed were the hopes of those who waved farewell to General McDowell's army as it passed·on into Virginia.

Meanwhile, President Lincoln delivered his first message to the special session of Congress which he had convened. In this document he completely neglected to mention slavery, which had been so important a part of his Inaugural Address. He now said that the Union must be saved. He explained the idea of democratic government which, without any very studied knowledge of the theory of government, he had chosen to adopt. It provided for a unified, centralized, all-powerful Federal state in which the states were mere geographical units, all united by common agreement and unable to get out of their agreement singly or *en masse*. He declared that the Southern idea of state's rights, state sovereignty, was entirely unjustifiable. He neglected to admit that the nation, prior to the outbreak of war, had been split in two by other than mere resistance to federal laws. The South had been almost a separate nation, with different ideals, different aims, different attitudes toward the systems of life. He preferred, like many others of his time, to believe that the South merely had decided upon a wilful and wasteful destruction of the Union in which it had endured for three-quarters of a century. Now he left slavery alone, as if to discard the last possible reason for believing that the South had a grievance. He begged Congress to give him for his disposal four hundred thousand men and four hundred million dollars to be used in the cause of liberty, for the preservation of the Union and the justification of the democratic ideal, in which he believed that the majority of people of all the states, including the seceded ones, had their hope.

Congress was but little moved and it did nothing immediately. It was too excited about the prospects of a great battle within commuting distance. Senators and Representatives were planning carriage parties and picnics in the wake of McDowell's victorious advance toward Richmond. Wives and families were to go along, to mingle with the crowds of camp followers, the hopeful contractors, the equally hopeful ladies of the back streets of Washington, the sutlers and stragglers which in the picturesqueness of gregarious emergency behind a moving army make up a part of the unhappy scene of war.

Abraham, with grave misgivings, and a humiliating sense of having allowed himself to be bowled over, remained at home. It was well for him that he did. As he drove alone in his carriage just before dinner on July twenty-first, Secretary Seward was looking for him with the sad news that General McDowell, after a reasonably well-planned attack, had allowed his great numerical superiority to be nullified by the courage and determination of the enemy leaders. The battle of Bull Run, the First Battle of Manassas, turned into a rout of the great new Union army, which, mixed with Congressmen, camp-followers, ladies and children, turned tail and rushed in a panic for the sheltering city of Washington. Abraham Lincoln's government paid dearly for its ill-considered action. It became plain that the military men were right, that you could not build an army overnight.

All that night, while Washington echoed with the feet of fugitives and the ominous sounds of rumor, Abraham Lincoln sat in his office, thinking hard. The curious shifts of consciousness which went on within him were as they must always be with the truest men, concerned chiefly with his emotions. And those emotions, calm and unruffled as the outer shell of him appeared in this crisis, boiled and roared so fiercely that they

penetrated that shell at last and made him break into the world
of action with his inner self. The action took the form of the
resolve to appoint a new Commanding General, a Democrat for
good and sufficient reason, and to formulate a definite war policy
without asking anyone's advice. The General was the young
George B. McClellan. The policy was as yet untried, but its first
step was the calling out of an additional lot of volunteers, these
to serve not for months but for three years. It was no longer
possible to stake everything in a sudden blow that would crush
the Southern states.

CHAPTER THREE

DISASTER

ONE day in February, 1862, Abraham Lincoln stepped out of a room in the White House and closed a door behind him. On the other side of that door lay his youngest son, Willie, with eyes closed in death. Never again would the gay, clever, spoiled, adorable child romp in his father's office, slide up and down the halls, bump into office seekers, steal cookies from the pantry, or run away with the hats of official visitors. The finger of what Abraham could not persuade himself was not fate, had once more pointed at him, and this time the point had pierced very close to the torn edges of his heart. Once more the dreadful sense of unhappiness which made everything seem futile had taken possession of him. Believing in the quality, not of mercy, but of unmerciful fate, the child of the Illinois prairies that had never quite grown into the man, believed that he was singled out as the instrument of human suffering, not that he was God, but that he was a doomed son of God. The death of his son seemed to him in the largest sense a symbol of the death of human hope. Darkness came into the world through the breast of Abraham Lincoln. Everything was now chaos which he, the chosen man, was to bear without complaint. And what he had to bear was so much heavier and sharper because of the simpleness of his nature and the absence from it of the protective whorls of rationalization which stood between terror and the emotions of lesser men.

As Abraham walked in that great mansion with its formal evidences of a life purely circumspect and public, the purely private and heedless pain of being a man contracted like a rope about his heart. Things ran through his head like stampeding cattle and he winced as each element of the stampede went by. He saw the vague glory of his election, the apparently clear and reasonable issue which separated what he had supposed to be a wilful conspiring minority in the South and the rest of the Constitution-loving nation. He saw the disquieting rumors which had made his trip to the capital uneasy, the frightful strain of breaking into the newness of official life that hurt his whole body like a gigantic but still too small pair of shoes. He saw the resistance which facts and events and states of mind other than his own had offered to his unsatisfying though honorable avoidance of the real issue. He saw again the gradual and ominous withdrawal from Congress of the Senators and Representatives of the cotton states, the apparently arrogant convention to which they had repaired and out of which had come the Confederate States of America, a name and a thing which might be read in the papers but which might not be spoken. He saw the hesitancy of Virginia, opposed both to himself and to the seceding states, her effort to save the Union and to preserve her identity. He saw with a trace of bitter anger how he had doubted her sincerity, how, in the very moment of doubting, Fort Sumter had been attacked and so had taken all value from his doubts. The call to arms which had followed the fatal blunder of Charleston harbor had hurt him terribly but he had listened to the voice of his one god, the people, and had heard them in their ignorance crying for revenge. It seemed that since then everything had slid downhill as if on a tilted board and heaped up upon his breast, stifling him, making him want to burrow down into the earth

to get away. What could be in command? What could be directing these calamities, tying his honest hands, nullifying his
passionate sincerity? What could have blamed him so that it had
to punish him with a death more cruel than his own would have
seemed? Could he be wrong and fatal, even in the midst of truth
and belief? Was there poison in his well-meaning touch? No
one else was so right, no one else was so straightforward, no one
else in such close and intimate contact with the sense of life
which lived in the common man, the broadcast seed of the
nation. Was there, then, some power, as yet unrecognized by his
genial consciousness, which singled him out, for his very excel-
lence, to bear the cross?

Why had he, Abraham Lincoln, been given such a scourge as
the Congressional Committee on the Conduct of the War?
Perhaps for the same reason that he had himself selected a cabinet
which could not, by reason of its immiscible personalities, its
inherent belligerency, its very hostility to himself, be anything
but a scourge, a pile of hot stones to walk on, a hairshirt to wear.
Oppressed with his personal loss now, Abraham saw with a sinking of heart the ferocity, the wild hysterical bitterness which
actuated so many of those who were in a position to consider
themselves his advisers. The irreconcilable Senators of the dread
Committee, Wade, Chandler and Trumbull; the Secretary of
War, whose position in the cabinet was part of the reason why
Abraham had secured the Republican nomination, and who had
turned out to be something of a crook, as everyone had long
supposed him,* and who had consequently been fired when the
scandal over him grew ripe; the Secretary of the Treasury, a
good man, but a bitter disbeliever in Abraham; the man chosen
to take Secretary Cameron's place, that very Stanton who had

* Stickney, A. Organized Democracy, p. 118 ff.

insulted Abraham at Cincinnati in the Manny reaper case; all
these and others, were a kind of penitence for Abraham. Now
he felt the need of their lashes all the more, to assuage the opposite pain of feeling that his son had died for his father's sins.
But was there not something which he did not quite understand
that led the members of Congress to grow ever more bitter
against him, to arrange power that could force his hand, to try
to drive him toward action in which he did not know how to
believe, toward open avowal of abolition principles, toward a
vengeful method of conducting a foolish war? And was there
not something, knowledge of which was as yet withheld from
him, that brought to his door such disasters as Bull Run; the
factional split within the Republican party at a time when the
very Republican Lincoln was honoring himself by trying to make
a government of all parties; the unpleasant mess in which the
quixotic General Frémont had allowed himself to be concerned
in Missouri; the unrest in England over the attitude of the North
which had been aggravated by the famous Trent affair and had
not entirely been dispelled by the government's return of the
Confederate Commissioners taken from a British ship? And
what of the impossibility of satisfying the public demands for
military victory?

Here was Abraham torn by a personal sorrow that seemed
to have no sense in it, supposed to be running a government
that did not want to be run, supposed to be guiding a people
that persisted, he believed, in misunderstanding him, faced with
the undeniable fact that the states which had seceded and set
up a separate government and which no one would admit had
seceded were now in the position of having won the only important military engagement of the war, of having threatened
the national capital, of having enlisted the sympathy and aid,

and almost won the recognition of several European powers. And these were the states which Abraham and most Northerners had fondly believed were being ruled by a little willful group of serious capitalists. Now in this hour of trial it was perfectly plain that to the last man they were united, and united as the remainder of the original United States had never been.

The death of Willie was very nearly the last straw for the President. He began to show signs of a return of that hysterical collapse with the aid of which he had tried to escape from Mary Todd twenty years before. But Abraham had grown, late as his development had been. Much as he still inwardly yearned to sink into the unexacting peace of the maternal bosom of madness, he could not let himself go. He went about with a sting of pain in the inside of his cheeks, and the beginning glitter of tears in his eyes, trying to concentrate upon things which must be done, saying nothing, speaking to no one that could be passed by without speech. But he could not help thinking, and he could not keep the thoughts from hurting. There was the matter of General Stone, condemned by the monster Committee on the Conduct of the War for some vague reason connected with his conduct of a skirmish at Ball's Bluff. Stone had not been tried, had not been told what charges were brought against him, although it was permitted the public to know that he was assumed to be a traitor who had led his soldiers into a deliberate slaughter by way of helping the Confederacy. The General had been thrown into prison and remained there for a long time. Nothing was ever done about him. He was never cleared of the charges, though he was eventually freed. Abraham could not forget that he had made no protest against this absurd injustice nor made any effort to exercise executive clemency. In fact he had announced, for the sake of taking upon himself the blame for all acts of the administration, that he alone had been responsible for the General's arrest and confinement. He knew that he had done this because Stone was displeasing to the Irreconcilables in Congress and was distrusted by the abolitionists. Abraham would not support the abolitionists, but he would do things to placate them. But now to his tender mind, newly bruised, his treatment of General Stone must have seemed monstrous. Two years later it would have been impossible.

And in the gloom of the White House rooms was the ever present worry about the army. Seven months before, after the fatal battle of Bull Run, he had called General McClellan to be General-in-Chief of the military forces, displacing the field General McDowell, and the aged Staff General Scott. Seven months had passed in agony. The Congress and the people clamoring for action, the General declaring that the enemy was too strong for him and that he must drill and strengthen his force more and still more before attempting any aggressive campaign. Abraham had hoped for McClellan, but he had constantly allowed himself to be swayed by the pestering and ill-advised opinions of the Committee and of public men. He had issued orders which hampered the necessary freedom of the General, which were based on political rather than military judgments. And he had made himself very unpopular with McClellan and extremely inimical to the Committee by his retention of that General in command.

Yet he had appointed McClellan, more than for any consciousness of his military qualifications, because the General was a Democrat, and it was necessary for a minority President, as Abraham was, to have the support of his chief opponents. In supporting their Democratic General, the members of that party would support the administration and its war. Unfortunately

for Abraham, and a thing which came home to him very painfully now, the bitter members of Congress who opposed Mc-
Clellan because he was a Democrat, so terrified Lincoln that to
conciliate them he issued orders which laid him open to the
charge that he was deliberately hampering McClellan's work.
The President was thus between two fires. In giving McClellan
his support he infuriated the immoderate Republicans of Congress. In modifying that support he infuriated McClellan and his
followers. And yet the war must be won. Was Abraham doomed,
by his very sense of mediation, his infinite and painstaking, if
often ill-advised care to be fair to everyone, to destroy the thing
he loved, the security of that mysterious mass which he supposed
to be the American nation? And was it not enough for everything he did to hamper his dearest objects, but that everything
must also have an overtone in his personal life? Shutting his
eyes the harassed and weary man could see the silent tragic darkness of that upstairs room where his little boy lay dead. His
little boy. Yes, his. Was he not in spite of his official and rather
monumental position, a man of flesh and blood, subject to pain
and sorrow, despair? There was nothing to help him, unless he
should confess humble obedience to the power that held the whip
above him and worship, as so many do, the somber darkness of
his particular scourge.

And how would that help? Abraham thought of the war.
The continuing delays of General McClellan, whose army must
be fairly well trained by now. He was beginning to have misgivings about McClellan. He remembered a call that he and
Secretary Seward had made at McClellan's house in the previous
fall. The General was out. The President and Mr. Seward sat
down to wait. When McClellan came in he was told that the
President was in the house waiting to see him. He went upstairs.

Half an hour later, the callers, having heard him come in, again sent word that they were waiting. A servant returned with word that the General had gone to bed.* It stung Abraham's cheeks even now to remember a thing like that.

Evidently people were still at their old tricks of trying to prove him a lout, "a coarse and vulgar fellow." They were, were they? Now what was McClellan going to do? Abraham had told the people of his strange country that he was going to do so and so in the matter of military affairs. After long hesitation, he had delivered himself of a definite program. As a consequence of it he had ordered McClellan to move forward on all his front on February twenty-second. Abraham did not know just what all McClellan's front was and he was himself a very amateurish tactician, but he knew what the people were crying for. McClellan, grown quite arrogant in his malicious resentment of presidential interference, did not like the order and insisted that he was not ready. He as much as refused to obey the rather absurd order of his chief. Abraham, feeling perhaps that he had exceeded his authority, weakened his position by backing down. Abraham felt now that he needed a father, a real father, someone who could advise him and whose advice he should instinctively know was trustworthy. There seemed to be no such person on the earth or in that reputed heaven above where the heavenly father of the theologians, hitherto a stranger to Abraham, had his seat. The nation, the nation, and no one to tell Abraham how to save it, how to use the instinct in himself which needed no telling but which he could not seem to bring into forceful play. And Willie was dead. That was bitter. It was unfair. But he would bear it if he could. If they would only let him alone.

But they would not let him alone. In the midst of his grief,

* Thayer, Wm. R. The Life of John Hay, Vol. I, p. 126.

his almost insane horror of the injustice of things, his bitter and tragic resentment at the crucifixion of his own ideals, his reluctant dread of the apparently inevitable admission that the evil in which he had never believed was not only real but also triumphant, in the midst of these tortures the fiendish Committee on the Conduct of War demanded a conference with him, even before his little son was buried. These gentlemen were out for McClellan's scalp and wished to serve notice on Abraham that if he so much as interfered with their wishes they would have his scalp too. In other words, if he did not force McClellan to move on Richmond, Congress would take the matter out of the President's hands. Abraham was practically, as he had been at several other points in his life, unable to attend to business, so torn was he by the personal disaster which had once more put its terrible bulk in between the real deep instinctive self that made the man, and the outer shell by which the man made timid and unsatisfactory contact with the world of action. But he did not immediately do what the Committee wished. He still clung to a faint hope that he could save the nation and yet be fair to McClellan. He was bewildered and vacillating, but he was not inhuman. He pacified the frantic Congressmen by reorganizing McClellan's army over the General's head in such away that the council of subordinate generals within it should be made up of the generals who were not personally favorable to nor influenced by the unfathomable but able "Little Napoleon." This was rather hard on McClellan, but it is doubtful if, given the state of mind that the General had come to at that time, anything could have given him the power of doing what must be done.

The President was still trying to play two games of cards at the same time. The crafty politician of the Illinois days, anxious for self and party advancement had largely been submerged in

the man broadened by sense of his great responsibility. But the
tendency of the natural man to be everyone's friend, offering
equal justice to all, regardless of the right to that justice, seeking
to save itself by saving its world, now led Abraham Lincoln into
one of the darkest and most terrible positions he had ever occupied. Almost simultaneous with the order which reorganized
General McClellan's command, went an order to that officer appearing to agree to his suggestion of sweeping on, instead of
directly toward Richmond, along the flank toward the sea. But
in this order Abraham had misgivings. He had felt a blow should
be struck at the Confederate armies concentrated in the locality
where the battle of Bull Run had been fought. He now, however,
for the moment, gave McClellan a free hand, free in sweep,
but rather constricted in the articulation of the fingers by the
various preliminary orders which had issued from the terrified
and muddled War Department, many of them at Lincoln's command. What McClellan did with this free hand was the last
straw. It broke the camel's back. The Confederates, anticipating
General McClellan's advance and feeling certain that he would
strike at Manassas, had already withdrawn from that point, showing plainly that it was considered untenable, although McClellan
had considered it impregnable. But what did the infatuated Union
General do? He immediately upon learning of the Confederate
retreat, advanced upon the evacuated position and then, immediately, like the King of France, returned whence he had come.
That was the end of the "Little Napoleon." Abraham, although
he did not understand what was going on or what had happened, was so bitterly disappointed at the loss of opportunity, and
the strange waste of time indulged in by General McClellan when
he had not the excuse of being definitely under orders, that the
President stepped out of character and in one of his rare rages,

returning to an earlier way of doing things, immediately removed McClellan from the chief command and gave him the
reduced command of the Army of the Potomac only. Not only
did this stroke leave the armies of the United States without a
Commanding General, a state of decapitation in which they unfortunately remained for four amazing months, but the deliberate
insult offered to the sensitive honest, loyal, able, if fundamentally foolish McClellan, turned out to have political as well as
military overtones. It precipitated the popular feeling that Mc-
Clellan was being unjustly treated, a feeling which had hitherto
been confined only to anti-administration Democrats but which
now began to bear fruit in other orchards.

In this late spring of 1862, with McClellan and his Army of
the Potomac conducting its slow if scientific siege operations before Yorktown and the points which threatened Richmond, with
the constant conflict of opinions and desires in the Federal administration, the South, united as it was, was not in such a good
mood. It would have comforted Abraham much to know how
the press of the seceded states was condemning Jefferson Davis,
and even the wise and far-seeing Lee, then military adviser to
the Confederate President. General Johnston, the Southern Commander, although he knew what sort of a fighter McClellan
was, had his trouble with his own President. They were the
same sort of troubles that McClellan was having with Mr. Lincoln. Conflicting orders, delayed actions, impertinent suggestions.
But with these handicaps Johnston did not have the strain of
imbecility in his nature which ruined McClellan as a Commander. His fears were not, like McClellan's, groundless, for the
enemy which faced him did greatly outnumber him, and might,
even in the hands of so slow and inept a tactician as the "Little
Napoleon" had proved himself, be a serious threat against the

Confederate capital. For the South, which in some ways appeared to be winning the war, having won the important engagements in Virginia, had also done some losing elsewhere. New Orleans had fallen into Northern hands. Missouri had been cleared of Confederate forces and was now unmistakably an element of the Northern Union. Kentucky, that border state and birthplace of Abraham Lincoln, land which its favored son was nursing with every power at his command, was being weaned away from its Southerly ties by the more or less successful applications of force administered by that capable General George Thomas. Ports in both South and North Carolina had been taken by the Federal navy. The hitherto unknown General Grant, whom the Federal War Department had done its best to snub, had struck a serious blow on the Upper Mississippi, taking Fort Henry and Fort Donelson and, in spite of blundering badly, had managed to repel a terrible Confederate counter attack delivered at Pittsburg Landing (Shiloh) in the doubtful state of Tennessee.

If the tortured Abraham, in his office at Washington, had been able to realize the state of mind of the Confederacy and to disregard the importunities of the various advisory groups which his over-elaborate gentleness had suffered to grow up about him, even so timid a warrior as McClellan might have been able to embarrass the Confederacy in a manner which would have hastened the end of the war. But to the President the instability of the Union administration, his own administration, as it was, seemed more terrifying than the difficulties in which the South found itself seemed pleasing. And even now, Abraham, much as he had learned, was unable to make up his mind on a point of activity. He wavered between feeling that he had been unjust to McClellan and feeling in terror of the Committee in Congress. He offered to send General McDowell in support of McClellan, and then after making the promise, becoming terrified by rumors of the whereabouts of the elusive "Stonewall" Jackson, recalled McDowell to "protect" Washington, which was exactly what the enemy had wanted him to do. This blunder permitted Jackson to fight with his Confederate comrades against McClellan in the Seven Days Battles along the Chickahominy. It not only allowed Jackson to join the Army of Northern Virginia, under General Lee, but, according to General Fitz-John Porter, one of McClellan's subordinates in the advance toward Richmond, it indicated a false position for the Federal forces, distributed in the expectation that General McDowell with forty thousand men was coming from Washington, as President Lincoln had advised. *

Something was happening to Abraham. The death of his son, the apparently destructive powers which rode rampant upon any decision he made or allowed himself to be forced into, the obvious inability of the paradoxical McClellan to succeed without believing in the possibility of his success, the hatred and bitterness of the leaders in Congress, the mistrust of the people whom he thought he knew and understood, were building up the apparatus of search in the unhappy President. He was beginning not merely to believe in himself but to wonder what he was really doing. His old system of listening to everyone and acting upon a part of each one's advice, was about to be weighed in the balance. Two days before the significant and disastrous battle of Mechanicsville, which set the Army of the Potomac retreating toward the James River the President made a hurried trip to West Point, where he was closeted with the aged General Scott. No one knows what conversation those two had.†

Whatever it was, the immediate result of it was the summon-

---

* Battles and Leaders of the Civil War, Vol. II, part 1, p. 319 ff.
† Nicolay, John G. A Short Life of Abraham Lincoln, p. 306.

ing from the West of a General who had made a name for himself in the Capture of Island No. Ten on the Mississippi, that
same John Pope, who as a Captain, had accompanied the President-elect on his journey from Springfield to Washington in the
previous February. General Pope, who was soon to prove himself
a trifle less competent than the preceding generals, was, in Abraham's new plan, to take charge of a new army, devoted entirely
to the defense of Washington.

In the meantime it was necessary to have more men. The Secretary of War, for some peculiar reason believing that the slight
advances made by the Union forces in the spring of 1862 foretold
an early end to hostilities had conveyed the impression that there
was not much need of further volunteers. Consequently, recruit-
ing had fallen off. Even on June twenty-ninth, when General
McClellan was in full retreat, badly beaten on the Chickahominy
River, Secretary Stanton had joyously assumed that the Union
army would be in Richmond within two days. It was now necessary, in order to counteract this dangerous impression, for Lincoln to send Secretary Seward on a visit to the governors and
prominent men of many of the Northern states from Massachusetts to Ohio, bearing a letter from the President in which he
indicated the need of one hundred thousand more troops to rein-
force the defeated McClellan without weakening any other front,
and thus make the capture of Richmond hypothetically possible.
"I expect," he said, "to maintain this contest until successful,
or till I die, or am conquered, or my term expires, or Congress
or the country forsake me: and I would publicly appeal to the
country for this new force were it not that I fear a general panic
and stampede would follow, so hard it is to have a thing understood as it really is."

The troops were promised. But there was no peace. Trouble

arose in Kentucky. There seemed no move possible for the recently defeated Army of the Potomac to make without reinforcement, no hope of adequate reinforcement for many months, no chance of affecting the strength of the Confederacy without a movement of the Army of the Potomac, only the need and ability to keep hammering away at the Southern armies in the West, to keep juggling the still doubtful states, to push work on the Pacific Railway in Missouri, to keep down the swelling tide of impatience in the North. This impatience was perhaps represented in an extremely aggravated form by a letter which appeared in the *New York Tribune* of August nineteenth signed by Horace Greeley and entitled, "The Prayer of Twenty Millions." In this extraordinary letter, Greeley addressed the President through the medium of his paper, and suggested for the benefit of the people that the administration was far too interested in sparing the feelings of Southern slaveholders, and that it appeared certain that most of the Northern army, officers and men, were more anxious to uphold slavery than to put down the rebellion. This was not the only thorn in the President's side, put there by the fact that he had deemed it wise to keep saying that the war was solely for the purpose of saving the Union. Liberal opinion in Europe had hoped that it really was a war for the extermination of an illiberal system, that of slavery, and in that hope had looked upon the North as a crusader. But Abraham's political insistence upon the contrary had done much to turn sympathy towards the South and to fortify the South's complaints of coercion. Now, the President had reached a point in his career at which it appeared that he would have to let go of the safety valve upon his own emotions and those of his people which he had been so carefully holding open. He saw that it was necessary for him to hint at a change of policy. He paved the way in his dignified reply to Greeley. " . . . If I could save the Union without freeing any slave, I would do it; and if I could save it by freeing all the slaves I would do it; and if I could do it by freeing some and leaving others alone, I would also do that. What I do about the colored race, I do because I believe it helps to save this Union; and what I forbear, I forbear because I do not believe it would help to save the Union. I shall do less whenever I shall believe what I am doing hurts the cause, and I shall do more whenever I believe doing more will help the cause. I shall try to correct errors when shown to be errors; and I shall adopt new views so fast as they shall appear to be true views. I have here stated my purpose according to my view of official duty, and I intend no modification of my oft-expressed personal wish that all men, everywhere, could be free." *

The abolitionists, who had been the most outspoken critics of the President, found nothing to sweeten their tempers in this. Meanwhile, events which were destined to throw Abraham into their arms were being prepared in the amazing battleground of Virginia. The clever flanking tactics of the Confederate General "Stonewall" Jackson, combined with the lowest ebb of Abraham Lincoln's judgment to produce a calamity of the first magnitude and to bring about the playing by the President of what he considered his last trump card.

Torn by the demands of the fiercest members of the Committee on the Conduct of the War, by his own uncertainty as to what McClellan was capable of doing, by his desire to get the Army out of McClellan's hands without hurting that General's feelings more than they had already been hurt, Abraham allowed himself to order the detachment of the main part of the Army of the Potomac and the assignment of it to the command of

* Lincoln to Greeley, Aug. 22, 1862. Works, Vol. VI, p. 123.

General Pope. On August thirtieth, it was made plain in what degree the poetic General Pope was to avail himself of the President's support. For on that day, almost on the very site of the first battle of Bull Run, within earshot of the Capitol at Washington, the Union Army, confused by the brilliant tactics of Jackson and outgeneraled by the sagacious and determined Lee, was almost totally ruined in a battle with the Confederates. Again, it appeared, in spite of Generals, in spite of volunteers, in spite of committees, in spite of the supposed righteousness of the Northern cause, Washington was seriously threatened. Something was wrong. When, in the face of all this, Congress, which believed that Pope's collapse was largely due to McClellan's supposed failure to support him properly, was informed that the President had called McClellan to take command of the forces in defense of Washington, it was aghast. The vindictive members of the Committee boiled with rage. The President explained to his Cabinet that although he did feel that McClellan had acted badly, there was no one else to turn to. This time Lincoln was not wrong. McClellan spent the next weeks whipping the disorganized and disgruntled Army into shape, forgetting as far as so petty a character could, his own grievances and the indignities which had been heaped upon him, entirely overpowering the old criticism which had had it that he was a traitor conducting all his campaigns in the interest of the South. But McClellan could not do more at this late date than faintly redeem himself in battle, whatever his services as an organizer. On the seventeenth of September he faced General Lee's forces at Antietam Creek, outnumbering the Confederates by about three to two. General Lee had invaded Maryland and seemed irresistible. A victory would have hurt the Union more than anyone can say. He was in a defensive position and McClellan, with a broken and spasmodic attack opened against him. The Union commander was unable to get much more than two-thirds of his men into action, preferring to remain certain that he was outnumbered and needed reserves. Such was not the case. McClellan did not succeed in driving the enemy from the field, but he did succeed in making it necessary for Lee to withdraw. He thus saved Maryland for the Union, and by so much was it a Union victory, no more. That was not enough to save McClellan, but it was enough for Abraham. Five days after the battle the President threw a bombshell into a cabinet meeting.

He entered this meeting, the Secretaries bitterly wondering what was to come, dissatisfied with the battle of Antietam, puzzled by the new aggressiveness in the hitherto vague and conciliatory Abraham, and produced from under his arm the latest volume of Artemus Ward, from which, before proceeding to business he read aloud. Everyone except the Secretary of War laughed heartily, but the tension still existed. Then, looking very serious, very old and worn, the weary man rose to his full height and disclosed to the men about him his plan for consolidating the nation in a great effort to win the thus far disappointing war. Abraham said to the cabinet officers, in his solemn, shrill but earnest voice, standing without gesture as he spoke, that he had been for a long time thinking over the relation of slavery to the prosecution of the war and had come to the conclusion that now was the time to do something about that issue. The gentlemen would remember, he said, that previously he had read them a memorandum on the subject, of which they had not approved, and that the matter had consequently been dropped. Now, however, he made no pretense even of asking their advice; the changed and much more resolute Lincoln merely announced to them that, having at last secured something that looked like a Union military success in the battle of Antietam, not a very great success, it was true, he was about to issue a proclamation emancipating the slaves of those states which on the following January first should be in rebellion against the United States.* The cabinet officers looked at one another in amazement. They saw the uncertain, vacillating, driven, apparently dazed Abraham standing before them with a bitterly determined look on his face in so many words announcing to them, his chosen and hitherto important advisers, that from that moment on he was to be to all intents and purposes a virtual dictator. The President read the proclamation, with its contradictions of his previous attitude and its plain declaration that its pronouncement was merely delivered as a matter of military and political necessity. In this document the President declared it to be his intention to recommend to the next Congress (he had been very careful to wait until Congress had adjourned before issuing his proclamation) that they pass measures tendering pecuniary aid to states which had ceased to be in rebellion against the United States and which had adopted immediate or gradual abolishment of slavery within their limits. Irrespective of any action by Congress the President proclaimed with a disregard of actualities which well indicated the aggressive state of mind to which he had been driven, "that on the first of January, 1863, all persons held as slaves within any State or designated part of a State the people whereof shall then be in rebellion against the United States shall be then, thenceforward, and forever, free." He further declared that he himself would announce on January first, 1863, what states were in rebellion against the United States and that states which then were represented in the Congress of the United States by members chosen "at elections wherein a majority of the qualified

* Report of Am. Hist. Assn., Vol. II, 1902. The Diary and Correspondence of Salmon P. Chase.

voters of such State shall have participated shall, in the absence
of strong countervailing testimony, be deemed conclusive evidence that such State and the people thereof are not then in
rebellion against the United States." The proclamation further
called the attention of Congress to an act of the previous spring
establishing as a new Article of War that no one in the military
or naval service of the United States should be allowed to use
any of their commands for the purpose of returning fugitive
slaves. It also mentioned, significantly, an act approved in July
which practically suspended the operation of the Fugitive Slave
Law, hitherto warmly upheld by the President.

In this extraordinary proclamation, Abraham offered no precedent, no justification for the act which he was proclaiming, no
suggestion nor apology for the power he was assuming. Indeed
he could not have done so, and to have done so would have
weakened his position and made it too easy for the vindictives
who had wanted him to make an issue of slavery, to laugh at him
now and say that this was not the way to do it, that he was merely
making an emperor out of himself.

As if the Emancipation Proclamation, which—unless a great
deal had happened which was not likely to happen by January
first, could have no actual validity as far as freeing the slaves was
concerned—were not sufficient evidence of his new administrative
attitude, on the twenty-fourth of September Abraham issued
another proclamation suspending that time-honored privilege of
the free citizen of a free country, that of obtaining a writ of
habeas corpus in case of arrest. In this proclamation also there
was no suggestion of precedent nor of authority. It was the final
incident in the making of a new public man out of the private
misgivings and uncertainties of Abraham Lincoln.

In the darkness of his room, in the loneliness of his stolen walks about the nervous capital, the new note of determination boiled and surged in Abraham's unhappy mind. He had asserted himself, and that fact gave him strength and relief, but as must always be the case with a man tied to inward darknesses, no assertion can fail to have its undertow. What did it all mean? Abraham Lincoln was President; he had fiddled along accepting other people's ideas because he thought he had to; now he was not going to do it any longer. Could he sustain himself in that power which he was gathering to himself? Would the country give him its support, or would he still meet with the bitter violence of factional prejudice? Horrible as the inner ramifications of his new course might be, there was now no going back.

CHAPTER FOUR

THE LADDER IS BROKEN

THE Emancipation Proclamation, issued by the President as a means of uniting the nation, followed as it was by the tactless proclamation suspending the writs of habeas corpus, did not have the desired effect. The former manifesto united the South but failed to please anyone in the North except the Boston fanatics, who believed it a blow for freedom. The Democrats ignored the slavery side of the proclamation and insisted on the dictatorial power which it assumed. They gathered many new supporters to their ranks by frightening them with talk of imperial arrogance. And for the moment, so confident was he of his rightness, imperial arrogance was what Abraham intended. He knew that he could use it to good advantage, because he saw things as no one else saw them. Felt them, rather. Indeed that unwavering, unshaken power, was what he now felt that he must have. Why else should he have come around to these high-handed declarations of principles in which he had never believed? He had been forced into them by the necessity of having power. He had hoped that he could save the Union through kindliness and gentleness, but men and facts had shown him that it would not work. He had to be thrown very heavily to learn that lesson, and he was not happy in it, now that it was learned, but he was confident that he was now taking the only possible course.

But in November, 1862, after the elections of that year it seemed that even the only possible course was not to be a successful one. For the most important states in the Union, except Massachusetts, returned majorities against the administration. New York, New Jersey, Pennsylvania, Ohio, Indiana, and Illinois, Lincoln's own state, all went Democratic. They would not be deluded by talk of Emancipation, perhaps realizing how little benefit the slaves in the belligerent Southern Confederacy could get from a proclamation issued by a foreign government unable to do more than keep itself from military invasion. The people of the North wanted either a military victory or a sudden end to the war without any victory. And Abraham, who had been trying to fight the war without admitting that battle is not a democratic institution had failed utterly, because he had tried to believe that the democratic spirit could do anything. He had not realized, and was not soon to learn, that war is a business, essentially feudal in its necessary organization, and must be run, if at all, in the most hard-boiled, professional manner possible. The unfortunate thing for the President was that the Confederate States had already realized this and had adopted a military organization calculated to get the last drop of fighting out of a small and poorly supplied citizenry. That citizenry was now being drafted, and officered not by officers who held their places as political plums but by serious soldiers. And those serious soldiers, about eighty thousand in number, met the vainglorious plum-holders, and their retinue one hundred and twenty-five thousand strong on December thirteenth, 1862, for no reason whatever except that a battle would look well to the electorate. The result was one of the most crushing and tragic disasters of the entire war. General Burnside, who had replaced the dashing but dilatory McClellan, very nearly contrived to lose, for President Lincoln, the entire army entrusted to him. As it was, he was able to retreat across the Rappahannock with a loss of only thirteen thousand men, as compared with the Confederate loss of less than five thousand.

Nothing could have been worse for Abraham. The Committee in Congress was furious. They and many others in Congress as well, believed that the President should get rid of his cabinet, with the exception of the double-faced, though able, Secretary Chase. Many even insisted that the President himself should resign. Abraham shut himself up in his room and would see no one. He could not seem to hide his clear conscience from the accusing finger which pointed at him as bitterly as if his heart had not been pure. In the first place, it was he who had insisted, against the General's own wishes, that Burnside take up the military command where Pope had left it. Burnside had not believed in his ability to do the job. He had failed, and the hateful Congressional Committee took good care to publish to the country, after an examination into the cause of the slaughter at Fredericksburg, a statement of the fact that the President had forced General Burnside into a position which he felt unqualified to occupy. The Committee openly continued its hostility to Abraham and showed it in an effort to drive Secretary Seward, now Abraham's right-hand man, out of the cabinet. That would never do. The President had come to like Seward very much, but even more than that, Seward commanded an element in the Republican party which could not be let go. The administration needed its support and without Seward would not get it. Chase saved the day by getting himself into a hole. He had been trying to play two hands at once: to appear friendly in both the cabinet and the Committee, a very difficult feat. The Committee had announced that it believed Seward was exerting a malign influence upon the administration. Seward had offered his resignation, in reply. The Cabinet and the Senatorial Committee, unfor-

tunately for Chase, convened to talk the matter over. Chase
had to defend Seward. But in doing so, he saw in the faces of
the astounded Senators who had often heard him revile the same
Secretary, that there was a nigger in the woodpile. It was now
Chase's turn to resign. It seemed to be his only way of getting out
of the difficulty that would, by embarrassing the President, put
himself once more in favor with the Committee. That was all
very well. But the President refused to accept the resignation of
either of his unhappy Secretaries. Thus did the formerly docile
and easily influenced Abraham, assert himself in his rôle of
dictator, at the same time strengthening his own hand and
weakening the alliance between the Committee and the Cabinet. *

But for all his assumption of dictatorial power, Abraham was
in a terrible position. He had destroyed and thrown away as
useless the ladder of tricks, submissions, bargains, suspicions,
recriminations, half truths and chicaneries, by which he had formerly supposed it necessary to climb, and there was nothing left
for him to do but cut his way out of his ambush with such
weapons as he could find at hand. And the first weapon he
found was a very blunt and dilapidated one. It was General
Hooker, who, within the disturbed and ill-fated Army of the
Potomac had been scheming against the incompetent and nervous General Burnside, attempting, unbelievably enough, to disgrace the Commander and work his own way into the commanding position. He knew that he was at the time a popular figure
and that he had the support and confidence of the Congressional
Committee. He may have had some idea of accepting the Committee's hostility to Lincoln and of eventually working himself
in to the summit of national prominence by means of a military
coup d'état which should leave him Dictator. Abraham's friends

* Stephenson, N. W. Lincoln. An Account of His Personal Life, 1922, p. 291 ff.

did not hesitate to tell him that this was what would happen if Hooker were not suppressed. Abraham, remembering, perhaps, what he had said in his salad days to his intimate friend Joshua Speed, to the effect that he and Joshua were destined always to dream of a world impossible of realization, continued his penitential system of administrative control, hoping against hope that a firm hand, combined with humility and resignation, might do something to bring about a millennial state of affairs. In pursuit of this happy end, the President did two extraordinary things. He urged Thurlow Weed to go to Governor Seymour of New York, one of the recently elected Democrats, and the leader of the moderates in that party who favored the Union but did not favor Abraham's method of governing it, and to say to the Governor that he, Abraham Lincoln, would promise to do everything in his power to secure for Seymour the presidential nomination in 1864 provided that gentleman would now, without delay or qualification, bring his Democratic following into a coalition with Lincoln Republicans by way of forming a Union party, devoted solely to the prosecution of the war. * The second thing which the President did was to write a letter to "Fighting Joe" Hooker, announcing that he had been placed at the head of the Army of the Potomac and informing him that although this step was taken for what appeared to be sufficient reasons, the President was not perfectly satisfied with Hooker's previous conduct. Furthermore, Abraham announced to the General that he had heard some talk about a dictatorship, but that he was willing to take a chance on that if Hooker would first provide some military victories. "Only those generals who gain successes can set up as Dictators," said the President. If Hooker was surprised, he was also pleased, and soon became extremely inflated. While

* Stephenson. Lincoln, p. 300 ff.

the nation waited for a victory, the General announced that "The enemy is in my power and God Almighty cannot deprive me of them." Abraham, metaphorically, looked the other way and issued a proclamation very different from anything he had ever said previously, indicating the great change which had come over the relations between his inner and outer nature.

" . . . It is the duty of nations as well as of men to own their dependence upon the overruling power of God; to confess their sins and transgressions in humble sorrow, yet with assured hope that genuine repentence will lead to mercy and pardon; and to recognize the sublime truth announced in the Holy Scriptures and proven by all history, that those nations only are blessed whose God is the Lord: . . . " *

But the Lord was not yet won over, for Governor Seymour would have none of the President's overtures, and General Hooker, though able and energetic, was not capable of organizing a victory. Lee and Jackson were too much for him. At Chancellorsville, ten miles west of Burnside's ill-chosen battleground of Fredericksburg, the Union armies once more met with disaster, disaster which again, as at Bull Run, came very near to being a rout. As if this were not enough to throw the President's manipulation of his precarious power off its balance, General Burnside, removed from the Army of the Potomac and sent to the supposedly harmless command of the quiet Department of the Ohio, again made trouble by arresting Clement L. Vallandigham, the leader in that state of the extreme wing of the Democratic party, commonly called "Copperheads," a group which sympathized with the South and believed in obstructing the progress of the war. Burnside, perhaps naturally, in view of the Presidential pronouncements about civil liberties in time of war, be-

* Works, Vol. VI, p. 270.

lieved that he was doing what the administration would have had him do. But maladroit that he was, he was wrong. His action threw the President and the cabinet into despair. They could not afford any such evidence of high-handed and presumably unconstitutional action, but neither could they afford to repudiate the actions of their subordinate. The country would have been down on them, in the first event, for over-severity, and, in the second, for weakness and too great lenience. The Lord almighty was indeed still estranged.

Abraham was now back where he had been before, his political strength very doubtful, one more General had turned out to be just another blue suit with trimmings, the ferocious Committee was still growling. The President was angry, and took refuge in a little unwarranted flippancy in the form of a "joke" played on the captured Vallandigham. Instead of the sentence of confinement which would have been natural in such a case, Abraham decided, with a slightly acid gesture, that he would banish the offending gentleman into the Confederacy, with which his sympathies were supposedly enlisted. Meanwhile, General Lee, resting after the terrible battle of Chancellorsville, which had once more proved how easy it was to beat a Federal Army, was formulating plans for a raid calculated to end the war in favor of the South. He planned to invade Pennsylvania and cause the withdrawal of the Union forces from Virginia, possibly even to do battle with them in Pennsylvania and, having defeated them, to advance on Philadelphia, cut off Washington and threaten New York.

When it became apparent that this was General Lee's plan, when it was recognized that the Federal forces had in two years of war given no signs of any ability to beat the Confederates in the Eastern theater of war, it became obvious that something radical must be done. The press and the public clamored for the restoration of McClellan to command, but Abraham, who saw more than military strategy involved, would not listen. Yet it was certain that Hooker, who wanted to attack Richmond while Lee was moving northward, would not do. For Hooker had gotten into a quarrel with the figurehead Commanding General, Halleck, in Washington, and had in annoyance asked to be relieved of his position. He was speedily accommodated by the President. It was taking a great risk to swap horses in midstream like that, but the President felt that it was taking less risk than would have been involved in urging Hooker to remain in command. For the situation was now serious. Lee had advanced into Pennsylvania, and with the usual timidity of a thing so heartless as finance, the stock market and government securities were both beginning to wobble. It is not the stomach upon which an army moves. It is the pocketbook. Something had to be done. On June thirtieth, 1863, the New York papers announced that General George Gordon Meade had been placed in command of the Army of the Potomac.

In Pennsylvania there was something approaching panic. No one thought that Philadelphia could be saved. The Governors of the adjacent states willingly supplied additional levies of troops; Governor Seymour of New York, who had rejected Abraham's political advances, replying with especial ardor to the military demands which the occasion made upon his state. It was plain that something was going to happen, and that that something would either unite or destroy the elements of the Union. General Lee, whom the North had reluctantly come to believe invincible, and who held no very high opinion of the Union Generals he had had to face, was having a comparatively easy time in Pennsylvania, until General Stuart, his dashing and picturesque cavalry leader, got lost behind the Union armies and ceased to be able to supply him with information. As General Meade was taking command, the advance of the Army of the Potomac located the Confederates at Gettysburg, Pennsylvania, where General Buford's Union cavalry had made an attack. The First and Eleventh Corps of General Meade's army engaged the Confederates on July first but were badly beaten, the Commanding General of the First Corps, Reynolds, being killed. It soon became apparent to General Meade that there was going to be a battle at Gettysburg whether he liked it or not. His corps commanders were already engaged in struggling for position at that point. The Confederates had been somewhat taken by surprise, as they did not know that the Army of the Potomac was concentrated so close to them. As there were, however, more Confederates than Federals on hand when the first fighting took place, the advantage was distinctly with the former. In fact, if General Lee had had more definite information as to the whereabouts of his enemy, he might have pushed his advantage of July first and prevented the Federal forces from taking up the very favorable position in Gettysburg which eventually, by its desirability and strength, secured the victory. It appeared that Lee, however, when he saw what he had to contend with and realized the success of his first day's battle, assumed that it was just the old Army of the Potomac all over again and that he would be able to go through them as a hot knife goes through butter, the result being a free road to the important centers of the North, as well as Washington, and a consequent end to the war.

General George Gordon Meade, whom the President had put in command of the Army of the Potomac just before the preliminary skirmishes at Gettysburg, was a man of rather higher character in many respects than his predecessors in command. He lacked some of the military instincts of General McClellan, but his training had done as much as it could with a sensitive, over-conscientious, tender-minded man, to make a general officer of him. Like almost all other Union generals, he lacked initiative. He seems to have shared with Lincoln that grave Old Testament inability to be forceful, to initiate, as if conscious always of some critical, vengeful presence in the next room. By the time General Meade appeared on the field at Gettysburg, at one o'clock in the morning of July second, his honest, homely face with its great eyes bore all the marks of absolute exhaustion. The General had had practically no sleep since taking command, so keenly did he feel his responsibility. He was not the kind to exult in the fas-cination of the difficult. There was little joy in his nature, un-like his patron in the White House. His sorrow and horror were unrelieved by the explanatory solvent of a keen and humorous understanding of the relationship of human nature to its world.

General Meade was nervous and apprehensive, but brave and determined. He had under him a far better trained, a far more finely integrated army than any of his predecessors had com-manded. He had the support and interest of his subordinates in a degree which had never been approached by McClellan, Pope, Burnside or Hooker. But he had the one great failing of the Northern American, a failing which was particularly in evidence among the men of Civil War times, due perhaps to the beginnings of that very nationalization of the people which was Abraham Lincoln's dearest interest. For General Meade, soldier that he was, was unable to believe in himself. At the close of the sec-ond day's battle at Gettysburg, on July second, after making a number of minor mistakes saved from being major ones by the swiftly changing attack of the enemy, he seriously considered a retreat from the field. He was voted down in a council of his officers, and remained to fight it out, to be given a victory which he perhaps deserved but which he had assuredly himself not earned, and which he could not appreciate when he had won it.

On the third of July, early in the afternoon, against the instinct and advice of his subordinate, General Longstreet, Lee ordered a charge against the Union center. He believed that the comparatively fresh division of General Pickett, advancing in column after a strenuous artillery preparation, could penetrate and hold the Union lines. The story of this charge, ill-fated from the start, with its heroic and needless slaughter, is too well known to need repeating. It is enough to say that it succeeded in penetrating the Union Lines at the cost of its very identity. Pickett's division was nearly annihilated and had to fall back. On both sides it was recognized that the tide of battle had turned. The Confederates knew what they had lost and feared that they were going to lose still more. But General Meade, over-cautious, failed to follow up the retreat of the assaulting column which his Army had successfully thrown back. He was content to have defended himself, a common failing in even great commanders. Lee had done the same thing at Fredericksburg after putting General Burnside to rout. It is not always easy to see the reason why, after a difficult battle, it would be well to urge the weary and poorly supplied troops who have secured a victory into a pursuit of their retreating enemy. There may have been reasons in General Meade's mind which we do not know. But it is certain that his failure to follow up his victory was a surprise to the enemy.

More than that, it was a source of great mortification to the all but despairing Abraham, now living at the bosky Soldiers' Home in the outskirts of Washington. More than a week after the battle, which even critics of the administration had to admit was a victory, when the Army of Northern Virginia under General Lee had safely retreated in good order across the Potomac, Meade was not near enough to molest him in the slightest. Although Abraham was probably wrong in thinking that the capture of a large part of Lee's army would have resulted in the immediate breakdown of the Confederacy, it is not hard to understand his exasperation at the timidity of his General. For on the Fourth of July, a rising officer in the West, Ulysses S. Grant, had compelled the surrender of the city of Vicksburg, Mississippi, after a prolonged siege, capturing thirty thousand Confederate soldiers, and opening the Mississippi River to Northern navigation from St. Louis to the Gulf.

Almost simultaneous with these two convincing victories of Union arms came, from the very heart of the nation, threats that all was not well. In many states of the Union, and especially in New York, the operation of the compulsory service law was resisted in fact as well as in spirit. In New York City, where it was felt that discrimination was being made in the draft against working men, especially those of foreign birth, Abraham's explanation of the manner in which the Civil War was a war on behalf of free labor, was for the moment forgotten. In his first annual message to Congress, delivered December third, 1861, when the war was young and its issues still in the formative stage, the President had said, " . . . It is not needed nor fitting here, that a general argument should be made in favor of popular institutions; but there is one point, with its connections, not so hackneyed as most others, to which I ask brief attention. It is the effort to place *capital* on an equal footing with, if not above, *labor,* in the structure of government. It is assumed that labor is available only in connection with capital; that nobody labors unless somebody else, owning capital, somehow by the use of it, induces him to labor. This assumed, it is next considered whether it is best that capital shall *hire* laborers, and then induce them to work by their own consent, or *buy* them, and drive them to it without their consent. Having proceeded so far, it is naturally concluded that all laborers are either *hired* laborers, or what we call slaves. And further, it is assumed that whoever is once a hired laborer is fixed in that condition for life.

"Now, there is no such relation between capital and labor as assumed; nor is there any such thing as a free man being fixed for life, in the condition of a hired laborer. Both these assumptions are false and all inferences from them are groundless.

"Labor is prior to, and independent of, capital. Capital is only the fruit of labor, and could never have existed if labor had not first existed. Labor is the superior of capital, and deserves much the higher consideration. Capital has it rights, which are as worthy of protection as any other rights. . . . " *

This was the opinion, sound enough in theory but not borne out by the facts, which had come into the sensitive and human, kind and common mind of the child of a prairie village who had shaken off the shackles, not of labor, but of too much earthiness. It was what he hoped was true, and what one hopes is as valuable to a stump speaker or a man in public office as what exists. But Abraham did not realize what the new industrialism, into which the labor of the North had been forced by that very development which he thought of as a striking evidence of national growth and dignity, had come to be. He could not have understood the state of mind of those who were writing to the New York papers in the summer of 1863, urging that only work-

* Works, Vol. V, pp. 407 ff.

ingmen should be drafted as the nation could get along without them but never without the business man who ran things. *

It was this spirit, failing to recognize the truth of Abraham's words, "Labor is the superior of capital, and deserves much the higher consideration," which had crept into the social organization of the metropolis of the North. And the laborer was unable to reconcile with those words, the fact that a provision of the Draft Law, allowed the man with capital to get out of military service (by the payment of $300) while the laborer could do nothing but serve. In New York City in certain congressional districts, chiefly the Ninth, there was a large proportion of laborers of foreign birth. In spite of the President's well-known anxiety to have foreign immigrants feel that they were welcome in the United States, these workers could not escape the feeling that Abraham's party was against them. With the help of local Democratic blandishment they soon concluded to espouse the cause of that, for the time being, headless party. In the elections of 1862, the Ninth Congressional District of New York, had for instance, returned a Democratic majority of three thousand.

On Saturday, July eleventh, the draft went into effect and drawings were made. On Sunday, the lists were published. The list for the Ninth District, containing almost entirely the names of workingmen with families to support, made good Sunday reading along Second Avenue. When Monday dawned, the feeling ran high. Rioting broke out at the headquarters of the Ninth District at Third Avenue and 46th Street. The building was set on fire and wrecked. The fire department, which was in sympathy with the rioters, let it burn. Mobs were forming everywhere. The Eighth District Headquarters was burned. The police found that they could do little or nothing. A great crowd

* *New York Times*, July 15, 1863.

rushed up Fifth Avenue to Forty-third Street where there was a large colored Orphan Asylum, and, believing that the colored race was the cause of its woes, set fire to the building. Fortunately the inmates escaped, but policemen, rioters and bystanders were killed and injured. The office of Horace Greeley's *New York Tribune,* being an abolition paper, was wrecked, from many New York lampposts hung the mutilated bodies of Negroes. Along Lexington Avenue, Second Avenue, Third Avenue, Broadway, blew the smoke of fires. Railroad tracks coming into the city were torn up. From Union Square to Fifty-ninth Street, the streets were cleared of almost everyone but rioters. The fourteenth and fifteenth of July passed with little abatement of the fury. The city was in the hands of the mob, which now numbered as many thugs and gunmen as it did indignant workingmen. But it had no leader, and by the sixteenth, with the arrival of some hastily detached soldiers who made a thorough job of cleaning up, the city was itself again. But the attempt of the federal government to substitute for the no longer active volunteering a compulsory form of service had caused casualties of more than a thousand, and property damage of considerably more than a million dollars.

Abraham Lincoln, isolated in the nation's capital among those who had never conceived that character could be found in a man who appeared to be at once lout, simpleton, vulgarian, and man of straw, must have felt very keenly the blow struck by the opposition to the draft in New York and elsewhere. It was as if he had solved a mathematical problem to his own satisfaction and then had suddenly been confronted with the fact that he had made a mistake in copying down the figures. Well, there was a troop of cavalry sitting about, with their horses saddled ready to fall into formation about Abraham wherever he tried to go.

How could he manage to get a moment to himself for thinking? Only among the bushes in the yard about the Soldier's Home, the "Summer White House" of that fearful summer. Abraham knew all the trees and most of the plants. He could walk about among them and look at them or not look at them as he wished. There was nothing to do but give New York a momentary respite from the draft and adjust any little injustice which might have crept in. The draft itself must go on. Men were not volunteering any longer. They wanted to believe that the war was over so they tried to believe it. They must be drafted. And if there had been too big a quota given to workingmen's districts in the big cities, that would have to be changed. It would not do to let workingmen think he was against them. For he was not.

The summer wore on. It was hot in Washington. Abraham, at night, when he was not at the telegraph office, would sit alone or with whatever members of the cabinet attended him, with his feet on the windowsill and his shoes on the floor. He tried to think of other things than the state of the nation, but it was hard. He read whenever he got time, chiefly in Shakespeare. James H. Hackett, the actor, had sent him a book. He relaxed himself by writing a letter of thanks. The gift was months old but there happened to be an evening in August when, reading it, he could think of the giver and thus take his mind from the field of battle, from the unknown quantity in the strange, McClellan-like General Rosecrans who was getting himself into trouble in Tennessee, from the silent, unquestioning, unanswering power of General Grant farther to the West, from the skillful if not aggressive Meade, facing Lee in Virginia.

" . . . For one of my age," he wrote to Hackett, "I have seen very little of the drama. The first presentation of *Falstaff* I ever

saw was yours here, last winter or spring. Perhaps the best com-
pliment I can pay is to say, as I truly can, I am very anxious to
see it again. Some of Shakespeare's plays I have never read, while
others I have gone over perhaps as frequently as any unprofes-
sional reader. Among the latter are *Lear, Richard III, Henry
VIII, Hamlet;* and especially *Macbeth.* I think nothing equals
Macbeth. It is wonderful.

"Unlike you gentleman of the profession, I think the soliloquy
in *Hamlet* commencing 'Oh, my offense is rank,' surpasses that
commencing 'To be or not to be.' But pardon this small attempt
at criticism. I should like to hear you pronounce the opening
speech of *Richard III.* Will you not soon visit Washington again?
If you do, please call and let me make your personal acquaintance."

There was a kind of warmth in Abraham as he wrote that.
He was truly escaping from the tortures of public life into the
life of the artist, which, strangely enough, he felt—rather than
knew—was his life. The artist in him had grown of late. It
was soon to have its performance. But now, he heard only pleas
for pardon of this and that deserter, some of which he granted,
others of which he refused. He heard protestations of interference and enmity from his generals, or queries from them as to
what they should do. He heard news of skirmishes and engagements which meant nothing but loss of life. He heard from
Mary Todd, his wife, herself suffering from the torture of knowing that Union bullets were thinning the ranks of her own
family, and not being happy in the thought that her husband's
was the patron spirit above those bullets. She was summering in
the North, at Manchester, Vermont, and among the purveyors
of silk and lace in New York. Abraham heard her writing
to know why he wanted her to come home, and was it not

dangerous with the hot weather, people said there was sickness in Washington, hadn't she better stay away a little longer. *

September nineteenth and twentieth had a sound very different from the opening speech of *Richard III*. Those days produced a hollow, empty rumble from the West where the hysterical General Rosecrans was suffering his army to be slaughtered, almost annihilated, because of faulty orders and the General's own panic, and only saved by the heroic and almost impossible resistance of General Thomas after Rosecrans had abandoned the field. In this battle the Confederate General Helm, Mrs. Lincoln's brother-in-law, was killed. It was just as well for Abraham that Mary was away, although he would have liked to have Tad to play with.

In October, in Chattanooga, Tennessee, whither General Rosecrans, busy, bustling, incompetent and nervous, had retreated after his mismanagement of the frightful battle of Chickamauga, the armies under his command were rapidly starving, cut off from supplies by the Confederate armies south of him and by the natural physiognomy of the hill country in which he was situated. Once more something had to be done. This time it was Grant, the hero of the West, who was put in command of the operations in Tennessee. Grant immediately displaced Rosecrans and gave the hero of Chickamauga, General Thomas, command of the dying horses and starving men in Chattanooga while Sherman approached with help and Grant himself hurried east to take command.

The army under Grant, directed by Thomas, looked very different from the assemblage of cripples and mendicants which it had seemed to be under the régime of Rosecrans. A general can translate his hysteria into the hysteria and despair of an army.

* Works, Vol. VI, pp. 418, 422, etc.

Another can calm a force of men and revive it as easily. Both Grant and Thomas were inspirers of confidence, and in their subordinate officers they were extremely fortunate. Grant found a plan already made; indeed part of it was Rosecrans'. There was nothing to do but wait for the arrival of Sherman with reinforcements.

When Sherman did arrive, Grant lost no time in putting his attack into execution. And in execution, the plan moved like the inexplicable elements of a dream, but a dream punctuated with the riotous thunder of heavy cannon, and the shattering, wave-like sweep of musketry, the cries of officers in exhortation and men in agony. The horrible losses and suffering on both sides were no dream, but the energy and agility with which the once-bewildered Union forces advanced under their clear-headed commanders would have seemed like a dream to poor old Rosecrans. In any case, Lookout Mountain, to the south, and Missionary Ridge to the east of Chattanooga, both strongly intrenched and fortified positions, were carried by the attack of the Union troops, and the Confederate States army, so long triumphant in Tennessee, was definitely driven back with severe loss. Furthermore, this victory led to the relief of General Burnside at Knoxville, where he had been threatened by General Longstreet.

Thanksgiving Day, 1863, thus made the first genuine Thanksgiving Day in many, many years. It was especially the occasion of thanksgiving to Abraham, who in the precarious exercise of the power which he had assumed had at last been granted something like real military success. And he needed military success, for without it he could not have maintained his position, could not have justified his course. As it now turned out, the President was able to reaffirm his policies and to feel strengthened in his support of them. The elections of 1863 had showed less of a Democratic trend in the North than had those of 1862. The Confederate armies had even in the East made no substantial advance which had not been nullified by counter-attack. In the West, the Mississippi had been opened, and the border states were being cleared. Congress had been adjourned since March, and Abraham had consequently been much freer than for some time from the bitter gnat-like voices of the Committee, perpetually alert, their owners athirst for his blood. The menace of England, sitting crouched like a lazy lion ready to pounce in and acknowledge the sovereignty of the seceded states as soon as the North was in a state not to retaliate, had been largely relieved by the victories of Gettysburg, Vicksburg, Stone's River, and finally Chattanooga. And they had, fortunately, been combined with the masterly tact of Charles Francis Adams, the American minister to the Court of St. James.

CHAPTER FIVE

THE ARTIST OF THE COMMON MIND

FOUR months after the battle at Gettysburg, Pennsylvania, when the many thousand dead were safely underground, brother and brother, and the astonishing violence of their hostility laid away with them, a gathering of people stood in the new military cemetery to listen to one of the most celebrated orators of the day, in an address of commemoration. Edward Everett of Boston had been invited to deliver this long address and had outdone himself in a scholarly, dignified and suitably pompous effort, to which the audience, with much weary shifting of feet and many yawns, listened in dutiful admiration. Not the least attentive of the orator's listeners was Abraham Lincoln, who had read Everett's speech some time before, the gentleman having kindly sent him a copy of it. When Everett was almost finished, Abraham took out his glasses and studied a paper which he held in his own hand. He shifted about nervously. When it came time for him to rise and face the throng on his own account he held the paper before him, his glasses slightly tilted downward on his nose. His great long body lifted its worn and aging face into the November air and spoke what its intuitive sense of arrangement had set down. The voice was high-pitched and shrill yet smoothed and abraded with the fine grit of tenderness. The stump speaker to whom it belonged, and whom everyone expected either to tell a jocose narrative or to harangue the crowd anent political issues, put off the stump manner and stood without gesture, speaking. The thrust of head and neck, the quick balance of throat to catch the shift of emotion in its muscle was the only gesture. Was this Lincoln, the politician, or was it the tragedian of a new theater? Was this the prairie boy grown old and slowed into solemnity, or was it the unlocated artist coming into his own, the artist of the common mind? It was all over so quickly, so few had had time to catch even a word, that no one knew. No one but Abraham, who for once had felt coming into him the amazement of emotional creation. Those two or three minutes of simple speech were the password which let Abraham Lincoln into his world. In their delivery, he must have known. The presidency and its powers, its requirements, its merely mechanical implications, its stress of surfaces, must have seemed to him something very small indeed, for perhaps the first time in his life. At last he had reached the height. He had been born again, he had found what he wanted most, and learned that he could do without it, having himself.

To the parasols, beaver stovepipes, flat derbies and flowered bonnets below him, the artist said: "Four score and seven years ago, our fathers brought forth on this continent, a new nation, conceived in Liberty, and dedicated to the proposition that all men are created equal.

"Now we are engaged in a great civil war, testing whether that nation or any other nation so conceived and so dedicated can long endure. We are met on a great battlefield of that war. We have come to dedicate a portion of that field, as a final resting place for those who here gave their lives that that nation might live. It is altogether fitting and proper that we should do this.

"But in a larger sense, we can not dedicate—we can not consecrate—we can not hallow—this ground. The brave men, living and dead, who struggled here, have consecrated it, far above our poor power to add or detract. The world will little note, nor long remember what we say here, but it can never forget what they did here. It is for us the living, rather, to be dedicated here to the unfinished work which they who fought here have thus far so nobly advanced. It is rather for us to be here dedicated to the great task remaining before us—that from these honored dead we take increased devotion to that cause for which they gave the last full measure of devotion—that we here highly resolve that these dead shall not have died in vain—that this nation, under God, shall have a new birth of freedom—and that government of the people, by the people, for the people, shall not perish from the earth."

There must have been joy in Abraham Lincoln's heart as he stepped away from the inattentive audience which had not quite understood him. He had joy of creation, that flowering in the simple mind of the empirical sense of life. Between this creation and its creator there was no long gap of modifying reason, no blur of metaphysical distance. It did not matter, now, what anyone thought, what enemies might do, Abraham had discovered the world, and it had neither past nor future.

As he puffed back to the capital in the horrible little train, he might well have thought, what did it matter if in performance he was wrong, so long as at any given moment he not only saw but was the thing which he experienced? If he could talk to the British Foreign Office for three minutes, there would no longer be anything to fear from England, victories in the field or no victories. If he could talk to all the people at once, Democrats, rigid Republicans, Union men, he would be the people and they would be, as he hoped they would be, united in him for the prosecution of the war, which now seemed to him as to many

others not in the military service to be on its last legs. And out
of the war must come that unity which, in his imaginative in-
ference, he had established as a reality already. But he could not
look into the eye of everything, nor shake its hand. Some things
had to be done through ambassadors, secretaries, generals, parties,
some things must be yielded to gain others, power must be assumed strings must be pulled, men and their vagaries must be
allowed for. Louisiana, freed from Confederate armies, must be
jockeyed back into the Union, Arkansas too. There were elections coming, and votes from new districts, that had not, in
1860, been Lincoln districts, must be secured. To foster and nour-
ish just the right sort of government in the border states which
had been doubtful or definitely Southern, whether by trickery
or plain dealing, would in the end be justifiable. If Louisiana and
Arkansas wanted to come in, and wanted to come in with a
Lincoln bias, why look too closely into the antecedents of the
new state of mind in those states? Get them in, that was the
point. If they were falsely gotten in the trouble could be rec-
tified afterwards. If they were not, so much the better. The artist
had to lift himself by the bootstraps and get these things done.

In December, 1863, the President issued a long proclamation of
"Amnesty and Reconstruction" in which full pardon was offered
to those persons who had participated in the existing "rebellion"
(with some few exceptions), with restoration of their property,
excepting slaves, provided that they would merely subscribe
to an oath to defend the Constitution and the United States, and
to support acts of Congress, relative to slaves, which had been
passed during the "rebellion," as well as proclamations issued
by the president during the same period. This document also
announced that whenever one-tenth of the voters of any of the
seceded states should get together and reorganize a state govern-

ment, that government would be recognized as the true government of the state and the state be accordingly considered back in the Union.

To the group in Congress which objected to everything about Abraham and believed that the seceded states should be punished and humbled before being allowed any privileges, this seemed pretty terrible. Congress considered a measure to take out of the President's hands all right to have anything whatever to say about the reconstruction of the Union. But some of Abraham's enemies resisted the passage of this bill in the Senate, preferring to wait for the man in the White House to twist himself up in his own rope and blunder into hanging himself. Abraham was quite ready to take a chance. In an extremely high-handed manner, and with very questionable authority he nursed the new government which was trying to set itself up in Louisiana. The House of Representatives countered by passing a resolution of censure against the President because he had not protested the arrogant and nationally insulting manner in which Napoleon III had made Mexico safe for the French. Abraham merely instructed his Minister in Paris to explain to the Emperor's representative that the acts of the House of Representatives were not the acts of the head of the American government and consequently not the acts of the government at all.

Abraham, thinking that the war was now nearly over, and realizing that his Emancipation Proclamation was a measure supported by neither legality nor inevitable effect, but merely by the fact of the nation's being in arms, understood very clearly that when those arms had been laid aside, the dignity and force of the Proclamation would be laid aside with them. Once the armies were disbanded, few people could seriously regard it as either constitutional or practical, in fact as anything but a political *tour de force,* a mere wind that had made the man who was going to shoot stoop to pick up his hat. Having lashed the country into such a fury of controversy over the why and wherefore of the war, having revised his own position, which had originally ignored the slavery issue, it would be necessary for him in some manner to preserve the dignity of his pronouncement and to give it permanent effect. He realized, and his few friends in Congress realized, that eventually it would be necessary to have a Constitutional Amendment abolishing slavery throughout the United States. Congress, as it existed, would never pass such an amendment by the necessary two-thirds majority. Hence Abraham's hurry to get the weakening southern states, who might desire to return, once more into the fold, their representatives with their votes seated in Congress. He must fortify himself. The opposition in Congress saw what he was up to, knew that he had no legal right to be up to it, and resisted him with a venom that was less attractive than his illegality. Abraham did not care any longer. He existed, as a man. He might well have said, *"Je suis l'état."* Except in so far as Abraham by virtue of his nature, his simple commonness, did spiritually represent the people, there was, early in 1864, no vestige of republican government in the United States. And until the national elections of November, 1864, there would be no way of telling whether or not Abraham really did have a mandate from the people. In any case, Congress, insulted singly and as a body, could not be expected to rejoice at the dictatorship. All it could do would be to continue its policy of waiting for Abraham to make a blunder with genuinely disastrous consequences. In the first months of 1864 that blunder looked very much on the horizon. In March, the useless figurehead, General Halleck, having been discarded, a shabby short little man, who walked as if the next step were going to send him flat on his face, and looked like a reformed drunkard reconsidering the value of his reformation, but in whose blue eyes there was a strange selfless light of determination, was given the revived grade of Lieutenant General and made Commander-in-Chief of all the forces of the United States. Immediately after his appointment, Ulysses Grant, born Hiram, took his cigars and moved into headquarters on the Virginia front, his plans largely made, his eyes fixed on one thing only. But he did not share either the President's or the people's confidence that with one great stroke he could win the war. * This rather tarnished-looking general, with his unpressed and stained uniform distinguished from an ordinary soldier's only by its shoulder bars, knew, like Abraham Lincoln, that he was one of the people and, unlike the earlier Lincoln, had no desire to be anything else. He did not care if there was hayseed in his hair. The only thing that he enjoyed anywhere near so much as domestic life, whisky, cigars and horses, was military activity. Not just military life. He hated that, and thought that no decent man could be a soldier in peace time. But war was like a good game of chess. And the Missouri farmer, once a West Pointer, who had fought in the Mexican War against his belief that it was a disgusting piece of national rapacity, had a peculiar power, a soft quietness of command, which was unlike anything the Northern armies had yet seen. The people took from their army a sense of confidence in him, the politicians of all parties trusted and admired him, perhaps chiefly because he knew how to keep his mouth shut. And Abraham's instinctive wisdom told him, without question, without examination or proof, that he had found a man of his own temper whose ways he could understand and trust. The result was that

* Richard H. Dana. Memoir, by C. F. Adams. Vol. III, pp. 271 ff.

the President, for the first time in his administration, gave his Commander a free hand.

When General Grant took command of the Armies of the United States he decided to locate his headquarters in Virginia, and with very good reason. He admired and trusted Lincoln, but he knew the President's ignorance of military matters and the value which, in Washington was put upon the political factors in the war. Grant wanted none of these, and he felt that his only salvation would be to be where he could throw all interference overboard the minute it cropped up. Telegrams and promises could not keep an army from disaster, but a man without political ambition who knew what he was up to could do exactly that. There were in Virginia at this time, the Army of the Potomac under the capable General Meade, the victor of Gettysburg, who had learned much about the handling of a large Army in the past ten months, and the Army of the James under the unmilitary, bombastic and ambitious General Butler, the most unpopular in the South of all Union generals. In that proud region he was known as "Beast" Butler, not without some reason. The Army of the Potomac on the first of May, 1864, numbered approximately 120,000 men, of whom practically 100,000 were equipped and ready for fighting. The Army of the James, numbered at the same time approximately 40,000. Against the two forces were opposed the forces making up the defenses of the James River approach to Richmond, City Point and Petersburg, on the first of May numbering about 6,000, and the Army of Northern Virginia, which numbered less than 60,000, under General Lee. It was General Grant's plan that General Butler should drive on Petersburg through City Point and then sweep north toward Richmond, while he with the Army of the Potomac should, by a concentrated advance by his own left flank, attack the army of General Lee spread out north of Richmond. On the third of May the Army of the Potomac began its advance by crossing the Rapidan River into that uncharitable tangle of forest known as the Wilderness in the vicinity of which General Hooker had been so badly defeated at Chancellorsville a year earlier. Grant had hoped that, before Lee could discover his tactics, he would have succeeded in passing his entire attacking force through the Wilderness and thus would be enabled to bring to the inevitable battle the superiority of strength and equipment which in the tangles of the forest would have given him no advantages. But Lee found out what was in the wind. He was not afraid of Grant. He attacked the Union army in the depths of the Wilderness on the fifth of May and arrested its advance. The Confederate army, weakened by prolonged campaigning, threatened by imperfect systems of supply and by dissension in their government to a degree far greater than was realized by their opponents, none the less had the advantage of a keen knowledge of the ways of the Wilderness and of the type of fighting which the heavily wooded region with its dense undergrowth made necessary. Although outnumbered two to one, they managed to keep back the no longer frivolous but now bitterly determined body of professional soldiers, officered by men of military science, which was opposing them. They felt, they knew, that it was their last stand against the tyrannous misconception of their very nature which in the event of a Northern victory would dominate their government.

In the eyes of any other general than Grant, the battles of May fifth and sixth in the Wilderness would have been a Northern defeat. He had lost nearly 18,000 men in two days and had failed to advance according to plan. But the blue-eyed little man in the frowsy coat and battered hat was no McClellan. He did not, as General Lee believed he would, retreat from the field. In fact, cheered by his men, who yet knew how long their dead bodies might lie in that dismal thicket undiscovered, he renewed the advance, moving toward Spottsylvania Court House, to the south. On the eleventh, Generals Hancock, Wright and Burnside attacked a salient in the enemy's lines a few miles north of Spottsylvania. Again in two days' fighting the losses were frightful and, as the army itself and the Northern public realized, far out of proportion to the success attained. The Army of the Potomac was gaining a little ground, and most important of all it was not retreating. The officers of the Confederate army, hearing from prisoners of discontent in the Union ranks, discontent with the terrible and apparently unprofitable carnage, believed that in the end Grant, like his predecessors, would abandon his campaign. But he did not. Believing that he had been put in command to fight, he fought, with a tenacity which earned him the title of "butcher." Even after the "Bloody Angle," the salient north of Spottsylvania, he kept on, his men fighting hand to hand with bayonets and clubbed muskets against the Southerners, hungry and ill-equipped, who were, none the less, fighting on their own ground defending their homes. On the twelfth of May General Hancock was in possession of Spottsylvania Court House, and had, in spite of losses, taken many Confederate prisoners. On the eleventh, General Grant had wired to the demoted General Halleck, now merely the swivel-chair Chief of Staff in Washington, "We have now ended the sixth day of very heavy fighting. The result to this time is much in our favor. But our losses have been heavy, as well as those of the enemy. We have lost to this time, eleven general officers killed, wounded, or missing, and probably twenty thousand men. I think the loss of the enemy must be greater,* we having taken over four thousand prisoners in battle, whilst he has taken but few, except stragglers. I am now sending back to Belle Plain all my wagons for a fresh supply of provisions and ammunition, and propose to fight it out on this line if it takes all summer."

All summer! and twenty thousand men gone in six days! In the telegraph office at the War Department in Washington, where the anxious President was waiting for news, this seemed incredible, almost too much to be borne. Lincoln believed that Grant was right in using every effort to destroy, wear down, and capture, the army of General Lee. It was that, and not Richmond, which would ensure the downfall of the government which had challenged the government of the United States. But this slaughter was hard to bear. And it took General Grant far more than all summer. On the third of June, the Commander attacked in his front, in violation of all the laws of military strategy, the Confederate position at Cold Harbor, Virginia. Every man that went into that dreadfully ill-advised attack knew how little chance there was of his living to fight another battle. All had escaped the flanking volleys and thrusts of Lee in the Wilderness, they had come unscathed out of the flames of the burning woods that swept over the ground and destroyed the wounded, groaning among the ferns, they had cheered their Commander, and marched forward, in the teeth of an irresistible resistance. Now they pinned slips of paper to their backs, that those who found their bodies might know who they were and to what quiet home to the northward they had once belonged. The attack on Cold Harbor failed. Barely ten miles from Richmond the greatest army ever thrown into battle on the American continent was repulsed by a weary force of less than half its

*It was not.

size, fighting with tenacity and courage because it did not dare
to yield. General Grant's losses in the thirty days of his campaign
had now risen to nearly 60,000, a number as great as that of the
entire force which opposed him. He now knew that he had made
a mistake at Cold Harbor and determined to change the point
of attack. He moved his entire army to the south, across the
James River.

While this amazing struggle had been going on in the region
northeast of Richmond, General Sheridan with some 12,000
cavalry had made a successful raid within the Confederate lines
and had come to the very walls of Richmond, causing considerable dismay within the city. His advance did much damage to
the sources of supply of Lee's army and weakened the opposition
to Grant by that much, but it was not yet enough. South of
Richmond, General Butler, acting on a plan of his own which
he thought beautiful, had got himself into a perfectly safe
but perfectly useless position between Petersburg and the Confederate capital. Far to the south, advancing into the lower
Confederacy from Tennessee with an army of one hundred
thousand experienced men, Wm. T. Sherman had driven
forward with the same vigor and ruthlessness which characterized the movement of the Federal armies in the north.
He met with severe opposition, but advanced more rapidly
than did the army of the Potomac in the north. While
Grant was fighting at Cold Harbor, Sherman was taking up
a new position between Allatoona and Marietta in the wake
of the retreating, but not defeated, Confederate General
Johnston.

Except for Sherman's unquestionable advance, it seemed to
Lincoln, and he knew it must seem to his people, that there was
little Union success to show for the horrible slaughter of the

early summer. Counting Butler's Army of the James, and the forces under Sherman, at least 80,000 men had been lost to the Union forces in less than two months. Many were grumbling, the strangely unstable Horace Greeley was grumbling particularly. Within the cabinet, troubles were still acute. Secretary Chase, an able Treasurer, was being stirred about with the long spoon of blandishment in the hope that he might jell into a suitable leader for the opposition to Abraham in the elections of the coming autumn. The President had tried not to notice this, but he could not entirely ignore it. Even when a Kansas Senator issued a circular definitely suggesting that Chase would make a better President than Lincoln, the President refused to accept Chase's resignation. He was so sure of himself that he felt that he could afford a few thorns in his side. He was trying to win the war and to secure his own acts. He had successfully ignored and handled Congress. He could bide his time. But the biding, even to an Abraham Lincoln serenely come into realization of his powers, of the nature of his quality, was not easy. There were rough stones in his path. In the middle of May, with the Republican national convention only a few weeks distant, a fake proclamation, supposedly from the President's hand, announcing the practical failure of General Grant's campaign and proclaiming a day of humiliation and prayer, got printed in some of the Democratic papers in New York, notably the *World* and the *Journal of Commerce*. Although the editors satisfactorily explained the error and duly announced the hoax in their pages, Abraham, with the help of Secretary Seward, ordered the arrest and imprisonment of these men and the suppression of the papers. There could not have been a more dangerous move for the President to make at this time. But he made it, and so great was the confidence of the common man in his integrity and his ability, that the incident hurt him nowhere that he had not already been damaged.

Had it not been for the impatience of a certain radical group in the fringes of the Republican party who could not wait for the convention but got together about four hundred strong and nominated General John C. Frémont independently for the Presidency, Abraham might have been seriously threatened by a schism within the nearer ranks of his party. He was not popular in Congress, and the radical element, which had been so relentlessly opposed to him, would, perhaps, have controlled the coming convention but for the fact that they became frightened by the split which nominated Frémont and did not dare to break away. When Grant had failed at Cold Harbor and the Army of the Potomac once more stood shrouded in uncertainty, the enemies of the President in Congress got together and once more rebuked him by refusing to seat the Senators and Representatives from the State of Arkansas, merely because Lincoln had managed all by himself the reconstruction of that once seceded state. At the same time Secretary Chase turned in one of his recurring resignations. This time, so tense was the conflict between Abraham and his enemies, he accepted it. And in accepting it, a great weight was taken from his mind. Chase had been a skillful Secretary, but he had been difficult to handle. It was no longer necessary to handle him, and it was only necessary, in order to placate the hostile ones who supported Chase to choose as his successor, not a war Democrat or a Lincoln Republican, but a radical Republican friendly with the Congressional irreconcilables who at the same time should have ability. Abraham happily found this man in Senator Fessenden, a radical Republican and a gentleman cordially supported by the financial interests of New York. That was rather a stroke and it cost Abraham nothing, as Fessenden was an able man.

This appointment did not placate the wrath of the irreconcilables who were busy with their bill arrogating to themselves all matters of reconstruction in states wishing to return to the Union. Nor did what the President did to that bill, after its passage in both houses, help to make him a pleasant sight in their eyes. Abraham took the measure, which was handed to him shortly before the adjournment of Congress, looked at it and put it down again, remarking that the insistence in it by Congress that slavery be prohibited in reconstructed states was a matter in which Congress could not act, it having been steadfastly affirmed by the President even so far back as the Douglas Debates that Congress had no power to regulate slavery within the states or territories. The sponsors of the Reconstruction Bill were furious. They could not see how the President, who was advocating the same thing which he was forbidding Congress to ordain, had any right to take such power to himself. But Abraham was through with all considerations of legal right or wrong. He was now something more than a country lawyer. He was a national dictator. He was not only a dictator. He was a balance wheel. He saw himself now in the position of correcting and editing democracy when it went wrong, and in this vision of himself, this personal apotheosis, there was, strangely enough, no trace of the self-centered ambition, the tight-lipped individual struggle for eminence, which had characterized the days of his development. It is not strange that many about him, who saw in his face, in his great hands, in the high gentle stoop of his body, merely the flesh of a man, could not conceive how that flesh had been lashed and scourged into a semblance of deity, of sublimated arbiter over the heads of mere men, whom Abraham's flesh loved, understood, and pitied. Few of the President's contemporaries, indeed few men of any time, have had in them that oversensitive awareness of suffering which alone can teach the sufferer to profit by his pain, few have so richly lived with fear that they have sold their peace and tortured their flesh to cast out fear. Those few that have done so are artists in their kind, as Abraham Lincoln was an artist in the management of himself and the delineation through his actions of the genius, otherwise inexpressible, of the common mind.

What he worked out as a system of government, studied in its own light, was a direct contradiction of many of his own beliefs, a direct disavowal of constitutional democracy. It would not do for the average President to take Abraham Lincoln as a pattern. The reason that the United States has had so few distinguished and effectual Presidents is not that its government is wrong, for its government is flexible, but that it has had, as all the world has had, too few men honest enough to profit by their own errors and their own defeats, few men courageous enough to be unafraid of their own overthrow.

In the summer of 1864 Abraham Lincoln was confronted with the possibility of his own overthrow, for his stock was very low. Many who believed that they spoke for a majority of the people, believed that those people wanted peace at any price and that the President in insisting upon the recementing of the Union only in combination with the abolishment of slavery, was cheating a torn and wearied nation of its best desire, and in apparent willfulness. For Abraham had permitted two gentlemen to go to Richmond, with his sanction, and to sound out the Confederate government on the subject of peace with restoration of the Union, knowing that Jefferson Davis would refuse to negotiate on such terms and that the refusal could be used in refutation of the anti-Lincoln claims of the Democrats to the effect that the President did not want peace and would make no effort to secure it. Furthermore, Abraham had punctured Horace Greeley's personal bubble by sending him to Canada to see two Confederates who were supposed to be courting overtures of peace in that place. Greeley had said that the President should send an officer to negotiate with these gentlemen, but he had not thought that he himself would be sent. He went, he saw, and he got all mixed up. He ignored some of President Lincoln's stipulations and put himself in a very embarrassing position. The President immediately sent a note to Niagara Falls showing plainly that he would accept any peace aiming at and assuring a restoration of the Union and the abolition of slavery, but none under other than those conditions. The Confederate commissioners saw that Greeley had been deluding them. The Confederates published their report of the affair, thereby putting public opinion in the North into a more confused state than ever. No one could decide whether the President had merely played with the Southern commissioners or Greeley was just a plain fool. Greeley could have made the President's position perfectly clear if he had not preferred to take a smack in the mouth rather than see one small leaf of laurel settle above the brow of the man in the White House. Lincoln urged him to tell the truth about the Canadian fiasco, but to tell it without saying that he thought the war was hopeless. Abraham did not want the public to know that a man in public life, editor of a great journal, was in so despairing a state of mind. But Greeley would make nothing public without saying what he thought, so Abraham was left in the position of appearing to have made peace difficult of attainment. On top of this misfortune, undaunted by the possibility of personal loss, realizing that the armies must have more men if the war was to be won, Abraham issued a proclamation calling for the drafting of 500,000 more men. Two of the Congressmen most hostile to the President now issued, with the help of Greeley's *Tribune,* a paper which practically suggested to the nation that Lincoln was a dangerous tyrant and should not be allowed to be one. Of course Lincoln was a tyrant, and he had no legal justification for many of the public acts of his office. While professing the closest adherence to the principles of the Constitution he was perpetually overriding the Constitution and making a mockery of Constitutional government. But his reasons for doing so, legally unjustifiable, were in the last analysis better reasons than the more legal objections raised by his critics. Few of his bitterest enemies seriously believed that he was ruining the nation. They merely understood that the presidency was spreading over them like a lava flow and their political personalities were being obliterated. They wished to think that the high-handed tyranny of the President was harmful to the country and superficially succeeded in making themselves believe so. But they never convinced the voters that they were right. And after all, democracy or no democracy, the voters will follow anyone that looks like a leader, unless the systems and exigencies of economic warfare take all the spirit out of them and make them afraid of themselves—afraid of everybody and everything not nationally advertised. In Lincoln's day, fortunately, the tight lid of industrialism had not been clamped down upon the cauldron of the common mind. There was still a sense of life, of functional activity arising from it.

So it was that when the Republican Executive Committee, supposing that the tide of popular favor had turned against Abraham, marched to Washington for the purpose of asking him to withdraw as their candidate, they marched back again with a different idea in their heads. Abraham was able to convince them that the thing to do was to win the war without considering the how or why, and to make them understand that if anyone could do it, he could. He remained the Republican candidate, though by no means sure that he would be reëlected. In fact he planned only for the few months remaining of his first term. After that he supposed that it would be merely a question of coöperating with his successor.

But the President's firmness, the firmness of a man who in his time had learned all about vacillation, had gathered to his support the curious abolitionists of the North, a group which was all important to him. And the evidences of his increasing integrity had already earned him the support of the intellectuals of the North. Yet it was not the support of these groups that mattered most. It was the fact that just as the Democratic national convention was meeting in Chicago to nominate General George B. McClellan and to declare that the war had been an entire failure, news was received that General Sherman had captured Atlanta, Georgia, with his army substantially intact. The policy of determined ruthlessness, which the general had followed, had triumphed over an exhausted and depleted Southern army, and the proudest city of Georgia was taken from the Georgians with their pride. It was a splendid gift for Abraham Lincoln, whatever tragedy it may have been to many a true heart below the Mason-Dixon line. And it was not hard to understand that it brought the end of the war much nearer. For it was consequent upon the capture of Mobile by Admiral Farragut, and the dashing raids of the Federal cavalry under Sheridan in the Shenandoah Valley of Virginia. It did not matter that General Grant, determined as ever, still sacrificing men on what looked like a hopelessly unresponsive altar, was failing dismally before Petersburg, Virginia, and that Lee's army was still in safe control of Richmond.

The victories turned the tide. At the November elections Abraham was treated to a clear and definite expression of the esteem in which his capacities were held. He received the largest electoral vote which had been given since the establishment of the government. Evidently his people trusted him, who had learned so much, and his strong-arm tactics were approved. They could have hurt no one but the people and now the people said, "It does not hurt. Save us."

CHAPTER SIX

VINDICATION AND OPPORTUNITY

ABRAHAM LINCOLN regarded his triumph calmly. To him it was not a personal triumph, but merely an acknowledgment by the people whom he governed, of the fact that there truly was a nation called the United States of America. Many in his political party regarded the election of 1864 as purely a Republican party triumph. They did not see, as the President saw, that the Democratic party had failed, not because its members had gone over to the Republicans, but because circumstances had made it impossible for the Democrats to vote the Democratic ticket without appearing to destroy the nation. The great number of Democratic votes which went to Lincoln were, then, not Republican votes, but votes for the maintenance of the Union. They were the expression of a feeling which had been growing in the North for many years, a feeling that whatever the origins of the nation had been, whatever its originators had intended, there had appeared in its development an unnameable factor, guided by neither party nor individual, but by that larger individuality which is compounded of the inapprehensible cells and factors of social life on earth. It is this individuality, this collective organism, which is a nation, and which controls men and their economies and is not controlled by them, however high the moral strength which they exert upon time and place and life.

Abraham Lincoln, without clearly understanding this, at the

same time felt some sense of its truth. He himself remarked that he had not controlled events but that events had controlled him. It is plain that they had, and that, in the controlling, they had found him to be what few can be, malleable stuff capable of taking a high temper, despite the bed of ignorance, misconception, weakness, unwonted ambition, from which that stuff had been dug. The man who on the ninth of November, 1864, had stepped out on a balcony of the White House, his secretary standing beside him, sheltering a candle in his hand; the man who had lifted a face carven with darkness and light and said to those enthusiastic admirers standing below on the damp grass, ". . . I am thankful to God for this approval of the people; but while deeply grateful for this mark of their confidence in me, if I know my heart, my gratitude is free from any taint of personal triumph. I do not impugn the motives of anyone opposed to me. It is no pleasure to me to triumph over anyone, but I give thanks to the Almighty for this evidence of the people's resolution to stand by free government and the rights of humanity. . . ." that man was the same man who not many years before in the struggle to shake off the hateful origins which he felt clung to him like the smell of something rank, had resorted to all kinds of tricks, had cast aside friends, and played the dirty game of politics, merely to advance himself. He had advanced himself, and when he reached the greatest point of advance, partly by luck, partly by personality, partly by bargaining on the part of his supporters, he had suddenly realized that it was of no profit to a man to climb, except to reach something which was reaching down toward him, trying to enter him, to dissolve the net of circumstances woven by fear and shame, and to release the flood of the heart upon the levels of human life.

Abraham Lincoln, now elected for the second time to the

presidency of the world's most important republic, had served for four years the creative power of national life, guarding its interests with his most devoted belief. He thought of the nation as an individual, as a kind of self of which his own was the prototype. He shaped himself into this thought, with the consummate genius of his art, art created of that ramification of intelligence with the guardianship of which he was charged, made into a power, a serviceable limb. He contributed little or nothing—less than nothing to the science of government, the theory of the state. He overruled and destroyed many sacred principles, justified in his own eyes by the almost mystic confidence in his own rightness which after 1862 had seldom left him. In the few months left him of life, he had many struggles to go through, and now, doubly certain by virtue of the vote he had received that he had a mandate from his people, he went through those struggles with the utmost confidence and calm.

The vengeful members of Congress had not lessened their cries for vengeance and humiliating retaliation upon the states which had dared to assert their individuality and to set themselves up as a new nation. They were bent upon thwarting the President's schemes for the restoration of state government in the South. They took advantage of every illegality, every questionable act of the Chief Executive in fostering the little groups of men, especially in Louisiana, who had gotten together for the purpose of following Abraham Lincoln's call back into the Union from whose protection they had been estranged. And there were a number of things which, if emphasized in the proper manner, would seem to be mountains instead of the molehills that they were.

In December, 1864, Abraham had recommended to Congress the passage of that same Constitutional Amendment, abolishing slavery, which had been defeated before the election, defeated by way of rebuke to him. Now he gently, but very firmly, advised Congress that it would be well, in view of the results of the election, to pass that amendment by the necessary majority. In January, Congress had approved the amendment. Soon it was on its way to the state legislatures for ratification, to be saved by those legislatures which Abraham had so carefully been priming against the day. But one severe disappointment was in store. Congress would not recognize the government which Abraham had set up in Louisiana. They persisted in that. Undaunted, but not unhurt, Abraham went on with his hopes for humane and generous-hearted reconstruction. He submitted to his cabinet a message which he proposed to send to Congress, offering the South $400,000,000 as a compensation for the liberation of their slaves, to be paid, part on the abandonment of resistance to the federal government, and part on the ratification by each returning state of the new Thirteenth Amendment. But the cabinet, believing that such a measure would never pass Congress and would only serve as an antagonizing element, disapproved the sending of the message. The President was very much pained. He would have been more deeply pained than ever, could he have lived to see what the Congress was to do with that matter of reconstruction which was so dear to him, how it was to carry on the charitable intentions of the deep heart of Abraham Lincoln.

During the first months of 1865 the military side of the war was progressing slowly but surely in the direction of Northern victory, victory but hardly triumph. Grant, continually reinforced, continually attacking, plugging away at his job without molestation and without protest, was being ably seconded by the attrition of General Lee's forces, the lack of supplies in Richmond and throughout the South, and the fact that soldiers with empty stomachs supported by a government with an empty pocketbook, cannot do their best fighting. General Sherman, after the fall of Atlanta, had marched to the sea, destroying everything destructible and infuriating the citizens of Georgia and South Carolina with the roughness of his tactics. He was now pushing northward into North Carolina, only separated from the retreating General Lee by the force of the Confederate General Johnston, barely more than thirty thousand men.

Overtures looking toward peace had been made by the Southern government, on the suggestion of Mr. Blair, the father of Lincoln's first Postmaster General, and a sincere if self-centered lover of the Union. President Davis had sent three commissioners, among them Alexander Stephens, Abraham's most intimate friend in the Thirtieth Congress of 1848, to discuss the preliminaries to peace. The President, at the suggestion of General Grant, having now no fear that any dealings with representatives of the Confederacy would be deemed base and cowardly, met the Confederate commissioners with Secretary of State Seward at Fortress Monroe, Virginia, but as the gentlemen from the South had not been instructed to make any arrangements on any other terms than a recognition of the existence of two separate governments, North and South, the conference came to nothing. It did, however, serve as an opening wedge and convinced the President that the South would come round in time. Indeed if he had realized the terrible state of affairs in the Southern Confederacy, the hunger and privation which the proud people under Jefferson Davis had undergone in support of their armies in the field, he must have known that the end was in sight.

In March, General Lee let it be known that he would like

to have a conference with General Grant for the purpose of determining whether or not the difficulties between the belligerent nations might not be adjusted. Grant wired Lincoln for instructions and was told by the President, on the last day of his first term in office, that General Grant should have no conference with General Lee except for the purpose of discussing terms of the surrender of Lee's army. For the moment the second attempt of the Confederacy to save its life and identity by ending the war, was thwarted. On the following day, under circumstances very different from those of four years before, a very different man of the same name, stood up in Washington to receive the oath of office from a former member of his cabinet, a hostile and difficult person, whose infidelity had been rewarded by Abraham Lincoln with the Chief Justiceship of the Supreme Court. When Justice Chase had administered the oath, President Lincoln, the second, in a firm high voice, graver in tone than had been its habit years before, spoke briefly and honestly, with a dignity which he had never exceeded. The artist was celebrating his laureateship. This is what he said:

Fellow Countrymen: At this second appearing to take the oath of the presidential office, there is less occasion for an extended address than there was at the first. Then, a statement, somewhat in detail, of a course to be pursued, seemed fitting and proper. Now, at the expiration of four years, during which public declarations have been constantly called forth on every point and phase of the great contest which still absorbs the attention and engrosses the energies of the nation, little that is new could be presented. The progress of our arms, upon which all else chiefly depends, is as well known to the public as to myself; and it is, I trust, reasonably satisfactory and encouraging to all. With high hope for the future, no prediction in regard to it is ventured.

On the occasion corresponding to this four years ago, all thoughts

were anxiously directed to an impending civil war. All dreaded it—
all sought to avert it. While the inaugural address was being delivered
from this place, devoted altogether to *saving* the Union without war
insurgent agents were in the city seeking to *destroy* it without war—
seeking to dissolve the Union, and divide effects, by negotiation. Both
parties deprecated war; but one of them would *make* war rather than
let the nation survive; and the other would *accept* war rather than let
it perish. And the war came.

One-eighth of the whole population were colored slaves, not distributed generally over the Union, but localized in the southern part
of it. These slaves constituted a peculiar and powerful interest. All
knew that this interest was, somehow, the cause of the war. To
strengthen, perpetuate and extend this interest was the object for which
the insurgents would rend the Union, even by war; while the government claimed no right to do more than to restrict the territorial en-
largement of it. Neither party expected for the war the magnitude or
the duration which it has already attained. Neither anticipated that
the *cause* of the conflict might cease with, or even before, the conflict
itself should cease. Each looked for an easier triumph, and a result less
fundamental and astounding. Both read the same Bible, and pray to
the same God; and each invokes His aid against the other. It may
seem strange that any men should dare to ask a just God's assistance
in wringing their bread from the sweat of other men's faces; but let
us judge not, that we be not judged. The prayers of both could not be
answered—that of neither has been answered fully. The Almighty has
His own purposes. "Woe unto the world because of offences! for it
must needs be that offences come; but woe to that man by whom
the offence cometh." If we shall suppose that American slavery is one
of those offences which, in the providence of God, must needs come,
but which, having continued through His appointed time, He now
wills to remove, and that He gives to both north and south this terrible war, as the woe due to those by whom the offence came, shall we
discern therein any departure from those divine attributes which the

believers in a living God always ascribe to Him? Fondly do we hope —fervently do we pray—that this mighty scourge of war may speedily pass away. Yet, if God wills that it continue until all the wealth piled by the bondman's two hundred and fifty years of unrequited toil shall be sunk, and until every drop of blood drawn with the lash shall be paid by another drawn with the sword, as was said three thousand years ago, so still it must be said, "The judgments of the Lord are true and righteous altogether."

With malice toward none; with charity for all; with firmness in the right, as God gives us to see the right, let us strive on to finish the work we are in; to bind up the nation's wounds, to care for him who shall have borne the battle, and for his widow, and his orphan—to do all which may achieve and cherish a just and a lasting peace among ourselves, and with all nations.

That utterance, almost biblical in style, showed how calmly now the ex-politician regarded the destiny of himself and his nation. He saw the dream of his later years approaching reality, a united nation proved strong enough to save itself, a people made one through suffering and humiliation as he himself had been made one with his inner self through a similar ordeal. Happily for him, he saw only the blessedness of unity, and not the sinister balance of the economic factors of that unity. He saw a united nation, almost on the brink of victory. But he did not see how the very forces which had brought about that union and that victory, had contrived to consolidate the powers which should make of union a strength aligned against itself and of victory, a triumph of the few who should be fortunate. For the great production required of the North in order to supply the armies in the field had resulted in the production of a centralized economic force which would be more benefited than the common man by the saving of the Union. The sad man, who

Abraham Lincoln Entering Richmond, April 3rd, 1865

had seen his own foolishness and how it had hurt him, and who had outlived it, saw in his country now only the same triumph over evil influences. He felt himself the father of its integrity, but he did not realize, indeed had no way of realizing, that the very strength which he gave it in helping to save it would make of the United States of America an imperial state in which, so great would be the power of centralization, the common man would not only not be free but would lack even the power to wish himself so. But he is not to be blamed for that. Abraham Lincoln chose the side of power. That it turned out to be the side of economic imperialism is no fault of his. But it is a tragic circumstance.

On the third of April, 1865, Petersburg and Richmond, Virginia, were evacuated by the retreating armies of the heroic and indomitable Lee. A few days later, amid the flames of the Confederate capital, Abraham Lincoln walked almost alone, eager as a child looking at the scene of an accident, sitting in President Davis's chair, running his hands over walls, trees, that had for four years stood in sight of men willing to give their lives in defense of beliefs which to him seemed wrong. Lee was holding his line vigorously as he retreated. The Confederate government had taken its papers and fled. Sherman was advancing in North Carolina. And the smoke went up along the river from buildings that had graced Richmond when Washington and Jefferson were alive. On the ninth of April, unable to hold out any longer, the armies under General Lee laid down their arms. Grant, the stolid, determined fighter, by force of superior resources had won. But he had the dignity to know that he had won as he had, and he could not, any more than Lincoln could, exult. The officers of the Confederate government, interpreting Northern public opinion, were in flight. Sherman's imminent victory over

Johnston would end all trace of military resistance on the part
of the South. A brave and heroic struggle was closing. And it
was none too soon.

Although the war was over, and the military enemy was disbanded, there was still an enemy. There were still many men in
Congress who could not accept Abraham's attitude toward the
South, men who wished, having won the war, to knock the
supine states upon the head and leave them forever incapable.
Abraham now had to fight with these. And the fight was not
to be an easy one.

The vision of attainment, clear and beautiful, was before
Abraham now. He went about his work, planning the campaign
against the hostile congressmen, with a tranquil joy shining in
his heart and climbing up through the long-tense nerves into that
face which was so grievously lined and saddened. Now that the
worst was over, the horrible doubts and tortures of the last few
years were gone, leaving in their wake a sense of pressure removed, of inner springs released. The unconscious powers behind his conscious deeds burned in him now. Their flush showed
in the background of his mind. He dreamed often and strangely.
Dreamed of persecution, of fate striking him down. It seemed
to him almost a protest of his inner self at having won too much.
But he laughed at the dreams and kept to his work of planning.
He had never been so much at ease, at peace with himself, never
before.

CHAPTER SEVEN

VICTORY

WASHINGTON, in the spring of 1865, was a far gayer town than it had been in 1861. Everywhere men and women were busy trying to forget how many of their sons and brothers would never be with them again. The man in the street, though perhaps not in Washington, at least elsewhere in the North, was glad enough to see slavery abolished, but he would have been gladder had the abolishment of it not led to years of unsatisfying if glorious fighting. Now that the fighting, except for that of General Sherman, was over, and it appeared certain that the Confederacy was dead, it was hard to understand why it had all been necessary. Well, there were always great deeds to think about, great men to steal glimpses of as they went about their business. There was the exciting sense of victory in the air that gave to the ordinary routine of civilian life a holiday aspect. There would be soldiers coming home, speeches, bands, balls, hospital fairs. Everything would be unusual and disturbed. Everyone would be a little off his head. They would be riding after Jefferson Davis and his cabinet sooner or later. That would be fun. Those fellows thought they were pretty important, didn't they? Well, we showed them.

In the alleyways, behind the dingy rows of dwellings beyond Capitol Hill, coal black Negroes emptied swill for the cats and dogs to nuzzle in, coal black Negroes as free as air, free to do what no one else would do, free to do nothing else after four years of fighting. In the restaurants and hotels, champagne corks popped, and glasses were lifted in honor of a concluded war, of enemies overcome, of a nation preserved. In the North the wheels and spindles and gears of mills and factories and mines went on turning with the new energy which the exigencies of war had imposed upon them. They did not slow down to any peaceful jog, now that the war appeared over. They were destined never to stop, they were the new lifeblood of the nation, and in the pulse was the germ of a slavery destined for three-quarters of a century at least to have no public enemies. The slaves of the South had been freed and Southern capital destroyed. The slaves of the North whom Abraham Lincoln had in the depths of his heart believed he was honoring and helping by his course, were by the inevitable outcome of the days which had made a man of him, shackled the more firmly to their wheel. Northern capital had been saved.

On Good Friday, the fourteenth of April, 1865, Abraham Lincoln, having delivered his ultimatum to the irreconcilables of the nation to the effect that the new state governments which were being organized must be recognized, that, in so many words, reconstruction must be left in his hands, met his cabinet. General Grant, his work done, was present by way of added attraction. There was much apprehension in the air over the coming quarrel between the President and Congress, but as Congress was not then in session, Abraham was able to forget it. General Grant was anxious on another point. There was still no news from General Sherman. The President, with a strange light of happiness on his face, remarked, "I have no doubt that favorable news will soon come, for I had last night my usual dream which has preceded nearly every important event of the war. I seemed to be in a singular and indescribable vessel, but always the same and to be moving toward a dark and indefinite shore." The secret depths which arranged the images of that dream had perhaps guided his life and purpose more than he knew, causing both the unhappiness and the singular half-mystic joy. Now he talked of the seceded states, saying how fortunate it was that the war was ending while Congress was not in session so that there would be no danger for the moment of being hampered by the unpleasant elements of that body. No one could expect him, he said, to have vengeful feelings about the Southern officials, even the worst of them. Surely no one did. The days of the malicious and uncharitable Lincoln had long since passed into the Lincoln of the Second Inaugural.

In the afternoon General Grant said good-bye to the President and left for the north to see his children. The White House then, for a little while, ceased to be the official residence of the President and became the home of Abraham Lincoln. Weary but happy, the gigantic frame of that aging man, not yet sixty in years but several hundred in his emotions, went upstairs to talk things over with son Robert, enthusiastically returned from a sinecure on the staff of General Grant. Late in the afternoon, with no official guests, Abraham and Mary Todd went out for a drive. They talked over the past, Springfield, the strange train of events which had brought the boy of New Salem to this day and place; the days to come, when the duties of the Presidency would be over. Abraham decided that, with the money they had been able to save (it appeared like a saving as many of Mary's clothing bills had not been paid and Abraham did not know of them) they would return to Springfield and live in comfortable quiet, fortified by the pleasure and unhampered by the exactions of a small legal practice, with Billy Herndon as a partner.

After supper, the need of performing one public duty took

Abraham from his comfortable chair. A special performance had been arranged at Ford's Theater. It was partly pain and partly pleasure to go, for he wanted to be quiet and alone, but he loved the theater. General Grant had felt able to get out of going because of his children; why should the President be worse off? Well, the public would expect it. He might as well be reasonable. "Mother, I suppose it's time to go, though I would rather stay," he said to Mrs. Lincoln.

The party got into the carriage and drove off through the dark streets of Washington to the theater.

THE END

BIBLIOGRAPHY

Adams, Charles Francis. *Richard Henry Dana*. Boston: 1891.

Anti-Slavery Society. *The Constitution a Pro-Slavery Compact*. The Anti-Slavery Examiner, no. 11.

Baker, James L. *Essay on Slavery*. North Amer. Rev., Oct., 1851.

Barton, William E. *Abraham Lincoln*. Indianapolis: 1925.

———. *The Paternity of Abraham Lincoln*. New York: 1920.

Battles and Leaders of the Civil War. New York: 1894.

Beard, Charles A. *An Economic Interpretation of the Constitution of the United States*. New York: 1914.

———, and Mary. *The Rise of American Civilization*. Vol. I. New York: 1927.

Benton, Thomas H. *Thirty Years' View*. New York: 1886.

Beveridge, Albert J. *Abraham Lincoln 1809-1858*. Boston: 1928.

Bogart, E. L. *Economic History of the United States*. New York: 1916.

Brooks, Robert C. *Political Parties and Electoral Problems*. New York: 1923.

Browning, Orville H. *The Diary of O. H. Browning*. Springfield, Ill.: 1925.

Campaigns of the Civil War: Chancellorsville and Gettysburg; the Virginia Campaign of 1864 and 1865; Statistical Record; The Peninsula. New York: 1882-83.

Census Bureau. *Report of the Eighth Decennial Census*.

Chapman, John Jay. *William Lloyd Garrison*. Boston: 1921.

Chesnut, Mary Boykin. *A Dixie Diary*. New York: 1906.

Chickering, Jesse. *A Statistical View of the Population of Massachusetts*. Boston: 1846.

Cluskey, M. W. *The Political Text-book or Encyclopedia*. Philadelphia: 1859.

Cole, Arthur C. *Centennial History of Illinois* (vol. 3, *The Era of the Civil War*). Springfield, Ill.: 1919.

Coman, Katharine. *Industrial History of the United States*. New York: 1911.

Commons, John R. *Horace Greeley and the Working Class Origin of the Republican Party*. Pol. Sc. Quar., 1.24, no. 3.

Congressional Globe. Thirty-sixth Congress, 2nd Session.

Cooper, Thomas V., and Fenton, Hector T. *American Politics*. Chicago: 1884.

Crawford, S. W. *The Genesis of the Civil War*. New York: 1898.

Davis, Jefferson. *The Rise and Fall of the Confederate Government*. New York: 1881.

Davis, Varina Howell. *Jefferson Davis*. New York: 1890.

De Bow, J. D. B. *Industrial Resources of the Southern and Western States*. New Orleans: 1852-53.

De Bow's Review. Issues of 1860 and 1861. New Orleans.

De Tocqueville, A. *De la Démocratie en Amerique*. Paris: 1835.

Dewey, D. R. *Financial History of the United States*. New York: 1907.

Dodd, William E. *Lincoln or Lee*. New York: 1928.

Fish, Carl R. *Lincoln and the Spoils System*. Amer. Hist. Rev., vol. 8, no. 1.

———. *The Rise of the Common Man*. New York: 1927.

Fitzhugh, George. *Sociology for the South*. Richmond: 1854.

———. *The Wealth of North and South*. De Bow's Review, no. 23, 1857.

Fleming, Walter L. *The Buford Expedition to Kansas*. Amer. Hist. Rev., vol. 6, no. 1.

Fry, James B. *New York and the Conscription of 1863*. New York: 1885.

Fuller, Margaret. *Woman in the Nineteenth Century*. London: 1845.

Gerhard, Frederic. *Illinois As It Is*. Chicago: 1881.

Grant, Ulysses S. *Personal Memoirs*. New York: 1885-86.

Hall, Benjamin F. *The Republican Party*. New York: 1856.

Hammond, Matthew B. *The Cotton Industry*. New York: 1897.

Hart, Albert Bushnell. *Slavery and Abolition*. New York: 1900.

Helm, Katherine. *The True Story of Mary, Wife of Lincoln*. New York: 1928.

Helper, Hinton R. *The Impending Crisis of the South*. New York: 1860.

Herndon, William H., and Weik, Jesse W. *Herndon's Lincoln*. Chicago, New York: 1889.

Hill, Frederick Trevor. *Lincoln the Lawyer*. New York: 1913.

Holst, Hermann Eduard von. *John C. Calhoun*. Boston: 1888.

Illinois House of Representatives. *Journals*. 1832-1841.

Illinois Journal. Various dates, 1853.

Illinois State Register. Various dates, 1853.

Isely, W. H. *The Sharps Rifle Episode in Kansas History*. Amer. Hist. Rev., vol. 12, no. 3.

Johnson, Allen. *American Constitutional History*. Boston: 1912.

Johnson, Allen. *Stephen A Douglas.* New York: 1908.

Jones, Chester L. *Readings on Parties and Elections in the United States.* New York: 1912.

Lusk, David W. *Eighty Years of Illinois.* Springfield, Ill.: 1889.

McMaster, John Bach. *A History of the People of the United States during Lincoln's Administration.* New York: 1927.

Merriam, Charles E. *Four American Party Leaders.* New York: 1926.

Munro, William B. *Government of the United States.* New York: 1923.

Myers, Gustavus. History of the Supreme Court. Chicago: 1912.

Newton, Joseph Fort. *Lincoln and Herndon.* Cedar Rapids, Ia.: 1910.

Nicolay, John G. *A Short Life of Abraham Lincoln.* New York: 1906.

Nicolay, John G., and Hay, John. *Abraham Lincoln: A History.* New York: 1920.

Ogburn, W. F., and Peterson. *Political Thought of Social Classes.* Pol. Sc. Quar., no. 31.

Oldroyd, O. H. *Lincoln's Campaign, or The Political Revolution of 1860.* Chicago: 1896.

Olmsted, Frederick Law. *A Journey in the Seaboard Slave States.* New York: 1904.

————. *A Journey in the Back Country.*

O'Neil, Charles A. *The American Electoral System.* New York: 1889.

Ostrogorski, M. Y. *Democracy and the Party System in the United States.* New York: 1926.

Patterson, Robert W. *Early Society in Southern Illinois.* Chicago: 1881.

Phillips, Ulrich B. *The Economic Cost of Slave Holding in the Cotton Belt.* Pol. Sc. Quar., June, 1905.

————. *The Economics of the Plantation.* South Atl. Quar., July, 1903.

————. *Origin and Growth of the Southern Black Belts.* Amer. Hist. Rev., July, 1906.

Phillips, Wendell. *Speeches, Lectures and Letters.* Boston: 1892.

Raum, Green B. *History of Illinois Republicanism.* Chicago: 1900.

Rhodes, James Ford. *History of the United States, 1850-1877.* 7 vols. New York: 1906.

Rutledge, Archibald. *A Southerner Views Lincoln.* Scribner's Magazine, Feb., 1928.

Sandburg, Carl. *Abraham Lincoln: The Prairie Years.* New York: 1926.

Sangamon Journal. Various dates, 1837.

Schaff, Morris. *The Battle of the Wilderness.* Boston: 1910.

Schouler, James. *History of the United States.* 7 vols. New York: 1913.

Schurz, Carl. *Henry Clay.* Boston: 1909.

Schuyler, R. L. *Agreement in the Federal Convention.* Pol. Sc. Quar., vol. 31.

Schwab, John Christopher. *The Confederate States of America.* New York: 1901.

Seligman, Edwin R. A. *An Economic Interpretation of History.* New York: 1917.

Seward, William H. *Works.* 5 vols. Boston: 1884.

Sherman, William T. *Memoirs.* New York: 1889.

Simons, A. M. *Social Forces in American History.* New York: 1911.

Smith, William H. *A Political History of Slavery.* New York: 1903.

Speed, Joshua F. *Reminiscences of Abraham Lincoln.* Louisville, Ky.: 1884.

Spring, Leverett W. *The Career of a Kansas Politician.* Amer. Hist. Rev., vol. 4, no. 1.

Stanwood, Edward. *A History of Presidential Elections.* Boston: 1884.

Starr, John W. *Lincoln and the Railroads.* New York: 1927.

Stephenson, Nathaniel Wright. *Lincoln: An Account of His Personal Life.* Indianapolis: 1922.

Stickney, Albert. *Organized Democracy.* Boston: 1906.

Thoreau, Henry David. *Slavery in Massachusetts.*

Townsend, William H. *Lincoln the Litigant.* Boston: 1925.

Tracy, Gilbert A., edit. *Some Uncollected Letters of Abraham Lincoln.* Boston: 1917.

United States House of Representatives. Thirty-fourth Congress, First Session, Report. No. 200. *Report of the Special Committee Appointed to Investigate Conditions in Kansas.*

Watkins, Albert. *Douglas, Lincoln, and the Nebraska Bill.* Lincoln, Neb.: 1908.

Webster, Daniel. *Works.* Boston, 1903.

Weik, Jesse W. *The Real Lincoln.* Boston: 1922.

Weston, George M. *The Poor Whites of the South,* 1856.

Wheeler, H. G. *History of Congress, Biographical and Political.* New York: 1848.

Wilson, Woodrow. *A History of the American People.* New York: 1917.

Wright, Carroll D. *Industrial Evolution of the United States.* New York: 1901.

INDEX